It is my privilege to commend this
Communicating clearly and logically c
African life and the biblical text, Elizabe
and fruitful African hermeneutic. She s
biblical worldviews, offering foundations for contextualization in a way
that brings together the interpretive horizons. She also draws on the
most useful, proven approaches, such as attention to genre, narrative
development, and historical context.

Craig S. Keener, PhD
F. M. and Ada Thompson Professor of Biblical Studies,
Asbury Theological Seminary, Wilmore, Kentucky, USA

African Christianity has often been described as a "mile long and an inch deep," "Sunday Christianity," "Shallow Christianity," "syncretized Christianity," etc. The author of this exciting book, *African Hermeneutics*, has aptly referred to African Christianity as "dichotomized Christianity." To remove this split Christianity, Mburu proposes that African Christians must contextualize the interpretation of the Bible by using known African categories of interpretation. Her proposal is new, fresh, engaging and potentially revolutionary and paradigmatic. In my mind, this is a must-read for all African theological educators, missionaries, students and pastors.

Samuel Waje Kunhiyop, PhD
Professor of Systematic Theology and Ethics,
ECWA Theological Seminary, Kagoro, Nigeria
Author, *African Christian Theology*

African Hermeneutics by Professor Elizabeth Mburu is a comprehensive masterpiece in modern African biblical scholarship. It is broad, insightful, refreshing, innovative, creative, contextual and critical as it makes the African worldview central to making hermeneutics a biblical science relevant to Africa. The choice of "African worldview" as a worthy tool in biblical interpretation was deliberate, because of its value and significance in creating new biblical and contextual hermeneutics and interpretations. This new method will certainly become a sought-after model of biblical hermeneutics and African biblical interpretation. To this end, this book provides a fodder to enrich biblical and theological discourse in Africa.

Mburu has demonstrated that even as a young biblical scholar, she can use her new, emerging, creative and innovative hermeneutical skills, criticisms and scholarship to rejuvenate and impact contemporary biblical scholarship. This new book will certainly redirect the course of biblical scholarship, especially in Africa, where this new approach will resonate with African emphasis upon the traditional value of storytelling as a sure and valid tool of biblical interpretation. This book in the course of time will certainly mark out Elizabeth Mburu as an outstanding African biblical scholar in the making. Her commendable scholarship should encourage and motivate younger African scholars to aspire to greater heights in biblical and theological scholarship.

Yusufu Turaki, PhD
Professor of Theology and Social Ethics,
ECWA Theological Seminary, Jos, Nigeria

Elizabeth Mburu lays down principles for a four-legged stool model of an intercultural biblical hermeneutics in Africa and applies it to both Old Testament and New Testament texts. Her contribution deserves close attention from any reader who is interested in the development of intercultural hermeneutics in Africa.

Jean-Claude Loba-Mkole, PhD
Global Translation Adviser, United Bible Societies, Kenya
Professor of New Testament and Bible Translation Studies,
University of the Free State, Bloemfontein, South Africa

AFRICAN HERMENEUTICS

AFRICAN HERMENEUTICS

Elizabeth Mburu

HIPPOBOOKS

© 2019 Elizabeth Mburu

Published 2019 by HippoBooks, an imprint of ACTS and Langham Publishing.

Africa Christian Textbooks (ACTS), TCNN, PMB 2020, Bukuru 930008, Plateau State, Nigeria. **www.actsnigeria.org**

Langham Publishing, PO Box 296, Carlisle, Cumbria, CA3 9WZ, UK
www.langhampublishing.org

ISBNs:
978-1-78368-464-9 Print
978-1-78368-538-7 ePub
978-1-78368-539-4 Mobi
978-1-78368-540-0 PDF

Elizabeth Mburu has asserted her right under the Copyright, Designs and Patents Act, 1988 to be identified as the Author of this work.

All rights reserved. No part of this publication may be reproduced, stored in a retrieval system or transmitted, in any form or by any means, electronic, mechanical, photocopying, recording or otherwise, without the prior written permission of the publisher or the Copyright Licensing Agency.

All Scripture quotations, unless otherwise indicated, are taken from the Holy Bible, New International Version®, NIV®. Copyright ©1973, 1978, 1984, 2011 by Biblica, Inc.™ Used by permission of Zondervan.

British Library Cataloguing-in-Publication Data
A catalogue record for this book is available from the British Library

ISBN: 978-1-78368-464-9

Cover & Book Design: projectluz.com

The publishers of this book actively support theological dialogue and an author's right to publish but do not necessarily endorse the views and opinions set forth here or in works referenced within this publication, nor guarantee technical and grammatical correctness. The publishers do not accept any responsibility or liability to persons or property as a consequence of the reading, use or interpretation of its published content.

This book is dedicated to my husband, Caxton, and our three children, Bryan, Michelle and Paul. They have been an invaluable support throughout the research and writing of this book, often offering helpful suggestions and testing the material.

CONTENTS

Foreword xi
Preface xiii
Acknowledgements xv
Abbreviations xvii

Part I: General Principles of Hermeneutics 1
1 Introduction 3
2 The African Worldview: Theological Aspects 21
3 The African Worldview: Philosophical aspects 45
4 An African Hermeneutic: A Four-Legged Stool 65

Part II: Specific Principles of Hermeneutics 91
5 Understanding the Context of the Bible 93
6 Interpreting Stories 107
7 Interpreting Wisdom 139
8 Interpreting Songs 165
9 Interpreting Letters 191
10 Conclusion 211
   Further Reading 215
   Bibliography 217
   Index of Subjects 225
   Index of Names 229
   Index of Scripture 231

FOREWORD

Without communication there cannot be a relationship, and without relevance in communication there would not be meaningful relationship.

The African believer has been invited into a relationship with God, as expressed in the Scriptures. Yet the Scriptures have remained to a great extent without the desired impact. This raises the question whether those of us who have been called to teach or preach the Scriptures have managed to cross the boundary between the content of the Bible and the relationship to the everyday life of the African Christian.

Professor Elizabeth Mburu does not only raise this question in *African Hermeneutics*, she also provides a way forward on how to achieve this. She lays down for us a methodology that certainly will make a difference.

The four legs of a stool approach, as Mburu proposes, guards against syncretism while at the same time giving the African worldview the place needed if the Scriptures are to be made relevant to an African's everyday life experiences and challenges.

We cannot but agree with the author that a stool that is missing one of its legs will not serve the purpose it is meant for. The African preacher and teacher needs to appreciate the many contributions (most of them from the West) in the areas of theological, literary and historical contexts, but also to acknowledge that these three legs will not go far in passing on the message of the gospel to the African believer when the fourth leg, namely the African context, is neglected.

In this work, Mburu illustrates how this fourth leg needs to be brought in when dealing with the different genres in the Bible – whether it be narrative, wisdom literature, epistle, or even apocalypse. This is done with excellence in both handling the teachings of Scripture and drawing from the riches there are in the African beliefs and practices.

This is a book every preacher or teacher who desires to see the message of the gospel have the needed impact on the African continent must read, learn from, and build on. Mburu may not have said all that can be said (both the Scriptures and the African contexts are too wide to get all aspects covered in one book) but she lays before us basic principles we can all build on as we heed her call to bring the African believer to that level where life is not dichotomized but lived for the glory of God in its totality.

Samuel M. Ngewa
Professor of New Testament,
Dean of Graduate School,
Africa International University
November 2018

PREFACE

Interpreting the Bible is always a challenging task. To be more precise, interpreting the Bible *accurately* is a challenging task. And yet the Bible is meant to be understood and applied in the daily lives of believers if it is to be a guide for faith and practice.

African readers of the Bible face the additional challenge that most of the models and methods of Bible interpretation, or hermeneutics, are rooted in a Western context. This is not surprising given that Christianity came to Africa from the West, the churches and theological institutions that were founded were missionary led, and most of the theological resources are produced by Western writers. Millions of Africans therefore use "foreign" approaches to the interpretation of the Bible. This may be one of the reasons why many African Christians experience a dichotomy in their Christian lives. While the content of Christianity may be known and perhaps even understood, practice is not often consistent with this knowledge. This book is an attempt to address this problem by providing the reader with a contextualized, African intercultural approach to the study of the Bible.

Part I provides a foundation for this intercultural approach by outlining principles that address the issue of this dichotomy and provide a solution through a contextualized hermeneutic. Since Bible interpretation can never be done in a vacuum, this contextualized hermeneutic begins with an exploration of African worldviews. Part I also presents a four-legged stool model that guides the reader in examining the text using four interrelated steps. Specific application of the biblical text to the African context is viewed as the logical endpoint of this process. The review questions at the end of each chapter in Part I are intended to help the reader think more critically about the African contextual issues that affect accurate interpretation of the Bible.

Part II applies the principles developed in Part I to the main genres of the Bible. Each genre is addressed in a separate chapter, and specific literary techniques used in analysing African literature are woven into the interpretation of the text. An example from African literature is given in each chapter and a biblical text is then interpreted using the model developed in Part I. A key aspect of this approach is the recognition that the biblical writers wrote from particular theological, literary and historical/cultural contexts and that they intended to communicate a message to their readers. It is this message to the original readers that we must endeavour to understand and then apply in our own contexts. There are no review questions in Part II as it is assumed that readers will have examples from their own contexts that they can relate to the biblical texts.

Recent reports indicate that most Christians today live in sub-Saharan Africa. This means that the church of the future will be defined within the scope of African Christianity. If Christianity is to maintain its integrity as defined by biblical revelation, it is imperative that we endeavour to understand and apply the Bible accurately, as the authors of the biblical text intended. It is hoped that this book will contribute to this task.

Elizabeth Mburu, PhD
Associate Professor of New Testament and Greek

ACKNOWLEDGEMENTS

The people of Kenya have a Kiswahili word that truly expresses the essence of communal life in Africa. It is a word that is found in our loyalty pledge and that has been used for decades to identify activities that require community support. This word is *harambee*. It means "pulling together." A book such as this has only come to fruition because of the *harambee* efforts of my family, friends, colleagues and students. Many thanks go to my husband, Caxton, and my children, Bryan, Michelle and Paul, for the tremendous support they have given me in the years that it took to envision and write this book. In addition to their moral support, they patiently served as "test subjects" for the material and graciously gave me much needed feedback and encouragement. A special thanks to Caxton who shared and confirmed some of the content with the rural pastors he trains, and Michelle for her artwork of the African stool. I also wish to acknowledge Dr Kariba Munio who provided some of the African material. I owe him a debt of gratitude for his contribution. My heartfelt appreciation goes to the entire team at Langham Literature. In particular, to Pieter Kwant who heard my passion for contextualized hermeneutics and challenged me to write this book; to Isobel Stevenson who worked tirelessly to edit and refine the contents of this book from its inception; and to Dahlia Frasier who participated in editing the finished product. Any mistakes are entirely my own. I wish to convey my appreciation to all the students I had the honour of teaching (at International Leadership University, Pan Africa Christian University and Africa International University, Kenya) for their feedback as I tested the material on them in the classroom. And finally, I thank God for providing the resources necessary to write this book. My prayer is that it will be a useful tool for the growth of the church in Africa and beyond.

ABBREVIATIONS

Bible Translations and Dictionaries

CSB	Christian Standard Bible
GNT	Good News Translation
KJV	King James Version
NASB	New American Standard Bible
NIV	New International Version
NIDOTTE	*New International Dictionary of Old Testament Theology and Exegesis*
NRSV	New Revised Standard Version
TDNT	*Theological Dictionary of the New Testament*

Books of the Bible

Old Testament

Gen, Exod, Lev, Num, Deut, Josh, Judg, Ruth, 1–2 Sam, 1–2 Kgs, 1–2 Chr, Ezra, Neh, Esth, Job, Ps/Pss, Prov, Eccl, Song, Isa, Jer, Lam, Ezek, Dan, Hos, Joel, Amos, Obad, Jonah, Mic, Nah, Hab, Zeph, Hag, Zech, Mal

New Testament

Matt, Mark, Luke, John, Acts, Rom, 1–2 Cor, Gal, Eph, Phil, Col, 1–2 Thess, 1–2 Tim, Titus, Phlm, Heb, Jas, 1–2 Pet, 1, 2, 3 John, Jude, Rev

PART I
GENERAL PRINCIPLES OF HERMENEUTICS

The Bible has played a significant role in people's lives throughout the ages and has been read, interpreted and understood in various ways. While the message might have been clear to the original audience, it is not as clear to us today, in part because we are separated from the world of the Bible by factors such as time, language and culture.

Our goal as students of the Bible is to attempt to read and understand it correctly. To achieve this, we need principles that will guide us in our study as well as specific methods that aim at uncovering the message the biblical authors wanted to communicate. In other words, we need to understand hermeneutics, which is the art and science of interpreting the Bible. Hermeneutics involves both theory and practice, and like any art or science it requires the use of certain methods or techniques to produce reliable results

The first part of this book will provide general principles of hermeneutics and explain the importance of understanding our African contexts and worldviews and how these influence our interpretation of the Bible. It will also provide an intercultural model of hermeneutics that will help us arrive at a reliable interpretation of the Scriptures.

1

INTRODUCTION

Why is it that after more than one hundred years of exposure to Christianity, traditional practices such as witchcraft, ancestor worship and polygamy are still found in Africa? Why is it not uncommon to hear of pastors consulting witchdoctors to acquire more "power" for the pulpit and of Christians using witchcraft to grow their businesses? Why, if the statistics on corruption and unethical practices on our continent are to be believed, has there been so very little transformation of society?

The Challenge: Dichotomized Lives

One answer to the question posed above is that many Christians, including those holding leadership positions in the church, live dichotomized lives. In other words, we as African Christians seem unable to understand how our faith should affect our everyday lives. It is as if we keep faith and life in two separate compartments. Like a precious jewel, faith is kept securely locked up in a safe whose combination only the owner knows!

We are Sunday Christians, or at least we act like Christians when we are in the company of other Christians. However, when faced with choices that do not seem to be "spiritual," we respond like the world would. This is particularly evident when we are not in church-related contexts. Our behaviour shows that while we may know the content of our Christian faith, it has not been internalized. The result is that individual believers and churches are weak and Christianity has lost a great deal of credibility.

It is not enough merely to identify this split in our thinking; we also need to determine why it is there. Hillman offers a useful summary of what has been said about the source of our problem and how we arrived at this destination:

> When not deliberately trying to destroy them, the colonial processes invariably undermined the systems, values and views of entire cultural worlds. Stripped naked and taught, in schools and churches, to be ashamed of themselves, their "primitive" and "pagan" way, the people were coerced, morally as well as physically, into clothing themselves with the ways of the invading culture. The colonial incursions, although they brought literacy and antibiotics, made westernization the way of human "advancement." Many people came to believe the "progress" consists not in being themselves, but in imitating foreign ways.[1]

The result was, as Laurenti Magesa says, that many an African Christian "operates with two thought-systems at once, and both of them are closed to each other. Each is only superficially modified by the other."[2]

We as Africans are still trying to imitate foreign ways when it comes to reading, interpreting and applying the Bible in our everyday lives. Perhaps if we understood that the interpretation of the Bible was already being done by Africans almost two thousand years ago, we might change our perspective. Church history reveals that some of the most important early interpreters of the Bible were in Northern Africa. The list includes church fathers like Origen (who spent much of his life in Alexandria in Egypt) and Augustine (who lived and served in the region now known as Algeria). Even though most of the ancient Northern African churches have been overwhelmed by Islam, the ancient Coptic and Ethiopian Orthodox churches are still very prominent there. The church can therefore claim to have early African readings of the Bible!

However, in the nineteenth century when Western missionaries brought Christianity to Africa, they also brought their own Western readings of

---

1. Eugene Hillman, *Toward an African Christianity: Inculturation Applied* (New York: Paulist Press, 1993), 5.
2. Laurenti Magesa, *African Religion: The Moral Traditions of Abundant Life* (Maryknoll, NY: Orbis Books, 1997), 7.

the Bible. Consequently, although some of the early approaches to Bible interpretation originated in Africa, Western approaches are prominent in the African church today. Many African biblical scholars have been trained in the West and therefore follow a Western tradition of interpretation. Even though several faculties of religion, seminaries and Bible schools have been established in Africa to cope with the demands of the rapidly expanding church here, the question remains: Is there a critical mass of faculty who understand the African situation and can adequately address the African context?[3]

The Solution: A Contextualized Hermeneutic

People sometimes speak of hermeneutics as if it has principles that are set in stone. But is hermeneutics static, or is it dynamic in the sense that it can change as methods of interpretation are adapted to different cultural contexts? To answer that question, we need to look more closely at what hermeneutics does.

Hermeneutics is necessary because we cannot hope to experience genuine transformation, whether of self or of others, if we lack the knowledge and skills to effectively interpret the Bible. Such interpretation will always involve both theory and practice, for the methods we use must have a theoretical foundation as well as a practical application. If you think about it, you will see that this statement implies that hermeneutics must be linked to a particular place. If our hermeneutical models are all from the West, how can we derive practical applications in an African context? If we lack an understanding of the African worldview as well as the biblical one, how can we understand what the Bible has to say about daily life in Africa?

Scripture is meant to be relevant to the context in which it is being taught and applied. And yet millions of believers in Africa are constantly being bombarded with foreign ways of approaching the text of the Bible that ignore important aspects of the social, economic, political and theological culture of Africa. We need an African hermeneutic, one that

---

3. Elizabeth Mburu, "From the Classroom to the Pulpit: Navigating the Challenges," in *African Contextual Realities*, ed. Rodney Reed (Carlisle: Langham Global Library, 2018), 227–248.

raises questions that a hermeneutic from a different environment would not. Or as Byang Kato puts it, we need contextualization, an activity that he defined as "making concepts or ideas relevant in a given situation."[4]

One Westerner who has thought deeply about these issues is Eugene Hillman. He proposes that the best way to communicate Christian doctrine in Africa involves what he calls an incarnational model, using "culturally appropriate instruments of God's saving grace."[5] In other words, we should draw on aspects of African culture that facilitate our understanding of the practical implications of the Bible.

At this point, we need to ask, "What is culture?" Culture can be defined as the beliefs, behaviours, objects and other characteristics common to the members of a particular group or society. It is through culture that people and groups define themselves, conform to society's shared values, and contribute to society. Culture is both material and non-material. The material aspect consists of the objects or belongings of a group of people, while the non-material aspect consists of a society's ideas, attitudes and beliefs. Both material and non-material aspects of culture should be used as critical resources for hermeneutics. Ukachukwu, for example, draws on African folklore to show how this can be done.[6]

This approach to unlocking the African understanding of biblical texts is not new. It is doing what Jesus did, for he too used elements of his culture to teach, moving from the known to the unknown, particularly in his parables. This is an extremely effective instructional technique and is especially significant for African readers since the culture of the Bible resembles African culture in so many ways. Even with modernization and globalization, there are many elements of both cultures that intersect. Thus the hermeneutical gaps for African interpreters may be significantly less than those faced by Western interpreters, whose cultures are far removed from that of the Bible.

This is the philosophy behind the four-legged stool model proposed in this book. It is an intercultural model that is based on the concept of

---

4. Byang H. Kato, "Contextualization and Religious Syncretism in Africa," in *Biblical Christianity in Africa: A Collection of Papers and Addresses*, Theological Perspectives in Africa 2 (Accra: Africa Christian Press, 1985), 23.
5. Hillman, *Toward an African Christianity*, 5.
6. Chris Manus Ukachukwu, *Intercultural Hermeneutics in Africa: Methods and Approaches* (Nairobi: Acton Publishers, 2003).

moving from the known to the unknown. It therefore moves directly from theories, methods and categories that are familiar in our world into the more unfamiliar world of the Bible, without taking a detour through any foreign methods. It recognizes that parallels between biblical cultures and worldviews and African cultures and worldviews can be used as bridges to promote understanding, internalization and application of the biblical text.

Some have argued that modernization has eradicated traditional African worldviews.[7] This is simply not true. While obviously not coded into our DNA, worldview is so embedded in the social fabric that it is transmitted both consciously and unconsciously. We have all acquired the knowledge, values, morals, and skills we need to live harmoniously in our communities. This point was brought home to me at university when I had to write an assignment on worldview and culture. I discovered that although I had grown up in an almost entirely Western environment, I still retained traces of a traditional African worldview, picked up unconsciously over the years. I was, and still am, as I concluded in my paper, undoubtedly "an African in Western garb."

In developing an African intercultural hermeneutic that embraces contextualization throughout the process, certain considerations must be kept in mind:[8]

- Africans tend to have an inherently religious or spiritual worldview that is not lost when they become Christians.
- The philosophy and method used in an African hermeneutic must address issues that are relevant to African Christians.
- An African hermeneutic must ground abstract thinking in concrete realities.
- An African hermeneutic must be comprehensible to all Christians and not just a select group of intellectuals. The goal is for millions of believers who live in Africa to truly understand the biblical text and apply it in their lives.

There is one other key factor that must serve as a foundation for the entire process: All conclusions regarding the text must be rooted in

---

7. The subject of worldview will be discussed in more detail in the following chapters.
8. These insights are adapted (with minor changes) from Samuel Waje Kunhiyop, *African Christian Theology* (Nairobi: HippoBooks, 2012), xv–xvi.

an understanding of the culture and worldview of the Bible. Only by understanding both our African realities and biblical realities can we avoid the dichotomous approach that is found even among graduates of theological institutions in Africa.

What about syncretism?

Contextualization does carry a very real danger of sliding into syncretism. Syncretism occurs when religious and cultural forms are combined with the biblical message without any regard for whether they align with biblical truth. We have seen this in the work of some theologians who have attempted to relate Christian theology to the African context. The rapid growth of African Initiated Churches (AICs) also reflects attempts to join elements of African Traditional Religions to the teachings of the Bible. While this growth is often positive, some of these movements have mixed so many elements of traditional religions with elements of Christianity that the resulting blend can no longer rightly be called Christian.

We need to take care not to fall into this trap. As Kato noted many decades ago,

> Africans need to formulate theological concepts in the language of Africa. But theology itself in its essence must be left alone. The Bible must remain the basic source of Christian theology. Evangelical Christians know of only one theology – Biblical Theology – though it may be expressed in the context of each cultural milieu.[9]

At the time Kato was writing, there was a growing interest in the use of African religions as sources for an African theology. The danger he identified was the move away from a clear understanding of the unique nature of biblical revelation. This move led to other sources being viewed as equal to the Bible, so that Christianity lost its unique status as the only way of salvation. Kato's warning reminds us that while African religious and traditional beliefs can and should be used in some measure to formulate an understanding of the Bible from an African context, they must not be allowed to displace biblical revelation. Whatever one's

---

9. Byang H. Kato, "Theological Anemia in Africa," in *Biblical Christianity in Africa: A Collection of Papers and Addresses*, Theological Perspectives in Africa 2 (Accra: Africa Christian Press, 1985), 12.

hermeneutic communicates as far as relevance to different cultures and sub-cultures within Africa is concerned, it must be in alignment with the Bible's teachings.

A word about assumptions

There is no neutral reading of a text, as many scholars have pointed out over the years. Assumptions will always influence our understanding of Scripture. An assumption is something that we take as true or certain without necessarily having proof for it. Those who favour a reader-response approach, for instance, assume that everyone's interpretation of the text is valid and hence there are as many interpretations as there are reading communities, and sometimes even readers. Those who adopt a feminist hermeneutic assume that the biblical text will always have a negative message about women. Those who prefer a liberation hermeneutic tend to focus on those elements of the text that support liberation and freedom for the oppressed. Closer to home, modern African hermeneutics have generally been driven by sociological and historical interests, resulting in post-colonial readings of the Bible.[10]

Our culture and our worldview are also founded on certain assumptions. We must honestly seek to identify these assumptions and ensure that throughout the hermeneutical process, they do not influence us to make interpretive decisions that may be inaccurate. If we fail to recognize them, we are likely to read meaning into the text. When we do this, we lose sight of the original message of the author who produced the story, or poem or proverb.

It must also be pointed out that the context of the reader and that of the biblical text may sometimes share certain common elements, but they are not identical. Therefore, to understand the text, the reader must endeavour to step into the world of the biblical text and allow the text to speak for itself so that no faulty assumptions interfere with the interpretive process.

---

10. Gerald West, "African Biblical Hermeneutics and Bible Translation," in *Interacting with Scriptures in Africa*, eds. Jean-Claude Loba-Mkole and Ernst R. Wendland (Nairobi: Acton Publishers, 2005), 7.

An Example of Contextualization

To help you grasp what I mean, let us look at the example of Paul's speech in Athens (Acts 17:16–34) which demonstrates his great skill in building bridges of communication across cultures and worldviews through contextualization.[11] In this speech, Paul deals with common elements of culture that form the basis for a worldview. But as we read his words, we note that although he understands the worldview of his opponents, and even sometimes uses it to his advantage, he never compromises his own Christ-centred worldview. Yet he can still engage positively with the beliefs of his hearers.

Background

By Paul's day, the glory of Greece in the fifth and fourth centuries BC was fading, yet Athens was still a cultural centre. The city was full of sculptures, for in Athens, as in traditional African contexts, art was a reflection of worship. The numerous idols revealed that the people of this city accepted any and all foreign gods and even provided them with temples and altars. Ancient sources tell us that Athens had more idols and more sacred feasts than all the rest of Greece put together.

Paul found his way to the Agora, which was famous as the place where philosophers debated their views. It was therefore the perfect place for him to begin speaking. He soon attracted a crowd and became involved in a debate with Epicurean and Stoic philosophers. His ideas received a mixed response: "Stoics and Epicureans alike . . . looked on him as a retailer of second-hand scraps of philosophy . . . a type of itinerant peddler of religion not unknown in the Agora."[12] While some regarded him as a "babbler" with nothing constructive to say, others thought he was talking about foreign gods, for this was how they interpreted his preaching about Jesus and the resurrection (v. 18).

Paul's interaction was so engaging, and his teaching so new and strange, that some were curious to know more. After all, the Athenians

---

11. For a fuller treatment of this text in a different context, see Elizabeth Mburu, "Leadership – Isolation, Absorption or Engagement: Paul, the Paradigmatic Role Model," *Africa Journal of Evangelical Theology* 32, no. 1 (2013): 3–19.
12. F. F. Bruce, *The Book of the Acts*, The New International Commentary on the New Testament, rev. ed. (Grand Rapids: Eerdmans, 1988), 331.

loved to hear about new ideas. They therefore give him an opportunity to speak in the Areopagus, a place that was the equivalent to our city centre or city hall. It was where the magistrates dispensed justice and business was conducted. It was also a meeting place where learned men met to exchange ideas. No new gods could be worshipped in Athens without the approval of the Areopagus.[13]

The details of Paul's speech there provide us with a model of how to use culture and worldview when presenting and interpreting the biblical message. He uses several points of contact as effective bridges between his worldview and the worldviews he encounters.

First bridge: "An unknown god"

Paul begins his address in an unexpected way, given what we know of his emotional response to his surroundings. The narrator tells us that "he was greatly distressed to see that the city was full of idols" (v. 16). But he does not become angry or even criticize his hearers for worshipping idols. Instead, he compliments them on their commitment to religion (v. 22). Paul has spent his time in Athens well, observing the people of the city and taking note of their beliefs. His introductory words open avenues of communication and set the tone for the rest of the speech.

Paul then explains why he has complimented them. In looking at the objects of their worship, he had come across an altar inscribed, "To an unknown god." We do not know what exactly he was referring to. However, historians say that the Athenians had many altars inscribed "To the gods of Asia, Europe, and Africa – To the unknown god." The identity of the god is not relevant. What is relevant is that Paul uses this altar as his first bridge for introducing them to the true God. By doing so, he accomplishes at least three things: first, he offers to fill the gap in their knowledge regarding this deity; second, he appeals to their curiosity about the new and the strange; and finally, he dismisses any idea that he is introducing a new god. As Chrysostom points out, he shows that "they have anticipated what he proclaimed."[14]

---

13. Riemer Faber, http://spindleworks.com/library/rfaber/aratus.htm.
Last Updated: March 12, 2001. (Taken with permission from *Clarion* 42 [1993]: 13.)
14. Cited in *Ancient Christian Commentary on Scripture*, New Testament 5, Acts, ed. Francis Martin (Downers Grove: InterVarsity Press, 2006), 216.

Paul appropriately begins his speech with a discussion of their understanding of deity (v. 26). As will be discussed in the next chapter, this is the starting point of any worldview, the foundation for everything that comes after. Although the narrator of Acts does not explain what Paul's opponents believed, we can know a lot about it by studying the historical context.

The Epicureans believed that gods existed and were made up of atoms, just like human beings and animals.[15] Their gods lived in peace and tranquillity, completely removed from humanity. They did not become involved in human affairs.[16] Because religion was seen as a source of fear, not comfort, the Epicureans thought that banishing fear of the gods was one step towards attaining peace and a good life.

Stoics, on the other hand, believed that the world had been created by Zeus, who was not thought of as having any human form but was assumed to be of a fine and subtle substance known as *pneuma* (breath).[17] Zeus was believed to be a divine force that penetrated all things and united them in one universe. This divine force, also known as reason or *logos*, was viewed as being one with creation, leading to a pantheistic view of reality. (Pantheism is the belief that God is not separate from his creation but is one with the universe and nature.) While the Stoics were monotheists and believed in only one god, they did not discount other gods; instead "the various gods were seen as metaphorical expressions of the God at work throughout nature."[18]

Although it is never explicitly stated, Paul clearly knows about these philosophies and uses this knowledge as a starting point for introducing the Christian God. We have already seen his strategy of moving from the known to the unknown in his reference to the unknown god. He immediately identifies this unknown god with the creator God who is sovereign over all creation. Although this creator sounds similar to the Stoic god Zeus in that he cannot be contained in human temples, he is different from Zeus because he is distinct from his creation and rules it as

---

15. Anthony Kenny, *An Illustrated Brief History of Western Philosophy* (Malden, MA: Blackwell, 2006), 94.
16. Diogenes Laertius, *Lives of Eminent Philosophers* 10, 123–124. Translation from the Loeb Classical Library.
17. Kenny, *Illustrated Brief History*, 97.
18. J. C. Thom, "Stoicism," *Dictionary of New Testament Background*, 1140.

"Lord of heaven and earth." Paul goes on to speak about the life-giving power of this God who supplies humankind with all things but has no need for humankind since he is the origin of all things. Paul's language mirrors Old Testament language about God.

Unlike the Epicurean god, the God Paul preaches is interested in human beings and wants to be involved in their lives. He is personal, loving and just, a God who is both near to humanity and far from them. In other words, he is both separate from creation and present within it and he is not under any external compulsion to act in a particular way. This personal God has intentionally chosen to reveal himself in a way that human beings will understand.

Note how seamlessly Paul weaves in his assumptions about human beings. He regards all people, including his listeners, as the intentional creation of a divine being. This implies that all people have worth. But, as Paul argues, they are also in need of salvation. This salvation has been provided through a man, Jesus Christ. Moreover, not only is God the creator of humankind, he is also the one who determines human destiny. This God is completely unlike the Epicurean gods who had no interest in human beings.

Epicureans also believed that human beings have total free will and are therefore not accountable to the gods: "Since we are free we are masters of our own fate: the gods neither impose necessity nor interfere with our choices."[19] Paul disagrees, arguing that human beings are created with a yearning for God. St Augustine (AD 354–430) would agree.

> Augustine spent years in search of the final target of human longing. He called it the *summum bonum*, the "supreme good." . . . What Augustine knew is that human beings want God. In fact, humans want union with God. . . . Until it's suppressed, this longing for God arises in every human soul because it is part of the soul's standard equipment.[20]

Paul recognized this essential truth, and the fact that in the absence of true revelation this longing would express itself as idolatry.

---

19. Kenny, *Illustrated Brief History*, 94.
20. Cornelius Plantinga, *Engaging God's World: A Christian Vision of Faith, Learning, and Living* (Grand Rapids: Eerdmans, 2002), 6.

Second bridge: "We are his offspring"

Paul's message takes a surprising twist when he states, "for in him we live and move and have our being" (v. 28) These words probably derive from the fourth line of a poem by Epimenides the Cretan (c. 600 BC),[21] and would have been familiar to his Greek hearers. They also fit with Paul's Jewish background, for Genesis states that human beings were created by God (Gen 1:27–28). What is startling is what Paul says next: "as some of your own poets have said, 'We are his offspring.'" The poet Paul was quoting was a Stoic named Aratus, whose poem "Phaenomena" was evidently well known to Paul's hearers.[22] But Aratus was referring to the heathen god Zeus, whom the Stoics worshipped as the supreme God. Again, we see Paul using the strategy of moving his hearers from the known to the unknown.

Why does Paul defend God's sovereignty over humankind by quoting pagan poets? After all, what does paganism have to do with Christianity? Does God need external witnesses, witnesses outside the Christian faith, to prove his authority, his power, his very existence? Paul would have responded to that last question with a resounding "NO!" However, and this is where Paul's genius becomes most evident, Paul understood one essential fact. Every human being has an instinctive knowledge that a divine being exists and that this divine being is in some way responsible for all of creation, including people. Paul also realized that every society would express this belief in some way. He uses this understanding as another bridge. He takes his hearers back to their own poets and their expression of the nature of human existence in relation to a divine being to remind them that human beings are utterly dependent on the true God for their existence.[23]

When he quotes these two poets, Paul is not saying that he agrees with everything they say. Rather, he is using their poems to point out two things: First, the Athenians had exchanged the glory of the immortal God for images resembling human beings; second, they were ignorant of the true God.

---

21. Bruce, *Acts*, 339.
22. Bruce, 339.
23. Mikeal C. Parsons and Martin M. Culy, *Acts: A Handbook on the Greek Text* (Waco, TX: Baylor University Press, 2003), 340.

Third bridge: The world as God's creation

Paul's assumptions about the nature of the world have already been hinted at. He rejects any idea that it came into being by chance. He believes that God created the world and everything in it. He also believes that God continues to be interested in his creation and to rule over it.

The Epicureans' beliefs about the nature of the world were quite different from Paul's. They did not believe the world was created by any deity; rather, they regarded matter as eternal, uncreated and having no divinely given purpose. They also believed that everything that exists is material. In terms of the way the world functioned, they did not believe in a deterministic world. They believed that every person had the freedom to make choices and that these choices determined the outcome of their lives. In other words, they neither believed in fate nor that the gods controlled their lives.

What about the Stoics? Like the Epicureans, Stoics believed that everything was material, even the gods: "Nothing exists outside the world and its material principles; there is no spiritual world or world of ideas."[24] However, unlike the Epicureans, Stoics were deterministic and believed that fate governed all of life. They thought that human beings should live in accordance with Nature.

By going to the very heart of his hearers' worldview, namely their understanding of deity and of the nature of human beings and the world, Paul establishes a common starting point. Having done so, he then proceeds to add to their prior knowledge, effectively moving them from the known to the unknown.

Fourth bridge: Expanding the old context with the new

Having established a point of connection with his hearers, Paul goes on to explain the implications of being God's offspring. He reasons that if human beings were created by God, God cannot be a material object made of gold or silver or stone (v. 29).

Paul is cleverly building an argument, as one might build a house. He lays down the essential truths first and then adds stone upon stone to build his case. His logic is convincing. In a context where he is surrounded

---

24. Thom, "Stoicism," *Dictionary of New Testament Background*, 1140.

by idols, Paul argues that since human beings are the offspring of God, idolatry is ridiculous.

This is where Paul's assumptions about the nature of knowledge tie his entire argument together and bring it to a resounding close. Paul's basic assumption about knowledge is that the basis for all knowledge is God's revelation. This revelation may be general revelation, which is seen in the world around us, or special revelation, which God gives through his Word and, even more importantly, through his Son, Jesus Christ, who lived in this physical world, died, and was resurrected from the dead. Paul regards all truth as being from God. For Paul, faith and reason should be understood as complementary and must be used together to form a cohesive worldview.

Although the narrator does not allow us to see behind the text by telling us about Paul's hearers' assumptions regarding knowledge, Paul was clearly aware of these assumptions. As far as Epicureans were concerned, knowledge was purely empirical and observation was viewed as the basis of all reason. This is like the scientific approach today. They believed that the physical senses were sufficient to provide accurate information. If someone was misled about reality, the fault lay with the individual.[25] Stoics, too, believed that knowledge was gained empirically through the mind. Reason was a crucial tool in making decisions that would lead to a virtuous life.

What is the logical conclusion to Paul's argument? He declares that human beings have now moved beyond ignorance and received God's true revelation of himself (vv. 30, 31; see also Rom 3:25). The knowledge they have been given is not merely intellectual knowledge about God but "involves moral and religious responsibilities, and for lack of this knowledge, in the measure in which it was accessible to them, the hearers are summoned to repentance."[26] This revelation must lead to action – specifically to repentance since ignorance is no longer excusable.

Paul refers to his hearers' own context as he builds his case, thus ensuring that he has an audience that is receptive to his message and more likely to internalize it.

---

25. Kenny, *Illustrated Brief History*, 94.
26. Bruce, *Acts*, 341.

Putting it all together

Bringing in the gospel, which in itself demands a knowledge beyond the intellectual, Paul concludes by providing the reason behind his appeal to his hearers to repent. Judgement is coming. Paul declares the gospel message in the last few words of his speech, pointing out that God has appointed Jesus Christ as judge. The proof of this is Jesus's resurrection from the dead.

With the re-introduction of "resurrection," the narrator takes us back to the thought in verse 18. There Paul began by preaching the good news about Jesus and the resurrection. He now links the resurrected Christ with the sovereign God. Paul shows that what he has been talking about is not a new deity, but one approved by God. Having heard the message that idolatry is not reasonable, the decision is now theirs. Will they choose to act on what they have heard by starting to worship the true God, one who is not made out of gold or silver or stone, a product of human imagination? Or will they ignore Paul's message?

Outcome

The Epicureans believed that the soul was material and disintegrated at death,[27] so that there was no need for people to fear death or even the prospect of judgement. The Stoics, too, did not believe that souls were immortal. They believed that souls would only exist until the destruction of the universe. Thereafter souls would either be destroyed or absorbed into the divine essence.[28]

Given this background, it is not surprising that some of Paul's hearers find the idea of the resurrection unbelievable, even ridiculous. They decide not to listen to Paul any further (v. 32). It is likely that the Epicureans, given their assumptions about life after death, would have been in this group. However, others (the Stoics?), perhaps convinced by the logic of Paul's argument but not ready to do anything practical about it yet, want to hear more.[29]

Paul leaves them. However, his interaction with them is not in vain for in this very crowd God finds men and women who choose to put their

---

27. Diogenes Laertius, 10.124–5. Translation from the Loeb Classical Library.
28. N. Clayton Croy, *Hellenistic Philosophies and the Preaching of the Resurrection* (Acts 17:18, 32), *Novum Testamentum* 39 (1997): 32–36.
29. Croy, *Hellenistic Philosophies*, 38.

faith in him. The narrator specifically mentions Dionysius the Areopagite and a woman named Damaris.

When Paul debated with those who disagreed with him, he stepped into their world and based his argument on assumptions that allowed him to engage with their culture and worldview. In so doing he shows how knowing the background of those you are addressing can be used to construct a vital bridge when interpreting and communicating the biblical message.

What Next?

One assumption we have to make as we approach any passage in the Bible is that it is understandable and that its message can be proclaimed in a way that links to our culture and worldview, as Paul has demonstrated. Our task is to provide a means by which the biblical text can be read with understanding by the millions of Africans who live within the continent of Africa or in diaspora in the rest of the world.

A number of books have already been written on issues that relate to contextualization in Africa. For instance, Loba-Mkole and Wendland's *Interacting with Scriptures in Africa* focuses on Bible translation and contextual application of biblical concepts. It raises our awareness of some of the hermeneutical issues that arise in interpreting Scripture in an African context. They have this to say about their work: "It is hoped then that these diverse studies will serve to illustrate something of the considerable range and diversity that Bible translation in Africa manifests nowadays with regard to communicative technique, and *local, contextualized application*" (emphasis mine).[30] Their book therefore intersects with this work in a significant manner as it addresses some of the contextual questions that relate to developing an African hermeneutic.

There are a number of different approaches to hermeneutics. As long as the methods we use are based on sound principles, hermeneutical diversity should be embraced. In the West, it has greatly enhanced our understanding of the biblical text. For instance, where the grammatical-

---

30. Jean-Claude Loba-Mkole and Ernst R. Wendland, eds., *Interacting with Scriptures in Africa* (Nairobi: Acton Publishers, 2005), vii.

historical method has proved deficient, the narrative critical approach has provided answers. Diversity in method is not the problem; the problem lies with any failure to incorporate sound and consistent hermeneutical principles.

It is hoped that a contextualized approach will not only bring about a better understanding of the Scriptures in Africa but will also preserve the integrity of Christianity in Africa. As early as 1974, Kato warned against the growing syncretistic trend in Africa and reminded us of the supremacy of Christianity over all world cultures:

> Christianity stands to judge every culture, destroying elements that are incompatible with the Word of God, employing compatible modes of expression for its advance, and bringing new life to its adherents, the qualitative life that begins at the moment of conversion and culminates eternally with the imminent return of our Lord Jesus Christ.[31]

This concern lies at the heart of this book. It is possible to achieve understanding without corrupting the biblical message. This point is important, for several authors have written on the need to reclaim the Bible from missionary and colonial influences and attempt to read it from an African perspective or even to "decolonize" it. That is not the focus of this book. Neither is this book an in-depth analysis of African literature, whether oral or written. What this book does is attempt to provide a way for us as Africans to faithfully interpret the text of Scripture. Note that this goal does not in any way minimize the fact that much work has been done to lay a foundation for *why* this is necessary.

In writing this book, I have drawn on the literature of post-colonial East Africa, which in turn draws extensively from a prior oral tradition. It is important to recognize that African literature is not uniform but reflects the varied national and ethnic cultures within the continent. Nevertheless, there are certain aspects of African literature that reflect a similarity of character, thus making this book possible.

Finally, let me reassert that my approach is based on the principle of moving from the known to the unknown. As African readers of the biblical text, we must discover our cultures and worldview and apply them

---
31. Kato, "Contextualization," 29.

in our hermeneutics. When we do this, we are more likely to associate with, understand and internalize the biblical content and overcome the dichotomy I referred to at the start of this chapter. The ultimate goal is that we acquire a biblical worldview that guides us in our day-to-day living.

The next two chapters will provide a discussion of culture and worldview as a foundation for the intercultural hermeneutical model proposed in this book.

2

THE AFRICAN WORLDVIEW: THEOLOGICAL ASPECTS

When I was ten years old, my school class had to memorize a poem called "The Blind Men and the Elephant."[1] I remember being baffled by the idea of six blind men trying to "see" an elephant. I was even more perturbed as the poem unfolded, trying to identify with the experience of each of these men as they touched different parts of the beast and came to their own conclusions about its form. I thought them somewhat silly, since I, in my wisdom, knew exactly what an elephant looked like. After all, I had grown up in an environment where they were quite common. I remember giggling as one concluded, on touching its trunk, that the elephant was like a snake; and yet another, falling against its broad side, immediately concluded that it resembled a wall. Imagine my amazement when still another, touching its sturdy legs, insisted that it must be like a tree! And on it went, each of them voicing his opinion and indulging in an increasingly angry dispute. As the poem came to an end, I was forced to conclude with the poet that although all of them were partly right, they were all wrong. So powerfully did this poem impact me that I remember feeling saddened by it. While I had the whole picture, they did not and I had no way of sharing what I knew with them.

Because of our different worldviews, we all see things in different ways. This is true not just as regards elephants but also as regards the way we read the Bible. We all approach it from different perspectives.

---

1. John Godfrey Saxe, *The Poems of John Godfrey Saxe* (Boston: James R. Osgood & Co., 1873), 259.

Just as the blind men were confused by their different perceptions of the elephant, so we in Africa end up confused when we are fed a diet of Western perspectives on the biblical text. This confusion is compounded when we have been fed this perspective for so long that we no longer recognize that it is out of touch with the way we live. The result is the dichotomized life spoken of in the previous chapter.

In this chapter, we will look at the whole idea of what a worldview is and will examine some of the primary characteristics of an African worldview. It is important to do this because it will help us begin to recognize our own worldviews and start thinking about which aspects of our own worldviews are truly biblical and which are not. This self-examination will help us understand how worldview influences how we interpret the Scriptures.

What Is a Worldview?

None of us has a neutral perspective on life or the Bible. We all operate on the basis of certain assumptions that we can refer to as our worldview. A worldview can be defined as a set of beliefs and values that guide one's thinking about all of life. Wolters defines it as "the comprehensive framework of one's basic beliefs about things."[2] But this definition is too limited because it focuses only on our minds and what we consciously believe. It misses out on other aspects of who we are.

Some people try to use metaphors to explain what a worldview is. For example, they say that a worldview is like a set of glasses (or contact lenses) through which we view life. Each person is wearing their own glasses, and hence each of us sees life differently. Helpful as this metaphor is, it is inadequate because it implies that our worldview is something outside of us, something we can put on and take off. Yet as Sire notes, "There will be no time during the day or night, not even in my dreams, when my worldview will not be an integral part of who I am."[3]

Sire then offers a more holistic definition of a worldview, one that encompasses the whole person:

---

2. Albert M. Wolters, *Creation Regained: Biblical Basics for a Reformational Worldview* (Grand Rapids: Eerdmans, 2005), 2.
3. James W. Sire, *Naming the Elephant* (Downers Grove: InterVarsity Press, 2004), 108.

> A worldview is a commitment, a fundamental orientation of the heart, that can be expressed in a story or in a set of assumptions (which may be true, partially true or entirely false) which we hold (consciously or subconsciously, consistently or inconsistently) about the basic constitution of reality, *and that provides the foundation on which we live and move and have our being*.[4]

The question of whether we should want to have a worldview is irrelevant since everyone, whether they know it or not, has a worldview. Moreover, our worldviews are dynamic and are constantly changing in response to internal influences and the data we receive as we interact with our environment.

Christians, obviously, seek to have a biblical worldview. But what does this mean in practice? Many people fall into the trap of believing that just because they know the contents of their Bible and can quote Scripture and discuss theology, their approach to life and their day-to-day living is biblical, when in fact their lives are secular or rooted in spiritual beliefs that are part of their culture. They know the Bible, but their interpretation of it is based on unbiblical assumptions.

In order to have a truly biblical worldview, believers need to ground their entire orientation to life in a cohesive biblical base, based on biblical assumptions. Their worldview must be informed and shaped by biblical beliefs and values. In addition, it must be consistent with the entire story of the Bible from Genesis to Revelation, that is, with the biblical metanarrative. We can draw on Sire's definition, quoted above, to draft a definition of a biblical worldview that is holistic and an integral part of the self:

> A biblical worldview is the orientation of the self to all of life that is the foundation of the expression of our identities as redeemed human beings in relationship with God, others and the world. This expression of identity is primarily embodied through behaviour and is consistent with the biblical message in all its aspects.

---

4. Sire, *Naming the Elephant*, 122. Emphasis added.

Is a Worldview Individual or Communal?

The metaphor of a worldview as a set of glasses can be taken as implying that a worldview is unique to each individual. To some extent this is true, for individuals have beliefs and values that are uniquely theirs. However, worldviews also have a communal character because communities hold things in common. In Africa, the communal aspect of our worldview receives more emphasis because we tend to emphasize "us" rather than "me."

It is important to remember that our worldview is formed within the context of our cultural setting and is therefore the sum total of our interaction with certain elements of culture. All too often, people are not aware of the deep influence culture has on how they perceive and live their lives. Here we are using the word "culture" to refer to all the values and social mores of a society, as well as all the learned patterns of behaviour that make that particular society unique. Because culture influences the formation of one's worldview, it plays a role in determining one's ability to be aware of, understand and interpret all of life.

Most people in Africa today do not grow up in a single culture. Modernization, urbanization and globalization mean that people from a number of cultures live in close proximity to one another. Moreover, the effects of television, movies and the Internet mean that we are also exposed to distant cultures. The result is that our culture is shaped by influences from many sources, ranging from the traditional to the modern. In the next couple of chapters as we look at aspects of the African worldview, we will acknowledge the role of culture in both its traditional and modern embodiments.

Since we live within the context of our culture and cannot realistically remove ourselves from it, there is a mutually reinforcing relationship between our culture's worldview (with its underlying assumptions) and our interpretation. As Seto points out,

> Since cognitive structures such as language, symbols, thought patterns and worldviews are all culturally determined, people

cannot perceive, understand and apply truths apart from culture. Thus, eternal truths and cultural truths are inevitably linked.[5]

Because the fingerprints of culture are evident in every worldview, we cannot afford to ignore the effect of culture in biblical and theological interpretation.

Is There an African Worldview?

Some people question whether it is right to speak of an African worldview, given the variety of cultures and ethnic groups in this vast continent. The question is a valid one, for there are numerous African worldviews. However, I would argue that certain underlying commonalities make it possible to examine the African worldview as a single entity. So in this chapter and the next we will focus on key elements of the African worldview and how these compare to the biblical worldview, and the implications of these similarities for how we interpret Scripture. We will start by looking at the more theological aspects of our African worldview.

Ultimate Reality

The first essential element in any worldview concerns the nature of ultimate reality: What functions as god in the lives of individuals and communities? Is it a spirit that prefers to remain aloof? Is it the ancestors? Or perhaps science and matter? Could it be an impersonal spiritual force? Or even a personal being who reveals himself to us? Our understanding of ultimate reality forms the foundation for our lives and defines the path that our worldview takes.

Traditional understandings of ultimate reality
Every culture in the world has some concept of an ultimate reality. However, each culture understands it differently. In the African context, ultimate reality is defined as the Supreme Being. As is characteristic of

---
5. See Wing-Luk Seto, "An Asian Looks at Contextualization and Developing Ethnotheologies," *Evangelical Missions Quarterly* 23 (April 1987): 138.

African thinking, this concept of God is holistic. In other words, it "does not exist in isolation from other beliefs. . . . All are part of the same spiritual fabric."[6] There is no need to prove God's existence. This Supreme Being is assumed to be present everywhere in the sense that people can call on him for help wherever they are.[7]

The above paragraph is, of course, a generalization. While such an understanding is held in common, details about the nature of the Supreme Being differ from place to place and from culture to culture. Because of this, it is sometimes difficult for us to grasp the idea of one universal God that Africans can hold in common.[8]

How does this African worldview compare with the biblical worldview? There are similarities in that the biblical worldview also assumes the existence of a Supreme Being and sees no need to prove his existence. This we see from texts like Genesis 1:1: "In the beginning, God created the heavens and the earth." However, while the biblical worldview agrees with the African one that God is present everywhere, the God described in the Bible differs from the African one in that he is described in consistent terms in both the Old and the New Testaments. The biblical God is one (Deut 6:4–5) but he is also complex, a complexity that we understand in terms of the Trinity of the Father, Son and Holy Spirit (Matt 28:18–20).[9] God is the creator and the one who provides salvation for all. Summing up God's qualities, Nash says that he is "eternal, transcendent, spiritual (that is, non-material), omnipotent, omniscient, omnibenevolent, loving and personal."[10] While some of these characteristics may also describe the Supreme Being in the African worldview, the God of the Bible is clearly superior.

A crucial aspect of worldview is the understanding in some African cultures that the Supreme Being cannot be properly known because he is too far away. This concept is technically referred to as God's

---

6. Yusufu Turaki, *Foundations of African Traditional Religion and Worldview* (Nairobi: WordAlive, 2006), 54.
7. Richard J. Gehman, *African Traditional Religion in Biblical Perspective* (Kijabe, Kenya: Kesho Publication, 1989), 190.
8. Keith B. Anderson, *Introductory Course on African Traditional Religion* (Nairobi: Provincial Board of Theological Education, Church of the Province of Kenya, 1986), 138.
9. Graham A. Cole, "God, Doctrine of," *Dictionary for Theological Interpretation of the Bible*, 260.
10. Ronald N. Nash, *Worldviews in Conflict: Choosing Christianity in a World of Ideas* (Grand Rapids: Zondervan, 1992), 36.

transcendence. The consequence of this belief is that the Supreme Being is viewed as "remote from the everyday life of a traditional African."[11] However, God's transcendence must be understood in light of African holism and not as God isolating himself from his creation. Holism is the belief that life is interdependent and integrated and is governed by a law of harmony.[12] The Supreme Being is thought to assign duties and responsibilities to lesser spirit beings, gods, and divinities who then interact directly with humanity.

Some African cultures, on the other hand, believe that God is both far and near. This nearness is known as God's immanence. Because he is immanent, God is interested in and concerned with the affairs of humankind and can be known through worship. He can also make his will known, sometimes through the ancestors who "would be offended if any member of the community failed to conduct his life according to the will of God."[13]

When we look at the biblical worldview, we see that it too affirms the transcendence and immanence of God. God desires a relationship with his creation, but any such relationship is based on the understanding that he is both separate from creation and present within it. In certain passages, particularly in the Old Testament, it may appear that God is just as remote from daily life as in the African worldview. However, this perception is wrong. Scripture affirms that God is personal and has intentionally chosen to reveal himself to human beings in ways that we can understand (see, for example, Ps 19:1). It provides many examples of God's desire to be close to us, including the theophanies through which he revealed himself in the Old Testament, his direct communication with some individuals through dreams and visions, and the coming of Jesus Christ the Saviour in human form – all these examples dispel the notion that God is remote.

Returning to the African worldview, Africans believe that they can approach the Supreme Being, particularly in times of need. However, this can only be done in the context of community. Worship, like everything else in life, is a communal affair. This means that horizontal relationships

---

11. Turaki, *Foundations*, 29.
12. Turaki, 32–33.
13. J. N. K. Mugambi, *African Heritage and Contemporary Christianity* (Nairobi: Longman Kenya, 1989), 62.

with other people have to be established before a vertical relationship with the Supreme Being becomes possible. Sacrifices, offerings, prayers and supplication are also essential when approaching the Supreme Being. Consequently, although a traditional African could approach the Supreme Being on his or her own, there was no point in doing so. The Supreme Being would not listen without sacrifices of "clean" animals offered by intermediaries such as priests, elders or the ancestors.[14]

It is also important to understand that traditional African interactions with the Supreme Being are transactional as opposed to relational. There was a belief that if one lived wisely in the present, one would reap positive benefits in the future. On the other hand, unwise living resulted in certain punishment. As Gehman puts it, "the worship of God was utilitarian, seeking God for the help they might receive, rather than extolling the greatness and goodness of God."[15] Traditional African worship therefore focused not on God but on human needs and desires. This is one reason why the prosperity gospel has taken root in Africa. It presents a familiar way of relating to God.

How does this African worldview compare with the biblical worldview? The crucial difference is that the biblical worldview affirms that God, not human beings, is the centre of his universe. He demands worship from us. The biblical worldview encourages personal interaction with God, albeit through the mediation first of priests in the Old Testament and then of Jesus Christ in the New Testament. Moreover, although communal worship is a feature of the biblical worldview, there are many instances in Scripture, particularly in the New Testament, of individuals approaching God on their own.

As in the African worldview, intermediaries such as priests and a sacrificial system were key features of the religious system God put in place for his people. Sacrifices were offered only by particular people and served many purposes – to cleanse, to seek forgiveness, to seal a contract (particularly between God and an individual) and so forth. As we read throughout the Old Testament, and even in the New Testament, "without the shedding of blood, there is no forgiveness of sin" (Heb 9:22).[16] As Yarbrough points out, "Sacrifice as nothing more than a ritual

---
14. Jomo Kenyatta, *Facing Mount Kenya* (Nairobi: Kenway Publication, 1938, repr. 2002), 243–252.
15. Gehman, *African Traditional Religion*, 193.
16. Although grain sacrifices were also acceptable in certain contexts.

act did not excuse transgression. Rather it was to be the expression of a contrite heart, and appealed to God for the mercy that he, and he only, could provide."[17]

There is also a crucial difference between the biblical and the African worldview regarding the need for sacrifices. In the New Testament, a once-for-all sacrifice is provided in Jesus Christ. Consequently, approaching God personally is possible through his work of mediation.

Ultimate reality in modern Africa

What is the current situation in Africa? With the coming of Christianity, much confusion arose as to how we were to relate to the Christian God. There were several barriers. These included a foreign language that needed to be translated, the race of Jesus Christ which brought confusion because it appeared to match the race of the colonizers, and the foreign and confusing worldview of the missionaries that left us with "two gods," Jesus Christ and God.[18] Despite these barriers, Christianity has taken root in Africa. This is probably because the African understanding of the Supreme Being and other spiritual entities has many similarities with the biblical understanding. It provides a common point of reference since our spiritual orientation makes it easy for us to understand spiritual realities. Once we understand the nature and character of the Christian God, putting our faith in him is not difficult.

But traces of the traditional African worldview can still be seen. While many of us have a firm belief in God, our interactions with him may shift between transactional and relational. In most cases, the transactional element is more prominent. As modern African Christians, we frequently find ourselves doing good things so that God will reward us. The growing tentacles of prosperity theology have fuelled this perspective, so that prayers frequently consist of asking God for yet more "blessings," which translates to material things. When we are aware that we have sinned, we respond in a vastly different way – we wait apprehensively for punishment. Indeed, as we will see later, almost all suffering is viewed as a punishment from God. Moreover, in modern African Christianity, the balance between transcendence and immanence is sometimes lost. It is

---

17. Robert W. Yarbrough, "Atonement," *New Dictionary of Biblical Theology*, 390.
18. N. Onwu, "The Hermeneutical Model: The Dilemma of the African Theologian," *Africa Theological Journal* 14, no. 3 (1985):145–160.

all too easy for many of us to keep God at a distance from our everyday lives and only seek him during times of crisis.

While there is definite growth in the number of Christians in Africa, there is an increasingly troubling trend that is rooted in our utilitarian attitude to the Supreme Being. We are trying to hold on to two worldviews. We think that Christianity is good in so far as it works, but other methods of achieving our goals are also valid. If God is taking too long to bless my business or grow my church, then perhaps the witchdoctor can provide the solution. This mixing of traditional religious beliefs and practices with Christianity is known as syncretism.

Africa is also witnessing a growing secularism, that is, the belief that there is no religious or spiritual basis for life. A number of young people who have been disappointed with the church have chosen to walk away and become either agnostic (claiming that we cannot know whether God exists) or atheistic (asserting that God does not exist).[19]

Implications for hermeneutics

How does our African understanding of ultimate reality affect how we interpret Scripture? Let's look at Genesis 1:1:

> In the beginning God created the heavens and the earth.

Africans assume the existence of a Supreme Being, and so on one level we would read this text as saying that God exists and has existed from eternity past. This is a crucial point, particularly in this age of growing secularism where the existence of God is questioned at every turn.

At a second level, we would focus on the creativity of this eternal God. He alone is the creator of all things. The rest of Genesis 1 would confirm this initial interpretation. This is an important point of contact with African thinking, for many African myths deal with the creation of the world and humankind by a Supreme Being. While the identity of the God named in the text would have to be clearly defined to avoid syncretism, our African worldview works in a positive way to encourage an accurate understanding of this biblical text.

---

19. See Kevin Murithii Ndereba, "Youth Worldviews among the De-churched in Nairobi and Implications for Ministry" (Thesis, International Leadership University, Nairobi, Kenya, 2015).

On the other hand, our African worldview can also have a negative influence on our interpretation of a text. We can illustrate this from Luke 6:38:

> Give, and it will be given to you; good measure, pressed down, shaken together, running over, they will pour into your lap. For by your standard of measure it will be measured to you in return.

The traditional transactional understanding of our relationship with the Supreme Being has led many to interpret this verse as meaning that when you give monetary gifts, particularly in the form of tithes, offerings and gifts to the poor, God is obligated to bless you in return. We do not look for spiritual blessings but for financial rewards. The link to the prosperity gospel is clear. What we may fail to note is that interpreting the text this way leads us to give with the wrong motives – not because we love God and want to thank him for his faithfulness but because we want something back. Our giving becomes merely a transaction.

External Reality

If the first essential element in any worldview is the question of ultimate reality, the second relates to our understanding of external reality, of the world around us. Does the world consist only of what we can see with our eyes, or is there also a spiritual dimension? How did it come into being? Was it by chance or was there a creator who brought it into existence? Is there order in our world or are we living in the midst of chaos? How we view the world in which we live, whether or not our perception is accurate, determines how we choose to interact with it.

Traditional understandings of external reality

Many African cultures believe that the world was created by a Supreme Being, sometimes with the aid of some animal.[20] For instance, the Wapangwa of Tanzania believe that before the world was created, there

---

20. J. N. K. Mugambi, *African Christian Theology: An Introduction* (Nairobi: East African Educational Publishers, 1989), 127.

was only the wind, a tree and some white ants. Over these was the Word, which created everything. The ants defecated on a leaf of the tree, and as the pile of excrement grew, it hardened and formed what we now know as the world.[21]

The Bible, too, speaks of the creation of the world by God. But the world did not come into being by chance. Rather, God created it out of nothing and it had harmony, order and purpose (see Gen 1:31).

The traditional African worldview includes belief in a creator and in a host of impersonal powers and spirit beings, some of which are non-human while others are the spirits of the ancestors. These spirit beings can be ranked in order of importance. For those African groups that acknowledge divinities, these beings are thought to have created the world and rank directly below the Supreme Being, whom they serve. West Africans tend to have a large pantheon of divinities, but divinities are less common in Central, Eastern and Southern Africa (with the exception of certain kingdoms in Uganda).[22] Ancestral spirits (also known as the living dead) rank below divinities, as do nature spirits.

The Gikuyu (or Kikuyu[23]) of Kenya, for example, acknowledge two supernatural powers. The first and most important is the high god known as Ngai. He is the creator and giver of all things and works alone. He rewards human beings if they are good and punishes them when they are bad. The other powers are the ancestral spirits, who are not worshipped like Ngai. Rather, the Gikuyu live in communion with them, and ritual acts of communion bring back the memory and glory of their forefathers.[24]

Spirit beings are thought of as channels of the power delegated to them by higher beings. However, it is sometimes difficult to distinguish between the power possessed by the Supreme Being and that of lesser spirits.[25] The spirits are seen as good or evil, depending on whether they bring blessings or curses.[26] They are also considered to be more active and involved in people's daily lives than the Supreme Being. Specialists such

---

21. David Adams Leeming, *Creation Myths of the World: An Encyclopedia* (Santa Barbara, CA: ABC-CLIO LLC, 2010), 292.
22. Gehman, *African Traditional Religion*, 124.
23. Gikuyu and Kikuyu can be used interchangeably.
24. Gehman, *African Traditional Religion*, 265.
25. Turaki, *Foundations*, 65–66.
26. Turaki, 25.

as medicine men, rainmakers, mediums, diviners, sorcerers, magicians, witches and those with the ability to manipulate spirit beings serve as mediators between the human world and the spirit realm.[27]

The biblical worldview also affirms the presence of spirit beings, who are referred to as angels and demons. These spirit beings are affiliated either with God or with Satan and are associated with good and evil respectively. The activity of demons receives much attention, particularly in the gospels. All spirit beings, Satan included, are shown to be under the authority of God. The story of Job makes this quite clear. Without God's permission, Satan could not touch Job. However, unlike the African worldview, the biblical worldview does not include the presence and worship of ancestral spirits.

Numerous scholars have suggested that for Africans the world is a mono-sectional reality.[28] What this means is that Africans assume that God, the spirits, ancestors, human beings, and objects all inhabit one world. There is no separation of spiritual and physical reality – there is only one reality. Turaki refers to this belief as holism. Citing Steyne, he explains:

> This view of the world means that there are no clear boundaries between the physical and the spiritual dimensions of life. There is no clear distinction between secular and religious activities, between one's work and one's community responsibilities – they are "all knit together in a whole [so that man] feels at one with his world."[29]

This holism is associated with the law of harmony, which encourages living at peace with the physical and spirit world.

For traditional Africans, the spiritual realm is as real, if not more real, than the physical world in which they live. Given that they see no conflict between faith and nature, between the secular and the sacred, they assume that life's questions, particularly in times of crisis, generally have a spiritual answer.

---

27. Turaki, 26.
28. Mugambi, *African Heritage*, 78.
29. Turaki, *Foundations*, 32, citing P. M. Steyne, *Gods of Power: A Study of the Beliefs and Practices of Animists* (Houston: Touch Publications, 1989), 58.

How does this compare with the biblical worldview? There is a great deal of similarity. When we read the Bible, we realize that both physical and spiritual realities co-exist as part of God's created order. The presence of spirit beings is not questioned but is taken for granted. In addition, it is assumed that these spiritual beings are at work in the world around us. The spiritual realm is as much a reality as the physical one.

External reality in modern Africa

The introduction of Western education, especially in institutions of higher learning, has promoted a secular way of life that explains the world purely in physical terms. This has affected our understanding of the world. Many of us, especially those with higher education, have difficulty reconciling science and religion. Science gives a logical explanation for everything around us and does not consider the spiritual realm as being as real as the physical one. This orientation is completely opposite to the one we have known for generations. Because of our difficulty in reconciling these two ways of viewing the world, we live dichotomized lives, not allowing spiritual matters to interfere with physical matters and vice versa.

Despite this intrusion of a western worldview, the spiritual realm remains very real for most Africans today. Spiritual activity in our everyday lives is never doubted, and many of us have little problem recognizing the invisible dimension of our faith. A rationalistic explanation for the things that happen, particularly during times of crisis, is rarely the first option. The activity of angels and demons is a reality and many of us still believe in the power of witchcraft over our lives.

Establishing communication with the spirit world and even vying for power to control this unseen realm is common.[30] Since nature cannot be controlled, we cannot change our circumstances through our own power and must look for other options. Turaki draws out one implication of this for African Christianity:

> This view of the world as governed by a law of power creates a need for a theology of power if we are to address the traditional theological conception of power and also how this law of power operates in traditional Africa.[31]

---
30. Turaki, *Foundations*, 35.
31. Turaki, 35.

The focus on power offers at least one explanation for the blossoming of the more charismatic African Instituted Churches. They encourage believers to exercise power over the demonic realm through exorcisms and other rituals.

Implications for hermeneutics

How does our understanding of the nature of external reality affect our understanding of Scripture? We have noted that in African thought the spiritual realm is as much a reality as the physical one, if not more so. The presence (and sometimes the worship) of ancestral spirits remains a part of everyday life. It is not unusual to hear someone say jokingly, "Let's not forget the ancestors" as they pour out the dregs of their tea on the ground. Pouring a libation for one's ancestors was a part of everyday life and reinforced the belief that when one's ancestors died, they merely moved beyond a curtain while remaining part of the community. We can look at Hebrews 12:1 to see how this worldview influences interpretation.

> Therefore, since we are surrounded by such a great cloud of witnesses, let us throw off everything that hinders and the sin that so easily entangles. And let us run with perseverance the race marked out for us.

In Hebrews 11, the author holds up the heroes of faith as examples to the living. Who were these heroes? They were the long dead ancestors of the Israelites who were still remembered for their great acts of faith. In interpreting this text, some read it very literally. They claim that the ancestors who have died in the Lord are ever present witnesses, watching over believers in the realm of the living and cheering them on. Here our African worldview is working in a negative way since it undermines accurate biblical teaching about the afterlife. Physical death results in the separation of a person's body and soul/spirit. While the soul/spirit is destined to exist eternally, the body is not, and it decomposes after death (Gen 3:19). The dead await the judgement of God (Heb 9:27) – either to eternal life or punishment (Luke 16:22–26; Rev 20:13–15). In this state of death, a person is not aware of and cannot influence what is taking place on earth.

Human Relationships

How does an individual fit into the larger framework of their community? Should we view people as individuals or as members of a community? How should we understand human nature? Is a person simply a product of evolution or the intentional creation of God? What happens to us when we die? Do we join our ancestors and become objects of worship to those still living? These questions must be answered since our worldview has a deep impact on our interpersonal interactions.

Traditional understandings of relationships

Most African myths are in harmony with the biblical teaching that human beings were created by a Supreme Being. But that is often where the similarity ends. Whereas the African worldview put human beings at the centre, a biblical worldview puts God at the centre of life. The Bible tells us that human beings are made in the image of God. As the intentional creation of God, we are capable of thinking, feeling and forming relationships. We possess personality as well as creativity. However, soon after creation, human beings sinned. This event is known as the Fall. Because of the Fall, the image of God in human beings was damaged, although not destroyed. Because people possess the image of God, they are of worth. At the same time, because of the Fall, we all have a sinful nature and can therefore never be considered good. We need salvation (Rom 3:23). Because we were made for God, a desire for union with God is "part of the soul's standard equipment."[32]

How we view ourselves affects our thoughts and behaviour in relation to God, ourselves, and those around us. Yet questions about self are difficult to address in an African context given that we have traditionally believed that individuals exist only because others exist.[33] This belief is known as *ubuntu* and is difficult to define. However, its most basic expression – "I am because we are, and since we are, therefore I am" – captures African communal solidarity. Archbishop Desmond Tutu describes it thus:

---

32. Plantinga, *Engaging God's World*, 6.
33. John S. Mbiti, *Introduction to African Religion* (New York: Praeger, 1975), 175.

> Ubuntu is . . . to say, "My humanity is caught up, is inextricably bound up, in what is yours." . . . We say, "A person is a person through other persons." It is not "I think, therefore I am." It says rather: "I am human because I belong. I participate, I share" . . . What dehumanizes you inexorably dehumanizes me.[34]

Ubuntu is a unifying worldview in that it captures the essence of what it is to be human for an African.

We are all aware that human beings can never exist in isolation but must live in relationship with others. But how these interpersonal relationships are expressed varies from person to person and from culture to culture. There are cultures that discourage individualism and promote the idea that people should act and think alike. On the other hand, there are cultures that emphasize individualism at the expense of the community. Given our understanding of *ubuntu*, it is clear that for Africans closeness tends to govern relationships. Indeed, the community plays a critical role and relationships are central in all interactions.[35] Consequently, the idea of personal freedom and autonomy without regard for the community was once unheard of.[36] What is important for us is not so much one's individual viewpoint but the overall health of the community as people learn to live together in harmony. An individualist is regarded with great suspicion. In some African cultures the word used for "individualists" emphasizes their selfishness and signifies that such people are likely to end up as witches or wizards![37]

What, then, best describes our African way of life? It is "existence-in-relationship."[38] In other words, individuals have been expected to maintain a balance in all their relationships. This is important because, as noted earlier, in the traditional African worldview, horizontal relationships had to be established before the vertical relationship with the Supreme Being and other divinities and spirits could take effect.

---

34. Desmond Tutu, *No Future Without Forgiveness* (New York: Doubleday, 1999), 31.
35. Samuel Waje Kunhiyop, *Foundations of African Christian Ethics* (Nairobi: HippoBooks, 2008), 68.
36. Mbiti, *Introduction*, 175.
37. Kenyatta, *Facing Mount Kenya*, 119.
38. Gehman, *African Traditional Religion*, 52. Originally coined by Swailem Sidhom and cited in Dickson, 1969, 102.

Because relationships were so important, our behaviour was guided by this framework of community.[39] It was a great offence to do something that led to the breakdown of harmony in the community. As Mugambi points out:

> The strong belief in the maintenance of the balance of relationships also implied that any action leading to the breakdown of harmony – between God and man, spirits and man, ancestors and man, and between man and man within the physically living community – was considered to be an offence against all those beings who formed this network of relationships.[40]

One had to be very careful not to offend other members of the community, and it was taken for granted that one put others first. Anything that broke the established customs and prohibitions of the family, clan or community constituted an offence.[41] Living a morally upright life as defined by the community was the honourable path. Violation of community standards led to shame and dishonour. All traditional African cultures were driven by honour and shame. An individual was expected to conform to the values and morals of the community.[42]

Within this network of relationships, the extended family system deserves special mention. It is the extended family, not the modern nuclear family of father, mother and children, that serves as the primary unifying factor in society. The extended family provides social support and fellowship not only between individuals but also between families, clans, and entire communities.[43] An extended family consists of all those related by blood – a man, his wife (or wives), their children, as well as their grandchildren and great-grandchildren. When an extended family became large, it evolved into a clan, which included all the individuals

---

39. Geoffrey Parrinder, *Religion in Africa* (Harmondsworth, UK: Penguin, 1969), 89.
40. Mugambi, *African Heritage*, 62.
41. Mbiti, *Introduction*, 175.
42. Constance Bansikiza, *Restoring Moral Formation in Africa* (Nairobi: AMECEA Gate Publications, n.d.), 13.
43. Daniel Bitrus, *The Extended Family: An African Christian Perspective* (Nairobi: Christian Learning Materials Centre, 2000), 1.

linked by their common descent from one family group.⁴⁴ The practice of polygamy greatly facilitated the development of clans.

This kind of community structure has tremendous benefits. It promotes healthy co-dependence and peaceful co-existence. It provides an efficient way of guiding all of life and organizing the community.⁴⁵ It ensures that one avoids offending either humans or spirits. For instance, we naturally give older people greater respect. Age is valued since it brings the wisdom necessary to keep the community going. Children learn to respect their elders at an early age. Any rude or disrespectful behaviour towards an older person is treated as a great offence. Those in positions of authority are also regarded with great respect.

Because of the belief in the importance of the community, communal effort in the daily tasks of life was taken for granted. The bringing up of children was a community effort, thus ensuring that childish pranks and indiscipline were kept to a minimum. All work was geared towards providing for the family as a unit. Accumulation of personal wealth for personal gain was unheard of. Moreover, when parents grew too old to participate in work activities, the children were duty bound to provide for them. From an early age, children learned the value of hard work. It was a part of our worldview that "parents shall not suffer want nor continue to labour strenuously in their old age while their children can lend a hand and do things to give them comfort."⁴⁶ Even when it came to work, relationships were central. Getting the work done was not as important as maintaining good relationships within the work context.

All these elements of the traditional African worldview are very similar to the biblical worldview. In the biblical worldview, family and community were very important. The family was held together by traditional concerns that included employment and the education and socialization of children. Particularly in the Old Testament, we see that this social structure provided not only a religious identity for the members of the community but also security and support for family members (see, for example, Deut 25:5–10).⁴⁷

---

44. Kenyatta, *Facing Mount Kenya*, 1.
45. Turaki, *Foundations*, 37.
46. Kenyatta, *Facing Mount Kenya*, 113.
47. John W. Drane, "Family," *New Dictionary of Biblical Theology*, 494.

While family is still a central feature in the New Testament, the teachings of Jesus suggest that the family of believers takes precedence over one's biological family. A biblical worldview sees believers as part of a great tradition moving towards the fulfilment of God's purpose for his church. When Jesus presents us with a metaphor of what the Christian family looks like, he compares himself to a vine and believers to branches of that vine (John 15). This reflects mutual benefit and interdependence. Relationships among Christian brothers and sisters are therefore to be honoured and protected. It is within this context of community that the Bible encourages believers to develop and express their individuality. While community is important in the New Testament, it must be balanced against individuality. First, it is only through a personal relationship with God through Jesus Christ that salvation is possible. Second, believers must strive to grow in personal spiritual maturity and to bear fruit. The role that individuality plays in both these contexts should not be undermined.

The question of our relationship to people extends to the afterlife. The African worldview holds that death is not final but is merely a transition into the unseen world. The extended family thus includes the ancestors, who continue to be a crucial part of the community and provide guidance when needed.

How does this compare with what the Bible tells us about the dead? The biblical worldview reflects two somewhat different perspectives in the Old and New Testaments. When you read certain statements (e.g. in Psalms, Job and Ecclesiastes), it almost appears that the Old Testament has a different understanding of the afterlife. It states that the dead will end up in the grave (also referred to as Sheol, a world very much like the underworld of the cultures of the Ancient Near East in that it is "a realm of sleepy, shadowy existence in the depths of the earth").[48] What does the New Testament teach? It teaches that when someone dies, their physical body is separated from their soul/spirit. However, because of the resurrection of Jesus Christ, all believers will experience a future resurrection and eternity with God. The wicked will be condemned to eternal punishment while the righteous will experience eternal life in the presence of God. In the biblical teaching, the dead are completely separate from the living.

---

48. Philip S. Johnston, "Death and Resurrection," *New Dictionary of Biblical Theology*, 444.

Relationships in modern Africa

While the community framework described above is still evident in many rural African communities, things are very different in urban Africa. People have flocked to the cities where they are now connected by cell phones and the Internet. The result has been a breakdown of the community structure and the growth of individualism. The extended family is losing its place as the principal organizing factor in society and no longer stands as the primary provider of social support. It has been replaced by smaller family units. Urban society is characterized by nuclear families, single parent families, and blended families (due to increasing divorce rates). Many do not have close ties with their extended families beyond their birth family and in-laws. More recently, it has become apparent that the younger generation is shifting its support system from the family unit to members of their social network. The increasing influence of social media has radically changed how relationships are defined. Yet many still feel some loose connection with members of their extended family.

As people from many cultures gather in urban centres, the tribal unit is also breaking down. This is not altogether a bad thing. Inter-tribal and inter-racial issues are no longer as prominent as they once were. Tribalism and negative ethnicity (i.e. negative perceptions of those from other ethnic groups) are decreasing. On the other hand, there has also been a decrease in cultural diversity. Many of us have almost no concept of our tribal origins and the customs and practices that our ancestors strove so hard to maintain.

Living in an increasingly individualistic environment has had an effect on many modern Africans. Many have become very selfish, elevating their individual needs and accomplishments above the needs of the community. An individualistic approach to life leads them to assume that what they do has no impact on those around them. While this may be true in the West (although this is debatable), modern Africans who decide to go their own way are at a disadvantage. The shift from a communitarian to an individualistic framework of societal organization is not yet complete, and individualism has no inbuilt support systems. There is no doubt that what we do influences those around us positively or negatively, and so we cannot completely disregard the community.

Even though Africans are becoming more individualistic, it is still difficult for us to think of ourselves in isolation. We recognize that we are part of a community of people forever linked by the blood that flows through our veins. Consequently, while individualism may prevail in some areas, the extended family and the community at large are still a part of the everyday life of most modern Africans. This is especially evident during times of celebration or mourning, or when there is financial need. At such times, most of us feel duty bound to contribute what we can, materially or otherwise. So although our ties with extended family and the larger community are not what they traditionally were, we still feel the need to meet with them occasionally and to reaffirm our common ancestry.

Implications for hermeneutics

In Africa, those who are older as well as those who have positions of authority in the community enjoy the respect of other members of the community. We place a high value on guarding our horizontal relationships with other people. No one wants to risk offending a member of the community. Traditionally, this would have meant that one had also offended the Supreme Being, the divinities (in certain contexts) and the spirits and ancestors, thus incurring their wrath. This worldview has a great deal of influence on how texts that appear to protect those in authority are interpreted. For instance, 1 Samuel 24:3–7 tells of how David spared Saul's life when Saul was plotting to kill him. Many African spiritual leaders place great emphasis on verses 6 and 7, where, after cutting off the edge of Saul's robe, David feels guilty and says to his men:

> "Far be it from me because of the LORD that I should do this thing to my lord, the LORD'S anointed, to stretch out my hand against him, since he is the LORD's anointed."
>
> And David persuaded his men with these words and did not allow them to rise up against Saul. And Saul arose, left the cave, and went on his way.

This text is usually used to protect the positions of men and women in authority, who are considered the "Lord's anointed." It is said that if David himself did not dare touch the Lord's anointed, who are we to question what bishops, apostles, and other church leaders are doing, no matter how bad?

We need to understand the background to David's words. In its historical context, David was simply recognizing that God himself had appointed Saul as king over Israel. Moreover, he had not received any directions from God allowing him to do whatever he liked with Saul. The words do not mean that we should never criticize spiritual leaders. When they are interpreted in that way, our African worldview is working in a negative way by promoting an interpretation that sustains oppression and poor leadership.

Questions for Review

1. In what specific ways do you see the communal aspects of worldview at work in your family, church or community? Identify the aspects that promote Christianity and those that hinder it.

2. In one or two paragraphs, identify your own worldview with regards to ultimate reality, external reality and relationships.

3. In what specific ways do these aspects of your worldview influence how you interpret and apply the Bible (either positively or negatively)? Cite specific texts.

3

THE AFRICAN WORLDVIEW: PHILOSOPHICAL ASPECTS

In the previous chapter, we examined elements of worldview related to fundamental theological beliefs. In this chapter, we will continue our discussion of worldview, looking at our fundamental philosophical beliefs regarding knowledge, morality, suffering, history/time, and art.

Knowledge

The question of whether we can "know" has troubled philosophers through the ages. Can what we know be confirmed? How do we know? What are our sources of knowledge? Can we trust them? Is there objective truth or is truth totally subjective, based on an individual's experience and interpretation? What is the place of reason and does it clash with faith? These types of questions are important because knowledge affects human life and therefore forms a part of every worldview. Different answers to questions about knowledge lead to different ways of viewing life.

Traditional understandings of knowledge

The transmission of knowledge in traditional African cultures focused first and foremost on the formation of character and the nurturing of traits such as integrity, honesty, respect and hard work. Such knowledge has always been acquired in the context of community, and thus personal relationships were given priority. Individuals first acquired knowledge within the family circle, then within the local group or clan, and finally in the context of the whole tribe. Religious specialists were another source of knowledge, for they were held to be capable of discerning the spiritual meaning of events through dreams, visions, vision quests, divinations or ordeals. Even today, medicine men and women, diviners, ritualists, and spiritists, "hold an important place and position in African society, for people go to them to inquire about their own destiny, fate and welfare and about the destiny and well-being of individuals, families, clans or tribes."[1]

This process of acquiring knowledge focused on life experiences in the community, beginning at birth and ending at death. The content included the oral literature of the community such as folk tales, proverbs, songs and dances, as well as instruction in practical tasks and through initiation rites. The homestead was the school, and learning experiences, both formal and informal, were geared towards applying knowledge to practical situations and moving the individual up the social ladder. This ladder related to the various stages of life through childhood, adolescence with its initiation rites, adulthood with its related responsibilities of marriage and childbearing, and finally old age and what this entailed within the community.

This understanding of knowledge has some similarities with the biblical worldview in that it assumes that knowledge is passed on in the home and community and that it serves a practical purpose. Knowledge must be applied to life. When this happens, an individual is wise and is acting with wisdom. The purpose of knowledge is to live a life that reflects wisdom.

The difference between the African worldview and the biblical worldview emerges when we consider a verse like Proverbs 1:7: "The fear of the LORD is the beginning of knowledge; fools despise wisdom and instruction." The Bible traces all knowledge back to God. Wisdom is always a divine gift and never the result of independent human effort.[2] Consequently, a biblical worldview emphasizes God's revelation to humankind. He has chosen to reveal himself in two ways. The first is general revelation, which is seen in the created world around us. The second is special revelation, which is through the Scriptures, and even more importantly through Jesus Christ.

---

1. Turaki, *Foundations*, 46.
2. Eckhard J. Schnabel, "Wisdom," *New Dictionary of Biblical Theology*, 847.

Because in the biblical worldview all truth comes from God, truth is objective. It cannot be whatever we make it to be. The basic assumption is also that the biblical records are reliable and understandable. Moreover, faith and reason are complementary, and so must be used together to come to an understanding of truth. What this means is that thinking logically through biblical truth is valid as long as we do not put faith aside.

Knowledge in modern Africa

When Africans were exposed to European systems of education in the nineteenth century, things started to change. An emphasis on formal education led to the establishment of missionary-initiated schools all over the continent. Formal education became a necessary qualification for employment. Those with a formal European education enjoyed higher social status, and illiteracy was considered a mark of inferiority. Consequently, the process of acquiring knowledge through oral or folk wisdom was despised.

Little regard was given to the African mode of life or worldview. Thus whereas in the past, education was regarded as an investment that would build character and ultimately benefit the entire community, in modern Africa education has become an individualistic activity that, more often than not, benefits only the recipient.

Implications for hermeneutics

In the African worldview, formal and informal learning were not ends in themselves. Learning had very specific goals and was geared towards the application of knowledge to practical situations. This practical aspect of knowledge acquisition shows itself in a very positive way in biblical interpretation. Look at James 1:27:

> This is pure and undefiled religion in the sight of our God and Father, to visit orphans and widows in their distress, and to keep oneself unstained by the world.

The text is clear. Genuine worship of God has practical results. James is not merely making a suggestion about what believers should try to do to live out their faith. Rather, he is identifying a practical outcome of our faith that must be followed to the letter. In this case, our African worldview is working in a positive way to help us apply biblical truth.

Morality

Morality refers to one's basic values and way of life. Questions about what is morally right and wrong are no longer easy to answer. People are asking whether morality is relative. In other words, can we do what we wish regardless of the impact on those around us? Are there some basic standards that are a part of every culture? How are right and wrong determined?

Clearly, everyone has some concept of right and wrong, and all societies have moral codes that lay down how individuals should live and the society should operate. However, these codes may vary in different cultures. In some cultures, morality may be based on societal values and expressed in rules that govern behaviour in various contexts, while other cultures may be more individualistic so that people decide on their own moral codes.

Traditional understandings of morality

Scholars have identified four laws governing traditional moral beliefs in Africa.[3] The first is the *law of harmony*: All things should work together in harmony in a world in which the spiritual and physical realms are interdependent. Where an action leads to a disruption of this cosmic harmony, it is viewed as morally wrong. The second is the *law of the Spirit*: As seen above in the traditional understanding of external reality, all of life is seen through a spiritual lens. One's goal in life is to find spiritual meaning in alignment with the impersonal powers and forces, spirit beings, divinities and gods that must be kept happy. Any action that does not lead to this goal is considered morally wrong. The third is the *law of power*: Human beings have a need to secure power because of the impersonal, unseen and unpredictable nature of the world. This power is acquired from spirit beings, and the higher the spirit being from whom one obtains power, the more powerful one is. One's morality is in question if one does not deal with one's problems through acquisition of such power. The final law is the *law of kinship*: Individuals are part of an interdependent community with common goals. Morality is judged by whether or not one maintains or disrupts communal harmony.

---

3. Summarized from Turaki, *Foundations*, 43–49.

These laws mean that moral formation in African traditional societies focused on values that made for harmony in the community, including respect for authority and reverence for supernatural beings. Thus morality was governed by the values, manners and customs of the community[4] and the agents in this process of moral formation included the family, various age groups, and the ancestors.

Given that the community plays such a central role in moral formation, some authors have suggested that Africans are so absorbed by the community that they do not "own" moral values. In other words, Africans have no sense of personal responsibility. This is not the case. Traditional Africans recognized that the development of right values is difficult if an individual is isolated from other people and the community. One needs interpersonal, social interactions in order to develop a healthy value system. However, individual moral formation is also encouraged and everyone is assumed to have a personal moral consciousness. As Bujo writes:

> When the African respects commands and prohibitions inherited from the ancestors, when he or she observes their rites, words and gestures taught by the forefather's tradition, this is not done blindly or automatically; the inherited norms rather put before the individual the choice of life or death, the decision for good or for evil, that is for strengthening or for diminishing the life of the community. The individual is always bound to reflect on what is beneficial to himself or herself and to the whole community.[5]

So although individuals are expected to act in solidarity with other members of the community, they are also required to reflect on the values and own them.

Given the practical bent of the African worldview, Africans emphasize the link between morality and behaviour. For instance, traditional rules and regulations governed sexual conduct between young people. Among the Gikuyu of Kenya, intimate contact between young unmarried people, referred to as platonic love and fondling, was encouraged so that the

---
4. Parrinder, *Religion*, 89.
5. Benezet Bujo, *African Christian Morality at the Age of Inculturation* (Nairobi: St. Paul Publications, 1990), 97.

normal sexual instinct would not be stunted.[6] However, actual sexual intercourse between individuals who were not married was considered taboo. This taboo was enforced by social sanctions.

Every society uses sanctions (i.e. rewards or punishment) to exercise control and encourage individuals to do what is right. In Africa, these sanctions took the form of the approval or disapproval of the community, including the ancestors who were also part of the social unit. In the case of sexual intercourse outside marriage, for example, failure to observe the taboo brought shame not only on the individuals but also on the entire family and clan. This sanction was so effective that sexual intercourse and pregnancies outside of marriage were rare.

There are many similarities between the African and the biblical worldviews in regard to morality. As in the community model described above, sin has consequences and believers are accountable to one another within the community of faith. We see this clearly demonstrated in the story of Adam and Eve and their expulsion from the garden of Eden (Gen 3). Communal accountability is reflected in Paul's words to the Galatians as he urges the community of faith to restore those caught in sin (Gal 6:1). Moreover, the honour–shame value system is also a part of the biblical worldview. Breaking any of God's laws was considered dishonourable and brought shame not just on the individual but also on the community, as the story of Achan demonstrates (Josh 7).

But there are also several significant differences. The most important is the basis for morality. Whereas African morality derives from community values, biblical morality is rooted in the unchanging character of God and his commandments. Consider the Ten Commandments (Exod 20:1–17). The first four emphasize our vertical relationship with God; the remaining six, our horizontal relationships with others. Another key example is found in Jesus's restatement of Deuteronomy 6:5. Jesus reveals that the greatest commandment is to love God with all one's heart, soul, mind and strength and then one's neighbour as oneself (Mark 12:30–31; see also Matt 22:37–40; Luke 10:27). The order shows that morality is not just about human relationships but begins with our relationship with God himself.

---

6. Kenyatta, *Facing Mount Kenya*, 155.

A second difference between traditional African morality and biblical morality has to do with the universally authoritative nature of biblical morality. If our morality is rooted in the character of God, which does not change, it follows that there must be universal moral principles or laws that "must apply to all humans, regardless of when or where they have lived. They must also be objective in the sense that their truth is independent of human preference and desire."[7]

God's ideal standard for morality is based on his will for all human beings, which is revealed throughout Scripture (Rom 2:12–16). All human beings, by virtue of being made in the image of God (Gen 1:26–27) have an innate knowledge of what is morally good and what is not and there can be no true morality without God. Thus, contrary to popular opinion, morality is not relative.

Morality in modern Africa

With modernization and globalization, our social and cultural environment is changing rapidly. These changes also affect our relationships, and since morality in Africa has been defined largely in terms of relationships, any change in this dynamic also affects our understanding of morality. Moral agents such as the extended family are no longer effective because of the shift in the definition of family in modern Africa. The nuclear family has increasingly become the principal organizing factor in society and the primary provider of social support. The sanctions of morality appear to have become almost useless. The growing individualism in the society has resulted in a disregard for the approval or disapproval of the community. Without a framework of communal responsibility, the means to test and nurture norms and values has been weakened.

These changes have led to conflicts between values, traditions, beliefs, and practices, resulting in problems at both community and individual levels. The following sentiment, expressed by Jomo Kenyatta as early as 1938, demonstrates the dilemma in which we Africans find ourselves in a modern world:

> Moral rules are broken with impunity, for in place of unified tribal morality, there is now, as anthropological readers will be well aware, a welter of disturbing influences, rules and sanctions,

---
7. Nash, *Worldviews*, 42.

whose net result is only that a Gikuyu does not know what he may or may not, ought or ought not, to do or believe, but which leaves him in no doubt at all about having broken the original morality of his people.[8]

It is confusing to live in this modern era. We know that values such as integrity, honesty, a good work ethic, kindness and generosity, politeness and respect should be embraced and practised from a very early age, and yet even in countries with a high percentage of Christians, corruption and impunity appear to have taken over.

Our exposure to people with different value systems from various parts of the continent and the world, as well as the influence of the Internet and the media, also present us with mixed signals that often contradict our traditional values. In our eagerness to adopt foreign values, we seldom pause to assess their worth. Moreover, we often fail to recognize that foreign cultures have their own sanctions that govern behaviour, and so we end up living as if there are no moral sanctions on behaviour.

The lack of appropriate models for the younger generation, as evidenced by the numerous scandals within the church involving corruption, pornography, adultery, and drug-related issues, has worsened the problem. Many of us have found ourselves compromising. For some of us, this causes discomfort because we instinctively sense that morality is not negotiable. It is almost as though we realize that going against our values will somehow upset the balance of relationships and bring punishment. For others, however, this does not appear to raise any internal conflict.

Implications for hermeneutics

How does this understanding of morality affect how we interpret Scripture? A Bible story we can easily relate to is that of Achan, an Israelite who sinned by taking forbidden items from an enemy camp. As a result, Israel began to be defeated in battle. Under strict instructions from God, Joshua investigated who had brought this trouble on them. Achan's sin was discovered and severely punished:

---

8. Kenyatta, *Facing Mount Kenya,* 155.

> Then Joshua and all Israel with him, took Achan the son of Zerah, the silver, the mantle, the bar of gold, his sons, his daughters, his oxen, his donkeys, his sheep, his tent and all that belonged to him; and they brought them up to the valley of Achor. And Joshua said, "Why have you troubled us? The LORD will trouble you this day." And all Israel stoned them with stones; and they burned them with fire after they had stoned them with stones. (Josh 7:24–25)

The outcome does not really surprise us as African readers. First, as noted above, morality is never theoretical but always practical, so we know that Achan is in the wrong. Second, the failure to uphold moral values always upsets the balance of relationships and results in punishment. So, as we follow the story, we know that Achan's action will not escape notice. And finally, even though the communal framework in our communities is not as strong as it used to be, communal responsibility for offences is still very evident in some societies. The shame of one person in the community is the shame of all, and therefore communal punishment is not surprising. In this instance, our worldview has a positive effect as it helps us step into the cultural and historical context of the Bible so that we are able to read the text without negative judgement.

Suffering

Why does God allow suffering? Why do bad things happen to good people? Is God in control during times of suffering? Is he perhaps a cruel God who enjoys watching people suffer? These are questions that are often asked, and for which we have few satisfactory answers. Our understanding of ultimate reality and our worldview determine how we respond to suffering and hardship, and whether suffering leads to a crisis of faith.

Traditional understandings of suffering

In the traditional African context, suffering must be understood through the lens of relationships. If there is suffering in a community, some relationship must have broken down. In this worldview, offending anyone within the circle of relationships automatically offends the Supreme Being, arousing his anger and drawing punishment. For instance, angering the ancestors by doing or saying things that caused a rift in the family or community was bound to result in swift judgement in the form of disease or some natural catastrophe. So when misfortune came, the community would turn to diviners to find out who had offended God, the spirits, or the ancestors.[9]

Natural disasters such as famine, drought, floods and so forth, were regarded as direct punishment by the Supreme Being. The correct response was to offer sacrifices and prayers to obtain his blessing in the form of rain and a good harvest, or in ending the flooding. As Mbiti points out:

> National calamities such as drought, epidemics, locust invasions, wars and floods are beyond individual human cause or control. They are generally attributed to God's activity, or to a spiritual being. If God is thought to be responsible, it is often taken that He is punishing people for their mischief.[10]

Illnesses and accidents were also generally believed to have a spiritual and not a physical cause. They were seen as punishments for moral offences.

However, not all traditional African societies have the same understanding of suffering. Among the Akamba of Kenya, for example, suffering is attributed to witchcraft and not the Supreme Being.[11] Other cultures never associate the Supreme Being with evil since he is completely good. Evil is therefore associated with lesser divinities, spirits, and witches or sorcerers. Consequently, "death, lightning strikes, sickness, miscarriages, suffering and all other human misery are the direct work of these malevolent spirits, with whom some human beings may be in league."[12]

The retribution theology that shapes African thinking on suffering is similar to that seen in the biblical books from Deuteronomy to Kings. The general theme in these books is that sin results in punishment, and

---

9. Mugambi, *African Heritage*, 62.
10. John S. Mbiti, *African Religions and Philosophy* (Nairobi: East African Educational Publishers, 1969, repr. 1992), 44.
11. Gehman, *African Traditional Religion*, 80.
12. Kunhiyop, *Foundations*, 17.

repentance leads to reward. For instance, Deuteronomy 28 presents a stark choice between living in obedience and so enjoying blessing/life, or living in disobedience and enduring a curse/death. However, it is a mistake to read this chapter as a mechanistic application of punishment. Instead, what this chapter and the rest of these books portray is a relationship with the living God.[13] So what is actually common to the African and biblical worldviews is their stress on the importance of relationships, not the element of retribution. Thus the Bible makes it clear that suffering is not always a consequence of sin. The story of Job and of the man born blind (John 9) illustrate this truth. While we cannot always explain suffering, we can know that God is always in control and that suffering is part of his greater purpose.

Suffering in modern Africa

Poverty, conflict, disease, oppression – these are all familiar to modern Africans. Many of us now take suffering for granted, recognizing that it is simply a part of life. Yet retribution theology continues to define our responses to it. Many still believe that suffering is a punishment for displeasing God, and so our first response when suffering comes is to examine our lives for sinful attitudes or behaviour. This response may also reflect our transactional approach to religion. We do not interpret our experience in the context of a relationship but solely in terms of sin and punishment.

Undeserved suffering is sometimes viewed as an attack by evil spirits, set upon us by witchcraft. Consequently some Christians choose to consult witchdoctors to counter the attack, rather than relying on God. This belief is related to the law of power discussed in the section on morality. People urgently seek power in order to manipulate the spirit realm and thereby gain control over their lives.

Implications for hermeneutics

Our understanding of suffering as retribution greatly influences how we read the Bible. When we come to the book of Job, for example, we can understand the perspective of Job's friends who maintain that he must have sinned, because a good person always prospers while a wicked person

---

13. Mary J. Evans, "Blessing/curse," *New Dictionary of Biblical Theology*, 399.

suffers. So they argued that Job needed to seek God and commit himself to him. Then he would enjoy the traditional blessings of peace, prosperity, a large family, and a long life (5:8–27). But the book of Job challenges this assumption and forces us to think more deeply about the suffering of righteous or innocent people and the justice and love of God amidst what appears to be unfair treatment.

In this case, our traditional worldview works both positively and negatively. It helps us to understand the thought world of Job's friends, but it may make us less likely to accept the biblical truth that God sometimes allows us to go through suffering for his own reasons.

History and Time

Because we live in time, it is important that we try to understand our relationship to it. We are full of questions. What is time? Is the past important, or are we simply living for the future? Are we moving forward in time, or is life a cycle that endlessly repeats itself? And how is God involved with time in this world? Does he have his hand on human history or are we simply going through meaningless motions as we move forward in time? And how does our understanding of time influence how we live?

Traditional understandings of history and time

The traditional African understanding of time differs from the Western understanding of time. This has caused many misunderstandings. Westerners have even complained that Africans have no concept of time, but this is not the case. Time for us is not a matter of "chronometric exactitude," neatly segmented into hours, seconds and minutes.[14] So when scheduling an event, we focus on the event itself rather than on its exact duration. The social interactions that occur because of the event are seen as more important than when exactly the event starts and ends. As in all things African, what is most important is the building of relationships.

This understanding of time is similar to the biblical understanding of time. In the Bible, the word "day" is used to refer not only to a twenty-four-hour period but also to an event, place or person associated with

---

14. Mugambi, *African Heritage*, 79.

some stretch of time. For example, the prophets often spoke of "the day of the LORD." When referring to prolonged periods of time in the past or the future, the Bible uses vague terms such as "for a long time" or "eternity."[15]

When it comes to understanding the relationship of the past, present and future, some traditional African thought is two-dimensional: it acknowledges a long past and a present, but no future.[16] For others, the future exists but is merely a continuation of the present, so that it can be referred to as the potential present.[17] The Western concept of time as linear, with an indefinite past, a present, and an indefinite future does not exist in traditional African thought.

How then are the past, the present and the future related? The past is by far the most important, for present circumstances can always be explained by looking to the past. The cause of every calamity lies in an individual's past – nothing happens without a reason. Consequently we lean heavily on tradition. Our oral traditions use mistakes in the past to teach us how to live in the present.

At the same time, fate is thought of as governing all of life so that certain events are predetermined. One's destiny is fixed and cannot be changed, although supernatural powers may hinder individuals from realizing their destiny.[18]

The idea of history progressing towards an ultimate goal is absent in African thinking. The universe was brought into being by the Supreme Being "in order to function according to regular patterns, rhythms and movements . . . As long as man maintains his proper relations with fellow men and with nature, the universe will continue as it has always done, unless of course, God chooses to change the course of events."[19] The future is understood as an extension of the present, and so those who live wisely in the present will be guaranteed a prosperous tomorrow. However, those who live unwisely, are sure to face the consequences of their choices in the near future.

---

15. Robert J. Banks, "Time," *New Dictionary of Biblical Theology*, 820.
16. Mbiti, *African Religions*, 78.
17. Mugambi, *African Heritage*, 83.
18. Turaki, *Foundations*, 40.
19. Mugambi, *African Christian Theology*, 127.

By contrast the biblical understanding of time is rooted in God's sovereignty over time. In other words, God is in control of human history and the past, the present and the future all contribute in some way to God's eternal purpose. Some see this progression as linear, moving forward from the past, to the present and into the future.[20] Others say that time is cyclical and that experiences and the mistakes of our past are continually repeated. It might be more accurate to say that while time does move forward, it does so in a cyclical, linear pattern, much like a spiral.[21] We may repeat the same experiences and make the same mistakes as our forebears, but we also progress in our ability to learn from our past. Biblical records bear witness to the fact that God was constantly referring his people back to the mistakes of the past as he encouraged them to make the necessary changes and move forward. We see this especially from stories about Moses, Joshua and the prophets in the Old Testament and in Paul's letters in the New Testament. Consequently, the past is important because we study it and apply it to the present and the future.

Unlike in the African worldview, the biblical worldview has no place for fate. While the world is orderly, it is not completely predetermined or preprogrammed – we can thus make real, significant decisions.[22] Consequently, time should be used wisely.

From a biblical perspective, history cannot be seen as a series of disconnected events that have no ultimate meaning. It must be seen as part of God's plan to bring all creation to a triumphant conclusion. Believers have a future hope because of Christ's sacrificial work. However, for unbelievers, the future holds only torment and punishment as they experience the reality of a final judgement (Heb 9:27; Rev 20:12–13).

History and time in modern Africa

The event-based concept of time is still very real in Africa today. While one might expect that urban Africa would be different, this is not the case. Instead, we live with a divided or dichotomized view of time. In a professional environment, we value chronological time and so show up on time for work; in a social environment, we are happy to interact with

---
20. Sire, *The Universe Next Door*, 43.
21. This is a view that was first suggested to me by Dr Jack Willsey during my studies at Corban University School of Ministry (formerly Northwest Baptist Seminary).
22. Sire, *The Universe Next Door*, 32.

people regardless of how long the event takes. It does not matter whether a social event begins "on time" because we expect delays. The time spent waiting is not wasted because it provides an opportunity for valuable interactions and building relationships with others attending the event.

Implications for hermeneutics

John 14:2–3 provides a good example of how African understandings of time affect our interpretation of Scripture:

> My Father's house has many rooms; if that were not so, would I have told you that I am going there to prepare a place for you? And if I go and prepare a place for you, I will come back and take you to be with me that you also may be where I am.

Jesus was speaking to his disciples towards the end of his life. He was encouraging them to hold firmly to their faith because their faithfulness would be rewarded. But here an African view of the future works in a negative way. While we may be able to visualize a future reality in which Jesus has prepared a place for us to inhabit, this prospect is not likely to be a strong motivation for the present life. Given our traditional lack of interest in the future, the reward appears to be too far away. This is one reason African Christians may have problems interpreting texts that have eschatological significance, that is, texts that speak of our future eternal destiny.

The Arts

The final category of worldview that we will examine is the arts. How do songs, stories, the visual arts, the dramatic arts, and so forth, reflect and affect how we view life? Can one conceive of a reality where these do not exist? Does God care about beauty, or is he only concerned with making things work? This category has been largely ignored in worldview discussions, but to do so is to miss out on an important element since the arts are part of our daily experience. They play a powerful role in any worldview, since they demonstrate that a worldview consists of more than abstract ideas or theoretical concepts.[23] The arts allow us to express human values in a concrete way and are consequently an integral part of life.

Traditional understandings of the arts

Music and dance, oral traditions such as stories, legends, myths and proverbs, and visual arts such as sculpture, carving, and painting have long been very important in Africa. They were the means by which ideas were passed on from one generation to the next. By examining them, we catch a glimpse of our African worldview. Their importance is yet another example of the way in which African processing of information differs from the Western approach. African thinking, like most non-Western thinking, is holistic, seeing the whole more clearly than the individual parts. A Western approach tends to be analytical, separating out the individual elements.

Within the community context, narrative or storytelling was central and was often dramatized with songs and dances. It was one way of communicating theological beliefs and worldview. As Mugambi notes, "theology in the African heritage was articulated not in treatises and manuals but in descriptive names and phrases, myths of origin, blessings and curses, greetings and expressions of gratitude, rituals, prayers, informal religious sayings, and in ordinary comments and explanations."[24] He does not explicitly mention other genres such as narratives, songs, riddles and proverbs, but they would certainly fit into his list.

Stories were often used to communicate moral values. The whole story was the moral, and everyone in a community understood the nuances that formed the whole picture. But if you were not a part of that culture, you might miss the finer details. Consider the following common story:

> One day, tortoise challenged hare to a race. As you might expect, hare was very amused because he knew that he was much faster than tortoise. However, he agreed to it, and on the appointed day, he and tortoise set off to race. What hare didn't know was that tortoise had asked his family members to

---

23. Leland Ryken, "The Creative Arts," in *The Making of a Christian Mind: A Christian World View and the Academic Enterprise,* ed. Arthur Holmes (Downers Grove: InterVarsity Press, 1985), 105.
24. Mugambi, *African Heritage,* 59.

help him. They positioned themselves all along the path the race was going to take. So, much to hare's surprise, no matter how fast he ran, every time he turned a corner he saw what he thought was tortoise ahead of him. In what was an upsetting turn of events for hare, he lost the race to tortoise.

What does this story teach us? Westerners might think it is about trickery and deception, but that is not the case. For Africans, this story is about the value of cooperation. Tortoise solicited the help of his family whereas hare opted to run on his own. So the point of the story is all about solidarity versus individualism. This is not a point that is made clear by only one part of the story – the ending – so that we can say at the conclusion "And the moral of the story is. . . ." Rather, the moral is brought out throughout the entire story.

How does a biblical worldview in relation to the arts compare with what we have in Africa? As Sire points out, "Artistic inventiveness is a reflection of God's unbounded capacity to create."[25] To start with, the Bible is itself literary form that has been written under the guidance of the Holy Spirit.[26] Within its pages, we see that the arts were a significant part of the worldview of the people of the Old and New Testament. As in Africa, the arts were considered a normal part of everyday life. The architecture of the tower of Babel is a good example (Gen 11:1–9). While it was a misguided project, it bore witness to the artistic creativity of human beings right from the beginning of time. Music and dance were an integral part of worship. The psalms express the life experiences of individuals and the community through poetry and song. Solomon hired artists to work on architectural projects, and the aesthetic aspects of their workmanship receive much emphasis. The Bible talks about individuals gifted in the creative arts. David, for instance, composed numerous psalms and it is recorded that he danced exuberantly before the Lord (2 Sam 6:14). The books of Job and Isaiah include both narrative and poetry. In the New Testament, various biblical writers use poetry and song to express their message. We read Mary's Magnificat and the doxologies of Paul. Jesus himself used artistic genres in communicating

---

25. Sire, *The Universe Next Door*, 35.
26. Calvin Seerveld, "Art, the Bible and," *Dictionary for Theological Interpretation of the Bible*, 63.

his message through parables.[27] Believers are exhorted to sing "psalms, hymns and spiritual songs" (Eph 5:15–20). Indeed, the Bible reveals that the ability to recite, sculpt and sing is given by God himself.[28]

The arts in modern Africa

With the coming of the missionaries, the traditional African arts were discouraged as it was thought that these would interfere with Africans' ability to truly embrace the Christian God. In addition, Western education introduced a scientific approach that began to influence our patterns of thinking. The result was that we began to demonstrate a more analytical approach to life that placed less emphasis on the arts. This statement is confirmed by research showing that in Kenya urban students have a more analytical pattern of thinking than rural students.[29]

Yet some of us have not abandoned our African orientation to the arts, but have complemented it with a Western education. While recognizing that the Bible does contain propositional truth (i.e. facts that can be itemized) we do not reduce it to a dry theological handbook designed to give instructions for every life situation. We find great value and enjoyment in the narratives in Scripture. We read them not just for the purpose of extracting principles, but for the joy of being a part of the story. Moreover, worship for us is a dynamic experience of exuberant singing, clapping and dancing. Without this total involvement of body, mind, will and emotions, we sense that there is a vital element missing in the worship of God. The arts therefore continue to be an integral part of our lives.

Implications for hermeneutics

Our African appreciation of the arts has positive implications when it comes to interpreting Scripture. When we read the Bible, we have a deep appreciation for the various art forms we encounter because they are an essential part of our worldview. The rhythm and figurative language of the Psalms, for instance, strikes a chord in our hearts that draws us deep into the text. Consider Psalm 51:8–12. This is a psalm of repentance sung by David after Nathan confronts him about his sin of murder and adultery.

---

27. Seerveld, "Art, the Bible and," 64.
28. Seerveld, 64.
29. Wilbur O'Donovan, *Biblical Christianity in Modern Africa* (Carlisle: Paternoster, 2000), 9.

> Let me hear joy and gladness;
>> let the bones you have crushed rejoice.
> Hide your face from my sins
>> and blot out all my iniquity.
> Create in me a pure heart, O God,
>> and renew a steadfast spirit within me.
> Do not cast me from your presence
>> or take your Holy Spirit from me.
> Restore to me the joy of your salvation
>> and grant me a willing spirit, to sustain me.

The figurative language, the tone of repentance, the complete brokenness and anguish that we detect behind the words, all climax in a powerful message that goes beyond mere verbal communication. As we are drawn into David's pain, we become aware of the character of a holy God who does not tolerate sin. We find ourselves identifying with David, inwardly pleading for his restoration. This way of reading, made possible by the poetic character of the text, is not foreign to us. We automatically orient ourselves in such a way as to understand both the artistry and the words of the text, recognizing that both make up the message.

Conclusion

These two chapters have demonstrated that worldview does indeed influence how we interpret Scripture. To go back to the poem about the elephant with which the previous chapter began, Christians from Africa, Europe, America and Asia must realize that although the parts we touch may have different shapes, the texture and the smell of the elephant are the same! For us, the elephant represents the biblical metanarrative, or the whole story of God, as it unfolds in the Bible. Our task is to work out how our perceptions fit into the bigger picture of the whole "elephant." To do this, we must have a control belief, that is, a basic truth that serves as the test for all the ideas discussed in these two chapters. A good control belief for the Christian worldview is the "existence of *God revealed in Scripture*" (emphasis mine).[30]

---
30. Nash, *Worldviews*, 52.

Finally, a biblical worldview begins with the understanding that we are part of one story. We have an intimate connection not only with believers who exist in the same place and time as we do but also with those who have gone on ahead. Once we understand this, we will realize what is more important than how we express our Christian faith is that this expression should be truly biblical. Rather than focusing on differences in cultural perspectives, we need to focus on getting rid of the inconsistencies where our own worldviews clash with the biblical worldview. In this way, we will be closer to a more accurate interpretation, understanding and application of the biblical text.

In the next chapter, we turn our attention to a hermeneutical model that will show us how an understanding of our African worldview can assist us in biblical interpretation.

Questions for Review

1. In one or two paragraphs, identify your own worldview with regards to knowledge, morality, suffering, history and time, and the arts.

2. In what specific ways do these aspects of your worldview influence how you interpret and apply the Bible (either positively or negatively)? Cite specific texts.

3. Contextualization means that the expression of the Christian faith looks different in different cultures. Explain how you would identify and correct a syncretistic doctrine or practice.

4

AN AFRICAN HERMENEUTIC: A FOUR-LEGGED STOOL

So far, we have been discussing how fundamental elements of our worldview affect our understanding of the biblical text, and have shown that these effects can be both positive and negative. It is now time to start systematizing our approach by developing a hermeneutical model that works for us as African readers of Scripture.

As noted at the beginning of this book, hermeneutics is the art and science of interpretation and involves both theory and practice. Like any art or science, it requires the use of certain methods or techniques in order to produce reliable results. A method that works well in an African context can be described using the metaphor of a four-legged stool. In this chapter, we will explain how this metaphor (which we will call "a model") works in the process of interpretation, and then in subsequent chapters we will apply this model to different kinds of biblical texts.

A stool is a familiar object in Africa, both in the past and in the present. Just as a good stool is stable and supports our weight, so the hermeneutical stool will be one we can put our weight on, confident that it provides a stable or accurate interpretation of the biblical text. To do so, it requires four legs, which in this case are (a) parallels to the African context, (b) the theological context, (c) the literary context and (d) the historical context. These legs support the seat, which represents the final stage of interpretation – the application.

Seat – Application

Leg 4 – Historical and Cultural Context

Leg 1 – Parallels to the African Context

Leg 3 – Literary Context

Leg 2 – Theological Context

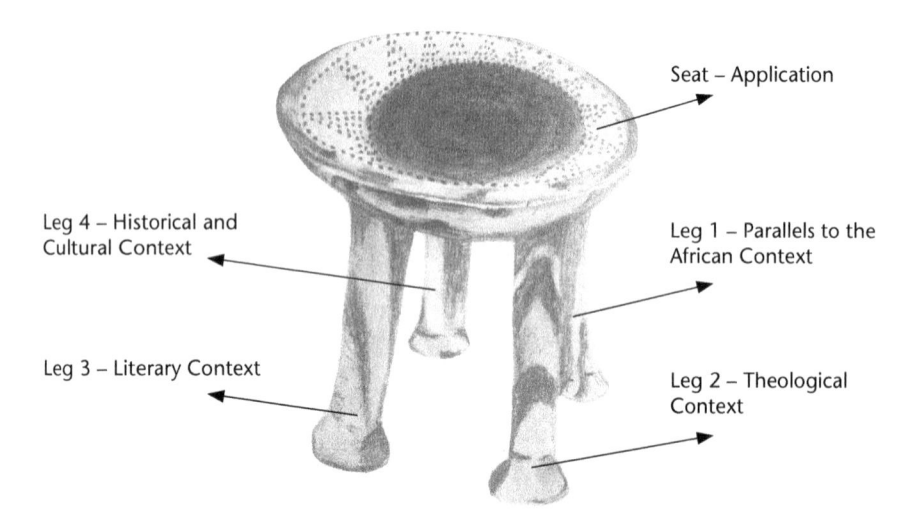

When we begin our process of interpretation, we must always begin with leg 1 (the African context) because that is what we know, and having that firmly in place will enable us to move from the known to the unknown. Thereafter, we will move sequentially from legs 2 to 4. However, the legs are not independent of each other and we will find that we will be moving back and forth between them as we try to find the right balance. Each leg affects the other, and we will be making constant adjustments as we gain greater understanding of the passage we are considering. In the same way, a carpenter will adjust the legs of a wooden stool to make sure that they work together to support the seat, and that none of them is weak or misshapen.

Another image that is sometimes used to describe our growth in understanding of the biblical text is the hermeneutical spiral.[1] This image makes it clear that interpretation is an interactive, ongoing, continuous process. As we keep looking at different aspects of the text, we spiral closer and closer to its intended meaning. This is because as we gain more information, our assumptions about the text change and our understanding grows.

---

1. Grant Osborne, *The Hermeneutical Spiral: A Comprehensive Introduction to Biblical Interpretation* (Downers Grove: InterVarsity Press, 2010), 22–23.

Original assumptions

Assumptions informed by understanding

Let us now look more closely at each of the four legs of the hermeneutical stool.

Leg 1: Parallels to the African Context

The first leg of the stool, the place where we begin our search for understanding, involves identifying the theological and cultural contexts that are the primary contributors to our own worldview, as well as any relevant features of our social, political, and geographical contexts. The previous chapters established that our worldview is our framework for understanding life, and so also our framework for understanding Scripture. We saw that this framework sometimes helps us to understand the text, and sometimes gets in the way of understanding the text. Where our assumptions are not in line with the biblical assumptions that are the basis of a Christian worldview, we must put aside our own assumptions and give priority to the biblical worldview.

There are two reasons why this first leg is so important. One, it enables us to begin to understand the biblical text from a familiar position. This is important because hermeneutics involves moving from the known to the unknown. Two, examining our own worldview and context puts us in a position to recognize where our assumptions do not fit with the text. If we do not know what we are assuming, how will we even recognize when our assumptions are wrong?

Until quite recently, hermeneutics emphasized the historical context of the Bible and paid little attention to the context of the reader. It was wrongly assumed that the context of the reader did not contribute either positively or negatively to interpretation. However, scholars have increasingly come to recognize the two-sided nature of historical conditioning. What does this mean? It means that while the Bible stands in a historical context and tradition, so does the reader. The Bible's context and the reader's context are in constant engagement with one another,[2] as we saw in the previous two chapters.

Ukachukwu speaks of this in terms of shared mutual interests. He points out that in oral cultures there can be no accurate communication and understanding of a story without certain commonalities between the narrator and his or her listeners.[3] These mutual interests, which may or may not be explicitly stated by the narrator, are a crucial interpretive key for the listener. How so? They define the scope within which meaning can begin to be determined. A narrator cannot begin to tell a story that has absolutely no connection with his audience. The mutual interests guide the listener as to how to hear and interpret the story. These mutual interests also form the basis on which the narrator earns the right to be heard by his audience. How does this apply to our biblical texts? Without these mutual interests, the reader is left grappling in the dark, not fully understanding either the meaning or the application of the text.

The first leg of our hermeneutical stool therefore guides us in identifying points of contact with the biblical text. Consider the story of the woman caught in adultery (John 7:53–8:11). How does this story relate to our African context? We can identify two links.

First, the matter of adultery. Even though polygamy was a feature of traditional life, it was generally understood that sex outside a marital relationship was taboo. Indeed, adultery was a punishable offence that incurred severe fines and sometimes even physical punishment. Consequently, we can easily relate to a story that involves adultery.

Second, we can recognize the elements of the honour–shame value system that are present in this story. Even with the growing trend of urbanization, modernization and globalization, traces of this value system remain, particularly in rural areas that still have a vibrant community model. In an honour–shame system, adultery is regarded as not only

---

2. A. C. Thiselton, *The Two Horizons: New Testament Hermeneutics and Philosophical Description with Special Reference to Heidegger, Bultmann, Gadamer, and Wittgenstein* (Carlisle: Paternoster, 2005), 11.
3. Ukachukwu, *Intercultural Hermeneutics*, 25.

morally wrong but also shameful. Those who are guilty of it bring shame on their community and are themselves exposed to public shame. So we can understand something about what is going on when a woman who has been caught in adultery is exposed to public shame. We have mutual interests with the narrator of the biblical text.

Or take the story of Hannah (1 Sam 1–2), in which we see barrenness treated as a curse, something to be ashamed of, rather than as a medical condition. Even in modern Africa, we can identify with that idea. Here, too, barrenness is a source of shame. Here, too, some husbands choose to find another wife to vindicate their "manhood." There is no shortage of points of contact between this story and the African worldview.

In the above two examples, similarities between African and biblical cultures and worldview make it easier for us to begin to understand the texts. But what about cases where our worldview works negatively rather than positively when it comes to interpreting a passage? Take the example of Hebrews 12:1. The context makes it clear that the "cloud of witnesses" are people who have already died. This raises the issue of the African view of death. In traditional Africa, death is not an end but merely a crossing over into a realm in which the dead are separated from the living by a curtain. In this respect, there is some similarity with the biblical worldview, which also holds that death is not the end. But in Africa death is in a sense a continuation of life, and the dead are still in contact with the living. In fact the living dead play a key role in the life of the community. The Bible's teaching about the nature of life after death is very different and forbids any attempt to interact with those who have gone before. This means that as we continue with the process of interpreting this verse, we need to be cautious not to apply our African worldview about death to the biblical context. In this case, the first leg of the hermeneutical stool allows us to acknowledge our wrong assumptions about death and begin to correct them with the biblical perspective.

It is important to point out that we may not always be in a position to fully analyze our context and worldview at this stage. What is important, however, is to acknowledge that they exist and to consider them as we read the biblical text so that it begins to feel more familiar. Then we can turn to legs 2, 3 and 4 of the stool to investigate the specific context of the Bible.

To sum up: *The first leg of the hermeneutical stool is to consciously identify our own context and discover the points of contact between it and the biblical context. In this way, we can identify cues that will allow for a more accurate interpretation of the text through a process of comparing the two contexts and analysing the findings.*

Leg 2: Theological Context

The second leg of the hermeneutical stool is to seek to understand the theological emphases of a text and how these are expressed in relation to the section and book in which it is found, and ultimately in relation to the whole Bible.

Some may ask why we move straight to theological concerns rather than to the historical and cultural context of the text. The answer is that Africans tend to be very religious, even in modern Africa. The spiritual dimension of life is always a factor in our interaction with the world around us. Because of this orientation, most African readers initially focus on the theological emphases of the text and allow these to determine their interpretation of it. Simply put, when we as Africans read the Bible, we tend to look for issues that relate to God and faith and how these affect our everyday lives. At this level, therefore, some tentative points of application will already begin to present themselves. But we must not hold too tightly to these initial applications. We must allow ourselves to go through the entire process, examining all four legs of the hermeneutical stool, so that our application is informed by thorough analysis.

Gerald West is making a similar point when he says that in Africa biblical hermeneutics cannot be separated from theological reflection as the emphasis is generally on addressing contextual realities within African culture.[4] This emphasis has led to what is known as the fusion of the two horizons in hermeneutics. These "two horizons" are merely another way of talking about the two contexts mentioned above – the context of the Bible and of the reader. When these contexts are fused, we assume that the meaning of the text to the original readers is identical to what it means to readers today. Interpretation and application are conflated.

---

4. West, "African Biblical Hermeneutics," 4.

So, for example, rather than trying to understand what Paul was saying to his Ephesian readers, an African interpreter might say, "What Paul is saying to me is . . ." This approach is harmful to interpretation because we are ignoring the context of the Bible and prioritizing our own context.

Many scholars have pointed out that the Bible can be viewed as literature. By this they mean that it is a literary work that has lasted for centuries. However, even though it is a literary work, it is primarily a spiritual document. This is evident all the way through – from the Old Testament, which starts with the origins of all life and moves on to God's activity in the lives of humankind in general, his choice of a particular nation through which he will bring salvation, his activity in their lives through various agents, the continuation of this story of salvation in the New Testament through Jesus Christ and the church, and finally the last chapter of Revelation, which depicts the events that bring this life as we know it to its triumphant conclusion in judgement and redemption. God is present in every chapter and verse, whether or not his name is specifically mentioned. Moreover, the aim of the Bible is to bring unbelievers to faith and to build faith in believers so that they may live their lives in a godly manner. This is a spiritual concern. Therefore, one key to the process of interpretation is a correct understanding of the theological emphases of a text.

The parallels uncovered above in leg 1 constitute a crucial hinge in understanding the theology of the given text, for both similarities and crucial differences are considered. For instance, when we read Mark's gospel, we soon become aware of the major theological emphasis that Jesus is the miracle-working, authoritative Son of God. There are strategic references to his being the Son of God in Mark 1:1, 11; 3:33; 5:7; 9:7; 12:6; 13:32; 14:61 and 15:39. In fact the Gospel of Mark begins with this theme and ends with it. The opening verse declares that Jesus is the Son of God, and at the end a Roman centurion acknowledges, "Surely this man was the Son of God!" (Mark 15:39). The author is framing his narrative theologically in terms of Jesus being the Son of God. This is no coincidence since Mark's audience was the church in Rome. We know that around that time the Roman emperors were beginning to insist that they be referred to as gods. Mark therefore turns his readers' attention away from these false gods to the true Son of God. This theological understanding should guide our interpretation of all of Mark's gospel, for the other texts in this gospel add to this major theme from different angles. But if someone makes the mistake of assuming that the major theological emphasis of the Gospel of Mark is that Jesus is the Jewish Messiah promised in the Old Testament, they will read that understanding into the text. The result will be that some conclusions they arrive at will be wrong.

How so? While the concept of Messiah (*Christ* for Greek readers) is mentioned once as a proper name in Mark 1:1 and then as a title in 8:29; 9:41; 12:35; 13:21; 14:61; 15:32, the way the story unfolds does not place great emphasis on how a Roman reader would understand this term. Indeed, focusing on this aspect would be counterproductive since the Roman context was very different from the Jewish context. For instance, a text on healing like Mark 7:31–37 would not have the right impact if the author was emphasizing that Jesus was the Jewish Messiah. But when we look at the Roman context, we notice that it was generally believed that Roman emperors like Vespasian were divine and could heal.[5] The right understanding of the theological theme allows us to understand the story in the way the author intended. It is not meant to affirm the messiahship of Jesus but to challenge the Roman belief in the divinity of emperors.

It is important to be very careful when examining this second leg of the hermeneutical stool. We must not allow premature conclusions about the theological emphases of the text to dictate how we understand the other legs. In other words, while our interpretation must not contradict the theology expressed through the text, our assumptions about the theology of a specific text or of an entire book must not be allowed to dictate our interpretation without consideration of other contexts. A holistic approach is advisable. Theological Dictionaries are a good place to start.

To sum up: *The second leg of the hermeneutical stool involves ensuring that the theological context is identified before moving on to other aspects of interpretation. It is crucial that the theological emphases provide the guidelines within which meaning should be sought. However, the other legs of the hermeneutical stool must still be allowed to affect the conclusions arrived at here.*

---

5. C. A. Evans, "Mark," *New Dictionary of Biblical Theology*, 272.

Leg 3: Literary Context

The third leg of the hermeneutical stool is to identify the literary features of the passage we are interpreting. Because the Bible is not only a spiritual document but also a work of literature, we need to establish the genre of the passage we are reading, what literary techniques are being used, details of the grammar and syntax of the language being used, and how this passage fits together with the surrounding text. The initial interpretation and tentative application we reached as we worked on legs 1 and 2 will be modified and clarified as we engage with the literary context.

Literary genre

To identify the genre of a text is simply to assign it to a particular category of writing. For example, we may decide that what we are reading is poetry or a drama or a story. It is important to do this because once we know the genre of what we are reading, we have some idea of how we should approach the text in order to understand what the author is communicating.

This is not a terribly complex issue, for we already make use of genres in our everyday lives. When we want to communicate emotions, we use a song or a poem. If we want to communicate the importance of a particular character trait, we tell a story or a folktale. If we want to encourage someone to think critically about what they are doing, we simply remind them of a proverb. For example, when we see someone getting so attached to material things that they are at risk of making foolish or even immoral decisions, we might quote the Kenyan proverb, "Wisdom is better than wealth."

Just as we select specific genres to communicate specific types of information, so the authors of the Bible selected the genres that would best communicate their message. Hence, literary genre functions as a vital interpretive key in the hermeneutical process.

> In literary terms, a text that bears no similarities of structure, content, or the like with anything previously written cannot be understood by a reader. Not only is genre recognizable in the expectations of the reader, but it also directs authors as they

compose the text. It shapes or coerces writers so that their compositions can be grasped and communicated to the reader.[6]

Perhaps one of the best metaphors for understanding the role of genre in interpretation is that proposed by Hirsch. He suggests that genre should be understood as a game. There are rules that determine how games are played. For instance, many of us understand how football is played and know the rules that make it work. In the same way, there are rules that an author follows in writing. The reader is aware of these rules and expects that the author has followed them.[7] This metaphor helps us understand not only what genre is, but also how it helps the reader interpret the text in the way that the author intended. If you know how the game is played, then you can participate in it.

But imagine if someone were to assume that the rules of football also apply in rugby and cricket. They would be very confused when they saw what the players were actually doing on the field. In the same way, we need to know that different rules apply when interpreting different genres. We cannot approach stories in the same way as we do poetry, or even understand proverbs as we do prophecy.

While texts written in the same genre have certain characteristics in common,[8] it is also true that literary genres are not static or even universal since they change over time.[9] Motifs and vocabulary may also be borrowed from one genre and incorporated into another to make a new genre.[10] For instance, a growing trend in African music writing and performance is to blend hip hop with African rhythms. This has created a new genre known as African fusion. This point has an important application. We cannot always assume that our modern genres apply to ancient texts. For example, we should not assume that the gospels are written like modern biographies – they are in a different genre. So when we identify the genre of a piece of writing, we need to be aware of what genres existed at the time the piece was written as well as the literary "rules" that applied at

---

6. Tremper Longman III, *Literary Approaches to Biblical Interpretation*, in Foundations of Contemporary Interpretation (Grand Rapids: Zondervan, 1987), 77.
7. E. D. Hirsch, *Validity in Interpretation* (New Haven: Yale University Press, 1967), 72.
8. Larry Hurtado, "Genre," *Dictionary of Jesus and the Gospels*, 277.
9. Hurtado, "Genre," 227.
10. Margaret Davies, *Rhetoric and Reference in the Fourth Gospel*, JSNTSup 63 (Sheffield: JSOT, 1992), 69.

that time. So while we can find it helpful to consider traditional African categories as we begin identifying the different genres used in the Bible, we also need to consider what other writers were doing at that time and how they understood what they were doing.

Literary techniques

The literary techniques an author uses may vary depending on whether the material is to be presented orally or in writing. When something is for oral presentation, the narrator can use a variety of techniques including mime, songs and dramatic storytelling. Performance is crucial to the engagement between teller and hearer. Commenting on a West African dirge, for example, Finnegan points out that when it appears in print it is only a shadow of itself. We can still recognize some of its imagery and the way the words are associated with one another, but we miss the "expressiveness of tone, gesture, facial expression, dramatic use of pause and rhythm, the interplay of passion, dignity, or humour, receptivity to the reactions of the audience, etc., etc."[11] Without fully taking into account these devices, it may not be possible to get the full effect of the poem.

Another key feature of oral literature is that it involves holistic listening and interaction between the performer and the audience. As Scheub and Gunner state,

> The audience . . . becomes an integral part of the story by becoming a part of the metaphorical process that moves to meaning. And meaning, therefore, is much more complex than an obvious homily that may be readily available on the surface of the tale.[12]

Holistic listening entails at least three things:
- *Active listening*. Hearing is by no means passive. Hearers actively participate in the storytelling, not just by visualizing what is happening and giving the narrator their undivided attention but also with comments. This brings the narration to life as

---
11. Ruth Finnegan, *Oral Literature in Africa*, World Oral Literature Series 1 (http://www.oralliterature.org/collections/rfinnegan001), 5.
12. Harold Scheub and Elizabeth Ann Wynne Gunner, *African Literature* (http://www.britannica.com/art/African-literature#toc57038).

listeners become, as it were, part of the story. The literary devices are familiar and hearers know their role in propelling the narrative forward.

- *Community listening*: Listening is not an individual affair; rather, there is community or communal listening.
- *Responsive listening*: The various forms of African literature demand a response. A story does not end when the narrator falls silent. It lives on because the audience is expected to apply the various aspects of the story to their lives. For instance, a story emphasizing bravery encourages the hearers to develop that quality in their lives.

Style too is extremely important where oral stories or narratives are concerned. Features such as plot, setting and characterization play a major role in communicating meaning. There is constant repetition of words and of key themes, and also constant interaction between narration and dialogue, which ensures that the reader becomes part of the story, identifying with first one character, and then another.

The above features of African oral literature are important for us when interpreting Scripture, for much of it began life as oral literature, or as a text that was written to be read aloud in public settings rather than by a solitary reader. Like those who listen to African stories, those who listened to the stories told in the Bible were expected to respond in some way. For instance, whenever the exodus story was retold, the hearers would recall God's faithfulness to their forefathers and would be renewed in their own faith. Where idolatry had crept into their lives, this story was a reminder to abandon false gods and recommit themselves to the true God (see, for example, Josh 24:1–25).

Other literary devices to which we need to pay attention are imagery and symbolism (which may be realistic or fantastic). This is another point where African literary techniques intersect with the literature of the Bible. Both are full of imagery in the form of metaphors and similes. A metaphor is a figure of speech that compares two things that are unrelated but have some things in common. The aim is to express an idea or concept in a way that will connect with the reader better. A metaphor is not to be confused with a simile, which also compares two things but uses the words "like" or "as." The Bible has many examples of the use of imagery, particularly in the more poetic sections. For instance, the righteous man is compared to a tree planted by streams of water in Psalm 1:3. Symbolism is another common technique. The use of animals in particular is quite common in both biblical and African symbolism. Mugo wa Kibiru, a prophetic seer from Kenya, described the coming of the railway using the symbolism of a huge snake undulating through the country. In the Bible, animal symbolism is used in books such as Daniel and Revelation.

We should also note the vividness with which an author writes. In African literature, this vividness is enhanced by constant references to nature. Almost all African songs, poems, riddles, stories and so forth are told within a setting in which the images in the narrative are supported by earthy details. Understanding these details is crucial to understanding the meaning of the communication itself.

Another point at which African literary techniques overlap with techniques found in the Bible is that African stories tend to have a non-direct approach. They do not clearly identify the moral of the story, as some Western fables do. African stories are not purely linear, so that all we need to do is read the introduction and the conclusion. Rather, the whole story carries the message and every component has a role to play. This approach enables one to arrive at the meaning of the story from many different angles. Crucial interpretive keys are embedded in the very fabric of the story. Like precious gems, they must be mined and strung together to reveal the intent of the narrator as the story moves forward. Some of the stories in the Bible provide us with a good example of this. For instance, the story of Joseph in Genesis 37 tells of how he was mistreated by his brothers and eventually sold into slavery. Nowhere in the text do we explicitly read that this was wrong or that God was directing Joseph's future. It is only as we continue reading that we sense that the brothers will eventually have to account for the evil they have done and that, even more importantly, God has been in control all along (Gen 45:5, 8).

Language

It is vital that we pay attention to matters like grammar, syntax, and detailed word studies. As we all know, language consists of words that are combined in ways that communicate meaning. So, for instance, the sentence "The man has a dog" uses exactly the same words as the sentence, "The dog has a man," but their meanings are very different. Clearly it is not only the words that are important, but also how they relate to each other. Linguists refer to this aspect of a language as its grammar and syntax. The meaning of words changes depending on how they are used in the context of a sentence, and the meaning of sentences changes depending on their context within a paragraph, and so on. The words and sentences that are strung together to create a text are all part of a whole. We should never focus so much on individual words and details that we miss the meaning of the whole. If we ignore grammar and syntax, we run the risk of failing to grasp the full meaning of the text.

Where the Bible is concerned, analysis of language helps to clarify theological emphases and sharpens our understanding of a text. For instance, how should we understand Acts 16:30–31? In this text, the jailer asks Paul and Silas a specific question: "Sirs, what must I do to be saved?" They respond: "Believe in the Lord Jesus, and you will be saved – you and your household." Because of the emphasis on community in Africa (and the reference to a household), an African reader might conclude that believing is a communal act and that the approval of the group is needed before someone can decide to believe and be saved. This interpretation would fit with the African worldview in which individuals exist only because others exist. That worldview may appear to negate (although see discussion in previous chapter) personal freedom and autonomy, and it suggests that coming to salvation should be a communal rather than an individual decision. But was this what Paul and Silas were saying? When we look at the English text, the "you" could be either singular or plural, so that interpretation is possible. But when we look at the original Greek text, we see that the "you" is in the second person singular, and so is the verb. Paul and Silas were asking for an individual response of faith, not a communal one. Examples like this make it clear why we need to either know the original languages in which the Bible was written or have access to tools to help us interpret what we read. Bible concordances, dictionaries, and lexicons as well as electronic language tools such as BibleWorks are useful here. Commentaries that work with the Hebrew or Greek text are also useful tools.

Literary flow

African storytellers are extremely skilled in ensuring that there is no breakdown in the flow of a story. While the telling of a story may not be linear, there is a cyclical-linear development that allows the story to flow smoothly from beginning to end. The details that are necessary for understanding are provided when they are needed to enable the audience to interpret the story. Take the following example, which we will be looking at in more detail later in the book.

> The Gikuyu people believe that in the days of long, long ago, when the Good Lord N'gai made his plans for all the creatures upon his earth, he made the hippopotamus as an animal of the forests and plains. But the hippopotamus was greedy and, finding plenty of food all round him and no enemies to worry about, he grew fatter, and fatter and fatter. And the fatter he grew, the more he suffered from the heat of the equatorial midday sun.

This opening narration provides the setting of the story and begins to develop the character of the hippopotamus. We learn that he was greedy. This is an important insight as it helps us understand the rest of the narrative and the dialogue that follows. Consequently, when we come to the part of the story that shows the hippopotamus's negotiation with N'gai to allow him to live in the water with the fish, we are not surprised that N'gai demands proof that he is not going to eat them. The context has already prepared us for such a response.

Similarly, a basic principle of biblical hermeneutics is that "the intended meaning of any passage is the meaning that is consistent with the sense of the literary context in which it occurs."[13] In other words, the meaning of a specific text cannot contradict the meaning conveyed by the larger context. The literary context establishes the flow of thought and helps us to determine the accurate meaning of words.

In reading the gospels, the literary context is very important for helping us to determine the correct relationships between units of thought. For instance, when we compare similar stories (also referred to as pericopes), it soon becomes evident that the material that comes immediately before and after these stories, or in other words, the literary context, differs from gospel to gospel. So when we read a story in a gospel, we need to consider

---

13. William W. Klein, Craig L. Blomberg, and Robert L. Hubbard Jr., *Introduction to Biblical Interpretation*, rev. ed. (Nashville: Thomas Nelson, 2005), 214.

the point that is being made in the context of that gospel (the "vertical" reading). Only after we have done this can we set about comparing the way the story is handled in different gospels (the "horizontal" reading).

To sum up: *The third leg of the hermeneutical stool is to ensure that the literary context is identified and analysed. In uncovering the meaning of any text, it is crucial that the genre, literary techniques, language and flow of the text guide the process and begin to confirm the meaning of the text arrived at so far. Other factors that follow in the process will then reinforce or correct the conclusions arrived at in this stage.*

Leg 4: Historical and Cultural Context

The fourth leg of the hermeneutical stool involves understanding how the text we are looking at was informed and shaped by the socio-cultural, political and economic circumstances in which it was written and the mindset of the author. This applies to all texts. Writing about African oral literature, Finnegan comments:

> Far more extremely than with written forms, the bare words cannot be left to speak for themselves, for the simple reason that in the actual literary work so much else is necessarily and intimately involved. With this type of literature, a knowledge of the whole literary and social background, covering these various points of performance, audience, and context, is, however difficult, of the first importance.[14]

Thus, any interpretation must consider the historical and cultural context of the text. These factors are just as much a part of a story, riddle, proverb, or song as its theological and literary aspects. As we grow in understanding of this context, we will refine the application points we identified when working on legs 1, 2 and 3.

In presenting leg 1 of the hermeneutical stool, we talked about shared mutual interests. Historical and cultural contexts fall in this category, as it is assumed that the teller and hearer live in the same context. Indeed,

---

14. Finnegan, *Oral Literature*, 17.

they grasp historical and cultural issues almost instinctively since they are so familiar to them both.

They would also share the same understanding of the way language is used. In other words, language develops within a specific social context which those who live in that context understand. This relates to words and expressions that are used in that particular context that might not be used elsewhere. For instance, a common Kiswahili phrase used among friends in East Africa is *ume potea sana* [you are very lost]. This doesn't literally mean that you are lost; it means that the person speaking hasn't seen you in a long time. Outside of the social context in which this phrase has developed, it doesn't make sense. This socially conditioned nature of language must be considered as a crucial clue in uncovering historical and cultural backgrounds.[15] We must therefore make the effort to step into the world of the narrator if we hope to understand his or her communication adequately.

But this is difficult to do when it comes to the biblical text. We live in the twenty-first century, and the biblical texts were written many centuries ago in a culture that is different from our own. There are thus temporal and cultural barriers between us and the Bible. These barriers are likely to hinder our full comprehension of what was written, and so we as modern readers need to learn as much as we can about the world of the authors and their original audience. If our aim in interpretation is to understand the message intended by the author, then this context must be uncovered and explained in terms that we understand.

Porter notes the following:

> Any text no matter how artistic or literarily shaped has an inherent historicality, in terms of at least the fact that an author . . . wrote it in a particular place or time . . . , using a variety of language of some linguistic community and it was read at least initially by readers in a given historical context who knew or understood the language, or at least sufficient to think that they were making sense of it.[16]

---

15. Robert Mulholland, "Sociological Criticism," in *New Testament Criticism & Interpretation*, ed. David Alan Black and David S. Dockery (Grand Rapids: Zondervan, 1991), 302.
16. S. E. Porter, "Literary Approaches to the New Testament: From Formalism to Deconstruction and Back," in *Approaches to New Testament Study*, ed. Stanley E. Porter and David Tombs (Sheffield: Sheffield Academic Press, 1995), 116.

In other words, no text arises out of a vacuum. All texts arise from a cultural and historical context that needs to be understood if the text is to be interpreted accurately. Our task thus includes reconstructing the specific situations that generated the need for this text. We need to try to grasp the perspective and mindset of the author.[17] These are rarely made explicit in the writing since both the author and his audience lived at the same time and in the same cultural context, and so shared similar perspectives.

Which areas yield the most useful data for reconstructing this context? We can look at geography, politics, economics, and history, including wars, cultural practices, and religious customs. We can find valuable information in Bible dictionaries, encyclopaedias, atlases, and so on. We can also make deductions from comments ancient writers made about the Old Testament, from the ancient Jewish sources known as Second Temple literature, and we can consider parallels from Qumran, rabbinic, and Greek sources.[18]

Researching this background information may be fascinating, and so it is wise to be alert to the danger of placing more emphasis on the background than on the message communicated by the text we are studying. Yet when we fail to take the perspective of the author into account, we may well miss the drama of a scene and the point the author intended to make.[19] Take the foot-washing scene in John 13. It is helpful to know that foot-washing was customarily the task of non-Jewish slaves. People who were socially inferior washed the feet of their superiors: it was never done the other way around. Without the cultural understanding that this task was considered too degrading for Jesus's disciples, or even Jewish slaves, we miss the significance of Jesus's action when he washed his disciples' feet. He was demonstrating radical service to others, the kind expected of all his followers.[20] Another example relates to the exodus. Failure to understand the significance of the exodus as the central or pivotal event in Israelite history also affects our interpretation. It results in a failure to understand the Jew's orientation to God, their

---

17. These categories derive from Klein et al., *Biblical Interpretation*, 229–30.
18. See Osborne, *Hermeneutical Spiral*, 127–139.
19. Osborne, 127–139.
20. Andreas J. Köstenberger, "John," *Baker Exegetical Commentary on the New Testament*, vol. 4 (Grand Rapids: Baker Academic, 2004), 403–405.

relationship to peoples of other nations, and their identity as a nation. Texts read without this understanding cannot be fully understood. For instance, when we read the story of Jesus and the Canaanite woman (Matt 15:22–28), Jesus insists that salvation is for the Jews. It may seem strange to us that he appears reluctant to heal her daughter. However, knowledge of the history of the Jews, always understood through the lens of their physical deliverance through the exodus, gives us a basis for understanding their special place in God's dealings with humankind with regard to spiritual deliverance.

What about mindset? In reading a text, one tries to understand not just the content presented but also the purpose behind the communication, as well as the intended emotional impact.[21] There are details about the text that are incomprehensible unless we know something about the period. Take the discussion between Boaz and the man who is Ruth's rightful guardian-redeemer in Ruth 4:7–8. At the end of the discussion, the guardian-redeemer removes his sandal. We will not understand the significance of this unless we know that at that time the removal of a sandal legalized transactions related to the redemption and transfer of property from one party to another. Today we legalize a transaction by signing a contract, not too long ago a handshake was sufficient, but in the period in which Ruth was set, taking off a sandal served the same function.

Fee and Stuart provide an excellent example of how to relate to the mindset of the author in their retelling of the parable of the Good Samaritan found in Luke 10:29–37.[22] They retell it using modern categories that we as readers can more easily relate to. The man set upon by thieves is represented by a poor family stranded at the side of the road, the priest is represented by the local bishop, the Levite by the president of the Kiwanis club (a charitable organization that focuses on community development), and the Samaritan by a well-known local atheist. The shock for the reader is realizing that it is the atheist who shows compassion. This way of telling the story captures the effect of Jesus's parable. It was not the religious leaders who did the right thing but the hated Samaritan.

---

21. Klein et al., *Biblical Interpretation*, 230–231.
22. Gordon D. Fee and Douglas Stuart, *How to Read the Bible for All Its Worth* (Grand Rapids: Zondervan, 1993), 147.

Since language is socially conditioned, studying the historical and cultural background is the main way of uncovering the mindset of the author. Once we understand what the writer was saying and what his message would have meant to the original hearers, we can more accurately interpret the message of the text for our times. This is the task of application to which we now turn our attention.

To sum up: *The fourth leg of the hermeneutical stool involves recognizing that the Bible cannot be understood in isolation from its historical and cultural context. A crucial aim of our study of the Bible is to understand what the text meant in its original context. To do so, we must enter into the world of the author and allow that world to guide our understanding.*

Seat: Application

We have now looked at all four legs of the hermeneutical stool. These legs do not exist in isolation from one another. Just as with any carpentry project, the legs need to be constantly adjusted in relation to each other to make sure that they are well balanced and provide a solid base for the application that will rest upon them. Our stool must not wobble! All four legs must be in constant contact with the seat of the stool and must support the seat.

In our model, the seat is the application of the text in the context of the modern African reader. This final step confirms the tentative application of the text that we discerned as we worked on legs 1 to 4. Given the holistic African approach, application should be understood to be taking place subconsciously from the point we first begin to engage with the text. Indeed, the text should bring up not just a mental or emotional response but also a practical one. This last step is therefore only a confirmation of how the text ought to be rightly applied in our current contexts. It is in this final stage that application is refined, based on the data that has been uncovered in all the preceding steps.

As we noted above, we are separated from the author of the text by time and culture. This means that there are numerous unknowns, so that it is not always easy to determine what the author meant. However, if we have done the necessary work on legs 1 to 4 of our stool, it is possible to arrive at the probable meaning intended by the author. Note that one of our basic assumptions in this book is that a text can only have one intended meaning – namely the meaning that the author intended to communicate when he wrote to his original audience. This is known as the authorial intent. Meaning is therefore understood to be single and determined by the author of the text.

But meaning is not the same as application. Application refers to the significance of the text for a modern audience. This means that while a text can have only one meaning, it can have multiple applications. Once we understand what the author intended to communicate to his original audience, we can legitimately apply this message to our multiple contexts. Our model therefore makes a distinction between meaning (as intended for the original readers) and significance (as applied to the modern reader).

This distinction is observed in other modern hermeneutical theories. Hirsch defines it as follows: "An interpreted text is always taken to represent something, but that something can always be related to something else. Significance is meaning-as-related-to-something-else."[23] We, the readers, must therefore recognize that meaning is the determinate or fixed representation of a text for an interpreter, whereas significance is fluid.

In African storytelling, this distinction between meaning and significance is related to the authority a storyteller has earned during their career because the community has learned to trust them. Ukachukwu refers to this as narrative authority.[24] One implication of narrative authority is that listeners cannot impose their assumptions on a story or make it mean whatever they want it to mean, in a postmodernist kind of way. The listener must allow the story to reveal itself, to come out of its shell, to unfurl its wings in order to allow us to catch a glimpse of its true reality. The story means something, but that something cannot be construed outside of the narrator's intention. Even though we, the listeners, become part of the story, we do not make the story "in our image." We must allow it to first guide us to its true shape and form before applying it to our contexts.

Oral literature in Africa always arose in response to a specific context, and this context was understood by both the narrator and the hearers.

---

23. E. D. Hirsch, *The Aims of Interpretation* (Chicago: University of Chicago Press, 1978), 79–80.
24. Ukachukwu, *Intercultural Hermeneutics*, 26.

However, although the story or song or riddle was intended to be applied to a particular contemporary reality, it was understood that similar contexts might arise in the future and would benefit from a reapplication of this wisdom. In Africa, the present is always visualized within the context of the past. And although the connection between past and present may sometimes be so close that they appear almost collapsed, there is still always a distinction between them. This means that while the meaning of the text remains constant, the significance or present relevance of the text for different generations, cultural groups and even individuals may change.

How, then, should we approach this final task of application? As we noted above, meaning is communicated in a specific cultural form. Application therefore requires that we separate the message from the cultural form in which it is communicated so that we can understand what the text signifies in our modern African contexts. What we are doing here is contextualizing the biblical message.

> Contextualization is the valid application of Scripture in any time-space context so that biblical truth is practiced, demonstrated, formulated, or communicated with no change in content or meaning, in the cultural, linguistic and mental patterns of that context.[25]

Contextualization recognizes that to bridge the gap between the biblical world and the modern world, the interpreter must have a grasp of both. Hopefully, the hermeneutical processes engaged in above make this possible.

Note that contextualization is not the same as syncretism. As pointed out in chapter one, syncretism results when we mix biblical and cultural elements without preserving biblical truth. To avoid syncretism, we need to be alert to the difference between culture-bound and trans-contextual truths.

Certain truths are relative and applicable only in a specific biblical context. We refer to these as culture-bound truths. Many commands in Deuteronomy and Leviticus fall into this category as they applied only to the newly liberated people of God. Note for instance Deuteronomy 22:11

---

25. Jack Willsey, "Essays in Biblical Hermeneutics," Northwest Baptist Seminary, 2004.

(see also Lev 19:19): "Do not wear clothes of wool and linen woven together." To insist that Christians today ought not to wear polyester cottons because those are made with a mix of fibres is to completely misunderstand the application of that verse. Rather, one must look for the principle behind this command and apply that. Taken in the context of the list of other prohibitions, this particular prohibition was meant to be an object lesson, reminding the Israelites that God did not want his people to mix ideas from other religions with their worship of him. God was demanding holiness from his people.

Other truths, however, are absolute and apply to any culture at any time in history. We refer to these as trans-contextual truths. For instance, the Ten Commandments found in Exodus 20:1–17 are trans-contextual. Unlike culture-bound truths, trans-contextual truths may appear as though they can be applied directly to our modern societies. This is because they are phrased in general terms. For instance, Exodus 20:12 states: "Honour your father and your mother, so that you may live long in the land the LORD your God is giving you." The idea of honouring one's parents is a trans-contextual truth. However, the way this honour is expressed in modern Africa may not be identical to the way it was expressed among the Israelites. We must therefore seek to reframe the application in a way that is relevant to modern Africans.

When dealing with trans-contextual truths, we emphasize the reader's engagement with both worlds. Hence, it is important to understand that trans-contextual truths expressed in biblical cultural forms fit exactly into the biblical society but do not fit equally smoothly into African society. Therefore, these trans-contextual truths must be de-culturized or decontextualized from the biblical cultural forms and then re-culturized into specific African cultural forms in order to fit African society.[26] The same can be done for other contexts.

In terms of methodology, it is crucial to take the following steps when developing an application (we will continue with the example from Exod 20:12):

i) Distinguish the trans-contextual content of Christianity and its attendant forms and expressions in African culture.

---

26. Adapted, with some changes, from Seto's model of contextualizing in Asian society, Seto, "An Asian Looks at Contextualization and Developing Ethnotheologies," 138.

The trans-contextual content in this case is the concept of honouring one's parents (see also Deut 5:16). This concept is also known in traditional African culture, where honouring one's parents took the form of obedience, respect, caring for one's parents in their old age, and proper conduct so as not to bring shame on the family name.

ii) Attempt to disengage the trans-contextual or non-cultural doctrines of Christianity from the biblical cultural forms. In the Jewish culture, honour primarily had to do with obedience. For instance, a father had the right to give his daughter in marriage (see Deut 22:16; Josh 15:16; Judg 12:9). For her to refuse this union would be to dishonour her parents. This is one cultural form of this command.

iii) Reframe these trans-contextual truths in African cultural forms and expressions.[27] How do we reframe obedience as honour in a way that is relevant for Africans? For example, while the Jewish concept of arranged marriages is similar to the practice in African traditional culture, modern African culture is changing. Obedience to parents is still expected but, in general, women of marriageable age are free to choose their own spouses. Honouring one's parents would therefore not extend to accepting a spouse the father has chosen. However, eloping or failing to follow the prescribed formalities related to marriage would constitute dishonour. The parents can still expect that a bride price will be paid and that there will be formal visits to the man's home to initiate a relationship at the family level.

As we go about the task of application, we must be careful not to treat trans-contextual truths as relative or to make culture-bound truths applicable to all without regard for the fact that these truths applied to a particular situation in the lives of the original hearers. This is a further reason why we need to determine the meaning of a text to its original readers before we come to a final determination of its application to our present context. This application should be expressed in terms that we understand in African society.

---

27. Adapted with some changes from James O. Buswell, III, "Contextualization: Theory, Tradition and Method," in *Theology and Mission*, ed. David J. Hesselgrave (Grand Rapids: Baker, 1978), 103.

Conclusion

This chapter has attempted to provide a theoretical framework for an intercultural African biblical hermeneutic. The four-legged stool model proposes five steps in analyzing biblical texts:

Leg 1: Parallels to the African context

Leg 2: Theological context

Leg 3: Literary context

Leg 4: Historical and cultural context

Seat: Application

All these steps are necessary to uncover the original intended meaning of any given text and its application to the life of an African believer today.

In the second part of this book, we offer a brief overview of the context of the Bible as a whole before providing guidelines for interpreting various literary genres and fleshing out practical interpretations for each of them, using examples from African literature as well as the Bible.

Questions for Review

1. In your own words, explain the importance of understanding the four legs of the hermeneutical stool.

>   Parallels to the African context
>   Theological context
>   Literary context
>   Historical/cultural context

2. What are some of the dangers we might face in our doctrine and practice if we do not first seek to understand the text in its original context?

3. How would you retell the story of the Good Samaritan in your own context?

PART II

SPECIFIC PRINCIPLES OF HERMENEUTICS

In the previous section, we noted that many African Christians live dichotomized lives because they are unable to understand how their faith informs their everyday lives. Consequently our Christianity is corrupted by wrong cultural practices. As a solution to this problem, we proposed an approach to hermeneutics that incorporates the African context. We emphasized that knowing our African cultures and worldviews is a valuable first step in interpreting the Bible. We also recognized that our assumptions influence us either positively or negatively as we interpret the Bible. Using this knowledge as a foundation, we developed a model for approaching the text of the Bible. This four-legged stool model uses our African context as a bridge to move us as readers from our known world into the unknown world of the Bible.

It is now time to apply what was discussed in the first half of the book to the various genres of texts found in the Bible. Before we can do that, however, we need to understand what it is that we are studying. Having understood our own African context, we must also understand the context of the Bible to ensure accurate interpretation. Thus this section begins with a brief introduction to the context of the Bible before discussing the genres of stories, wisdom literature, songs and letters. While there are other genres we could have identified, these four broad categories cover most of them and lay a foundation for further study.

5

UNDERSTANDING THE CONTEXT OF THE BIBLE

This chapter provides a brief introduction to the context of the Bible – specifically providing a basic understanding of what the Bible is from a theological, literary and historical/cultural perspective. These three categories are closely related to legs 2, 3 and 4 of the four-legged stool model. We will thus be focusing only on areas that significantly enhance our ability to carry out the hermeneutical task using the model laid out in this book. We will look at how the Bible is organized, and how the three contexts (theological, literary and historical/cultural) contribute to a better understanding of its contents.

The Importance of Studying the Bible

The Bible is an ancient book that is still of great significance in twenty-first-century Africa because it is God's special revelation of himself. Thus the only way to know and understand what God intends for his people is to study his word. Much of this revelation is given in the context of God's dealings in the past, but the Bible also deals with our present and our future as believers. It thus has as much relevance today as it did in the past and provides us with answers for life's questions.

As we saw in Part I of this book, our African worldview influences our perceptions of life. Some of these perceptions may be right and some may be wrong, but the only way to identify which is which is to test them against the Bible. Studying the Bible forces us to confront our assumptions about life and start developing a biblical worldview. It also enables us to avoid syncretism in the practice of our African Christianity.

Finally, studying the Bible is a means of establishing and strengthening the community of faith. It enables us to connect with believers in our present as well as with our great African predecessors such as Origen and Augustine. We can and should continue their tradition of excellence.

The Old Testament

The Bible is divided into two parts, the Old Testament and the New Testament. The Old Testament comprises the Scriptures God gave to the Hebrew people (also known as Israelites or Jews) over the course of many centuries. The bulk of the Old Testament was originally written in Hebrew, although a few chapters in books like Daniel are in Aramaic. These writings were produced over a period of more than a thousand years from around 1200 BC to 200 BC. Much of the Old Testament is composed of stories from the oral traditions of the people who came to be known as Israel.[1]

Organization

The Old Testament is traditionally divided into five parts:

1. The Law (or the Pentateuch), which consists of the first five books of the Bible – Genesis, Exodus, Leviticus, Numbers, and Deuteronomy.
2. Historical books – Joshua, Judges, Ruth, 1 and 2 Samuel, 1 and 2 Kings, 1 and 2 Chronicles, Ezra, Nehemiah and Esther.
3. Poetic books – Job, Psalms, Proverbs, Ecclesiastes and Song of Solomon.
4. The Major Prophets, that is, the longer prophetic writings – Isaiah, Jeremiah, Lamentations, Ezekiel and Daniel.
5. The Minor Prophets, that is, the shorter prophetic writings – Hosea, Joel, Amos, Obadiah, Jonah, Micah, Nahum, Habakkuk, Zephaniah, Haggai, Zechariah and Malachi.

---
1. John H. Tullock, *The Old Testament Story* (Upper Saddle River, NJ: Pearson Prentice Hall, 2001), 5.

Given the number and range of the books it contains, we can describe the Old Testament as a library. Whenever we interpret a text from the Old Testament, it is important to identify the section from which it comes. This is very useful, particularly in identifying genre.

Theological context

The Old Testament is, however, more than just a library; it is also a spiritual document. It is spiritually authoritative because biblical writers and even Jesus himself acknowledged it as such when they referred to it. It is important that we grasp its theological emphases as these are an important guide to interpretation as we work on the second leg of our hermeneutical stool. We must be careful not to arrive at an interpretation of an Old Testament passage that contradicts the theology of the Old Testament.

Of the many theological themes in the Old Testament, at least six stand out because of their importance and because they constantly recur:

1. *God*: God is introduced in the very first chapter of the Bible. His existence is taken for granted and his role as creator is amplified throughout that first chapter of Genesis. The rest of the Bible reveals more about his identity, nature and character. He is shown as sovereign over his creation. His attributes include self-existence, self-sufficiency and self-sustenance, as well as omniscience, omnipresence, transcendence and immanence. His character is revealed in his holiness, grace and love.
2. *Sin*: Sin is also introduced in the very first book of the Old Testament. In Genesis we read of the entrance of sin, its nature and its consequences. The Old Testament also documents the continued escalation of sin as well as God's intervention and the promise of an ultimate solution to sin through the Messiah.
3. *Faith*: Throughout the Old Testament, biblical authors document the role of faith in the lives of God's people. Individuals such as Noah, Abraham, Moses, Ruth, David, Nehemiah, and Isaiah demonstrated faith by their actions and

teach us what it means to live a life of faith, particularly in the midst of testing.
4. *Promise/Covenant*: This is a theme that runs through the Old Testament. God is presented as a faithful God who covenants with his people, assuring them that his promises to them will be honoured.
5. *Exile and restoration*: The theme of exile reveals itself very early in the biblical text of Genesis. God warned his people that if they disobeyed him, he would discipline them by allowing enemy nations to rule over them and take them away as captives. However, he also promised that when they repented and returned to him, he would restore them to the land.
6. *Salvation*: The Old Testament speaks of both physical and spiritual salvation. In the opening book of the Old Testament, God promises to send a Saviour with the power to defeat Satan. This Saviour, who is revealed to be a king from the lineage of David, is mentioned in various places throughout the Old Testament.

Literary context

Genres of the Old Testament

The genres of the Old Testament can be categorized in different ways. In general, however, there are at least four main genres that make up the Old Testament: narrative, poetry, wisdom and prophecy.[2]

1. *Narrative*: Simply put, a narrative is a story. Much of the Old Testament consists of stories that tell of God's dealings first with human beings in general and then with the people of Israel, and by extension with foreign nations that had dealings with Israel. This genre is dominant from Genesis through 2 Kings. It is also found in major portions of the prophetic books including Isaiah, Jeremiah, Ezekiel, Jonah, Haggai, Zechariah and Malachi, and also in 1 and 2 Chronicles, Ezra,

---

2. See categories as listed by Klein et al., *Biblical Interpretation*, 323–397. While they also list law as a major category, it does not stand alone and is generally incorporated in narrative.

Nehemiah, Esther, Daniel, and Ruth. It is important to remember that labelling these passages as narratives or stories does not mean that they are not historical accounts.[3]

2. *Poetry*: This genre is dominant in Psalms and the Song of Songs. However, it is also found in several narrative sections of the Old Testament. For instance, Exodus 15 includes the songs of Moses and Miriam after the parting of the Red Sea. In addition, extensive sections of prophetic books like Isaiah incorporate poetry.

3. *Wisdom*: Wisdom literature could be categorized as a form of poetry, but because it addresses a unique subject it is generally treated on its own. Wisdom literature expounds on the theme of how to live wisely in the midst of competing and conflicting ideas. It is represented by books such as Proverbs, Job, and Ecclesiastes, but can also be found in other Old Testament books. This genre ranges from extended wisdom poems to one-line (in Hebrew) proverbs.[4]

4. *Prophecy*: Prophetic literature is prominent in the divisions of the Scriptures known as the Major and Minor Prophets. While the word "prophecy" may suggest that this genre of literature focuses on foretelling God's acts in the future, much of it focuses on "forthtelling," that is, on announcing God's judgements in the present or near future.[5] As with the narrative genre, there are several types of prophecy.

Literature associated with the Old Testament

Much of the literature associated with the Old Testament was produced by Jewish authors during what is referred to as the Second Temple period. This period stretches from the reconstruction of the temple in Jerusalem after the exile to the destruction of that temple by the Romans. Thus it covers the period between roughly 530 BC and AD 70. The writings produced in this period include translations of the Hebrew Scriptures as well as expansions and rewritings of these Scriptures. We know these works as the Septuagint (the Old Testament in Greek), the Apocrypha,

---

3. Klein et al., 326.
4. Tullock, *The Old Testament Story*, 3.
5. Klein et al., *Biblical Interpretation*, 359.

the pseudepigrapha and the Dead Sea Scrolls.

The first thing that must be emphasized is that, apart from most of the books of the Septuagint, this Second Temple literature is not canonical in the Protestant tradition. However, it does provide us with a glimpse of what was happening in the lives of the Jewish people in that period. It also enables us to appreciate the struggles that they were facing, particularly regarding their faith. This is valuable background for understanding the ministry of Jesus and the issues surrounding the founding of the early church. The literature also provides crucial historical and cultural data that is an invaluable resource in the hermeneutical task.

Historical and cultural context

Before the Old Testament came to be in the form in which we have it today, it went through a process known as canonization. The word *canon* is derived from the Hebrew word *quaneh*, which literally means a straight rod. It originally referred to a reed used for measuring, like a yardstick.[6] In time, it came to be used of the Old Testament, and biblical literature in general, to indicate a body of writing that served as a standard because it was held to be sacred. The canonization process of the Old Testament was a lengthy one that took place approximately between 400 BC and AD 90. The final form of the Old Testament canon was officially recognized by the Council of Jamnia (AD 90), but it is generally acknowledged that this council did not determine which books belonged in the Old Testament; rather, it confirmed the books that had been recognized as orthodox for generations.

The historical/cultural setting of the events recorded in the Old Testament is ancient Israel, which was part of a larger region known as the Ancient Near East. This region, which is also referred to as the Fertile Crescent, stretched from Mesopotamia in the north, through Syria-Palestine, and on to Egypt. Today, this region is known as the Middle East.

It is difficult to establish an exact chronology for the whole of the Old Testament, for it developed over a period of two thousand years and historians do not have sufficient data for precise dating. Both the historical

---

6. Bill T. Arnold and Bryan Beyer, *Encountering the Old Testament* (Grand Rapids: Baker Academic, 1999, 2008), 22.

and the cultural context vary greatly as one moves from Genesis to the later prophetic literature. The period covered spans great technological changes like the invention of writing and the rise of metal-working, and many changes in international affiliations. All of these changes influenced the social, economic, legal, political, military and religious life of Israel.

The New Testament

The New Testament is the second part of the Bible. In terms of content, it is much smaller than the Old Testament. It was written much later than the Old Testament and over a much shorter period of time. Most conservative approximations of the dates of writing range between AD 58 and AD 100. The New Testament is generally considered to be the primary source of doctrine for the church.

Organization

The New Testament has four major parts:

1. The four gospels – Matthew, Mark, Luke and John.
2. One historical book – the Acts of the Apostles.
3. Twenty-one letters, which can be subdivided into three groups:
    - Pauline epistles – Romans, 1 and 2 Corinthians, Galatians, Ephesians, Philippians, Colossians, 1 and 2 Thessalonians, 1 and 2 Timothy, Titus, Philemon.
    - Johannine epistles – 1, 2 and 3 John.
    - General epistles – Hebrews, James, 1 and 2 Peter, Jude.
4. One apocalypse – Revelation.

Theological context

Like the Old Testament, the New Testament can be regarded as a literary work with all the artistry and beauty that label implies. However, it too is far more than that – it is also a spiritual document that tells the story of the saving life and ministry of Jesus Christ, the establishment and growth of the early church, the challenges faced by the early believers, and the establishment of church government. It culminates in a promise of the future redemption and glorification of believers as God works out his purposes in history.

The following major theological themes emerge from a study of the New Testament:

- *God*: While the nature, attributes and character of God are explored in depth in the Old Testament, it is in the New Testament that the Trinitarian nature of God is more fully revealed. The birth of the incarnate Christ and the dramatic entrance of the Holy Spirit, particularly in Acts, flesh out in more detail the relationship between the Father, the Son and the Holy Spirit, and show how believers are to worship in light of this revelation. Jesus Christ represents God's special revelation of himself to humankind.

- *Salvation*: The very first chapter of the Old Testament describes the entrance of sin into the world with subsequent chapters and books documenting its explosive growth and effect on the relationship between God and human beings and on relationships between people. The Old Testament contains hints about the solution to sin. The New Testament expounds this solution, offering a salvation that bridges the gulf between human beings and God. This salvation, as we are told from the very first of the gospels, comes in the person of Jesus Christ. It is wholly God's work of grace in Christ through which he rescues human beings from eternal damnation and saves them from the penalty and power of sin.

- *Sacrifice*: The concept of sacrifice is introduced and expounded in the Old Testament, particularly in the book of Leviticus. The New Testament completes our understanding of sacrifice by highlighting the sacrificial death of Jesus Christ as the once-for-all atonement for humanity's sin, completely satisfying God's requirements and restoring our relationship with him. Believers no longer need to offer physical sacrifices; however, it is expected that as they grow in spiritual maturity, they will offer themselves as spiritual sacrifices.

- *Faith*: While faith in God is clearly seen in Old Testament narratives, it is in the New Testament that it finds its fullest expression. Faith in the person of Jesus Christ is a major theme of the New Testament. Indeed, it is essential, for as the writer of Hebrews states, "Without faith it is impossible to please God" (Heb 11:6). Faith is frequently contrasted with works, but as both James and Paul point out, works are the expression of genuine faith.

- *Sanctification*: Sanctification is one of the richest themes throughout the New Testament and is often understood in relation to holiness. Believers are encouraged to grow in spiritual maturity and to bear fruit that lasts. From the gospels all the way through to the letters of Paul and even extending into Revelation, there is a requirement that believers allow the Holy Spirit to work in their lives to convict them of what is not acceptable to God. The goal of sanctification is to grow in Christlikeness, allowing the Holy Spirit to transform every aspect of our lives. Sanctification is both a work of God and a human work.

- *Mission*: One of the key characteristics of the New Testament church is its emphasis on mission. Believers are not to hoard their faith but are to go out into the world, making disciples of all nations (Matt 19:28). This last command given by Jesus just prior to his ascension is reflected throughout the writings of New Testament authors. God desires to restore his relationship with the peoples of the world by reconciling them to himself through Jesus Christ.

- *New Creation*: While the Old Testament begins the theme of creation, the New Testament unveils the nature and means of God's new creation. It begins with the life, death and resurrection of Jesus Christ and culminates in his triumphant second coming, as described in the book of Revelation. Throughout the New Testament, the biblical writers make it clear that believers have a future hope and that this present life with all its trials and struggles will one day be done away with. God will surely make all things new.

Literary context

Genres of the New Testament

Like the Old Testament, the New Testament contains several genres of writing. The three main ones are as follows:

- *Narrative*: This is the major genre found in the gospels and the Acts of the Apostles. As in the Old Testament, this genre is used to communicate information in story form. In the New Testament, the stories focus on Jesus and the establishment of the early church.

- *Epistle (or letters)*: This genre dominates the New Testament. The letters tend to be contextual as they are generally written in response to a particular problem or situation.

- *Apocalypse*: The only apocalyptic document in the New Testament is the book of Revelation, which has such distinctive content that it deserves its own category. Apocalypses are primarily concerned with supernatural revelations from God, often communicated through visions. They are generally concerned with "impending upheavals that culminate in the end of this world and a new creation."[7] The book of Revelation is unique in that, while it is primarily an apocalypse, it is also a prophecy that is presented in the form of a letter.

Literature associated with the New Testament

As with the Old Testament, there are many works associated with the New Testament because they were written at much the same time and in the same culture. The most significant are the New Testament apocrypha and pseudepigrapha, as well as the writings of the Jewish historian Josephus. Others include various versions and expansions of Scripture, writings by the church fathers, rabbinic writings, and targums, as well as apocryphal and pseudepigraphical works.[8]

This associated literature provides valuable background to the cultural, political, social and religious contexts in which the New Testament was

---

7. John J. Collins, "Apocalyptic Literature," *Dictionary of New Testament Background*, 40.
8. David A. DeSilva, "Writing and Literature: Jewish," *Dictionary of New Testament Background*, 1289.

birthed. It also enables modern readers to understand the nature of the literature of the time, particularly with respect to genre. This provides some clues as to how this kind of literature was understood. Some of this literature, such as the New Testament apocrypha, also reveals the response of early believers to various situations. In addition, it provides crucial information about the struggles within Judaism that help us understand Jesus's ministry, as well as the struggles with competing Jewish groups that shaped the New Testament text and its theology.

Historical and cultural context

It is believed that before the New Testament as we know it came into being, early Christians assembled collections of Old Testament scriptures that they used to support their teaching and preaching. We see examples of these in Romans 9:25–29; Romans 10:18–21 and Hebrews 1:5–13.[9] They also seem to have developed their own creedal statements, hymns, confessions, and prayers. We can see evidence of this in Paul's reference to "what I received" (1 Cor 15:3), his use of the Aramaic prayer *marana tha* (1 Cor 16:22) and of what appears to be an early Jewish Christian creedal statement in Romans 1:3–4, and the quoted summary of Jesus's story in Philippians 2:5–11.[10]

At that stage, it appears that the message of the gospel was still communicated largely in oral form. However, with time the early Christians became aware of the need to put their message in writing (and eventually form a collection that was considered canonical). The following factors shaped their thinking:[11]

1. The deaths of the eyewitnesses and apostles sparked an awareness of the need to preserve their oral testimony to Christ's life and the growth of the early church.
2. Challenges posed by the distance in time from the historical Jesus may have raised the need for a written form of his teachings.

---

9. Witherington, *New Testament Story*, 14–17.
10. Witherington, 14–17.
11. Witherington, 100.

3. The church felt the need to preserve books that were considered valuable since they were written by an apostle or prophet.
4. Theological and ethical problems in the early church meant that believers needed to know which books should be used in the churches and which should not. For instance, as early as AD 140, the heretical Marcion accepted only limited sections of the New Testament canon and deleted portions that he considered unacceptable.
5. On the positive side, there was the missionary stimulus. The rapid spread of Christianity meant that the Bible needed to be translated into other languages. As early as the first half of the second century, the Bible was translated into Syriac and Old Latin.
6. Persecutions and politics ushered in the final phase of full and general recognition of the whole canon of New Testament writings. The persecutions under Diocletian and Maximilian (AD 302/303–13) provided a strong motivation for the completion of the canon. It would provide a standardized source for faith so that those under persecution would not fall into heresy.

The twenty-seven books that comprise the New Testament were formally recognized at the Council of Carthage in AD 387. However, as with the Council of Jamnia and the Old Testament, this council did not decide which books should be considered canonical, but rather confirmed the books that had been recognized as inspired and authoritative since the end of the first century. Canonization can be defined as the creative and historical process by which these books came to be acknowledged as sacred.

Information about the socio-political environment of the New Testament is invaluable when it comes to interpreting the biblical text. For instance, it is important to recognize that the events of the New Testament took place during the time of Roman rule. The Jews were not ruled by a Jewish king but were subject to a Roman governor and forced to pay taxes to Rome. They frequently rebelled against Roman rule as they awaited a physical deliverer. While Jesus came as a spiritual deliverer, many of his contemporaries did not understand that. Even his closest allies, his disciples, went so far as to ask (after his resurrection) if he planned to restore the kingdom to Israel, showing their continued expectation of physical deliverance (Acts 1:6).

Understanding the religious environment is also significant for the study of the New Testament. The Jews were not a homogenous group but included the Jews of the Diaspora (or Dispersion), Hebraists and Hellenists, as well as the scribes, Pharisees, Sadducees, and the common people. The most prominent groups in biblical literature are the Pharisees and the Sadducees, who opposed Jesus at every turn.

Conclusion

To ensure accurate interpretation, we must understand not only our African context but also the context of the Bible. This chapter has provided a brief discussion of this context, focusing on theological, literary and cultural-historical perspectives. These are the categories that are important when applying the hermeneutical model laid out in this book. In the next few chapters, we will use this understanding as a base as we apply the four-legged stool model to various genres found in the Bible.

6

INTERPRETING STORIES

Most people need no explanation of what a story is. As children, we were constantly exposed to stories at home and at school. If asked, you could probably easily identify a favourite story. You would also know that a story is not a poem or a song, although it may certainly include one of these in its telling. But when it comes to hermeneutics and the interpretation of stories, we need to be able to give a more detailed definition of what a story is, and of how and why stories are told. As Osborne says, "The interpretation of narrative has two tasks: poetics, which studies the artistic dimension or the way the text is constructed by the author; and meaning, which re-creates the message that the author is communicating."[1] This means that when we read or hear a story, we must account for the way it is arranged as well as the meaning it communicates. In this chapter, we will be looking at how this works out in practice in relation to African stories and to the stories in the Bible.

The Story Genre

If pressed to define what a story or narrative is, we could say that it is an artistic arrangement of specific content to communicate some meaning (and/or emotion) through the unfolding of scenes or episodes. This content may be fictional or it may reflect real events, and it may be presented in written or in oral form, the latter being more common in Africa.

---

1. Osborne, *The Hermeneutical Spiral*, 154.

A key element of stories is that they involve two distinct but interconnected worlds. There is the world of the narrator and listener (whom we could call the agents of communication), and the world within the story itself. In interpreting stories, one must understand how these two worlds function and interact to communicate the meaning of the story. Both help to move the story forward to its conclusion. So while we may talk about them separately, it must be understood that they are in constant interaction with one another.

The world of the agents of communication

The world of the narrator and the listener is more clearly apparent when we are speaking of oral stories, for we can all envisage scenes where a parent or community elder is telling stories to an attentive audience. Nevertheless, this world is also present in written stories like those we find in the Bible. Many of the stories we read in the Bible were originally oral stories treasured by the people of Israel. Other biblical stories may have been in written form, but they were written in a context where they would be read aloud to others (see, for example, Moses's instructions in Deuteronomy 31:11–13 and Ezra's public reading of the law in Nehemiah 8:1–8). Moreover, many Bible stories are still told in churches and Sunday schools to this day. So the agents of communication are still relevant when looking at the Bible.

The narrator

The narrator is the person who is telling the story. This person matters, for the authority of the storyteller is crucial for successful storytelling. Traditional stories could not be told by just anyone in the community. They could only be told by people of proven authority. Moreover, a narrator will have some purpose in telling a story, even if that purpose is only to entertain. It is important to note that in traditional African storytelling, a story can only mean what the narrator intends it to mean. We, the listeners, do not have permission to construct our own meanings but must allow the narrator to communicate the meaning through the vehicle of the story.

The listener

While the narrator does the telling, the listener does the listening. In most cultures, it is not only the social setting (the time and place where the story is told) that determines the kind of story and how it is told. The listeners, whether children, youths or adults, also play a role.[2]

The listener's role may be less obvious when reading a written story (although it is not absent – if readers do not become involved with the story, they will stop reading it). But it is impossible to miss the listener's role in oral storytelling. Listening in Africa is not a passive affair. As explained in chapter four, it is holistic or active and involves community listening, visualization, enthusiastic responses, and so forth. We see evidence of this in the Bible too when we see how the hearers reacted to Ezra's reading of the law (Neh 8:9).

The world of the story

The world of the story is concerned with what happens within the story itself, from its opening to its closing words (for stories have a defined beginning and ending). It includes the plot of the story, which revolves around the main characters and is the vehicle that drives the story forward from one point to the next until it arrives at its logical conclusion.

The world of the story also includes characterization, which is how the characters in a story are presented and developed. Some minor characters are barely mentioned, whereas other characters are developed quite significantly, so that we could call them full-fledged characters. Characterization is sometimes accomplished through the use of dialogue. Parts of the story may be told by a narrator in his or her own words, but at other times the characters in the story may speak for themselves.

Time is also an element within the world of the story. It may pass quickly or slowly, with events appearing to speed up at certain points and slow down at others, depending on what the narrator wishes the listener to focus on. Aspects of a story that are not viewed as crucial may be covered in a single statement ("a thousand years passed"). Or, the narrator may choose to slow down narrative time almost to a snail's pace

---

2. Naomi Kipury, *Oral Literature of the Maasai* (Nairobi: East African Educational Publishers, 1983), 10.

("Tick, tick, tick – Musa looked at the clock again. Only one minute had passed by, although it seemed like hours").

African Stories

For most Africans, stories and other forms of art are part of our daily lives and part of the way we learn how we should live. They serve many functions, including preserving the culture of a civilization, explaining natural phenomena, transmitting historical and social information, and teaching moral and ethical lessons.[3]

For our purposes, we can identify the following four main functions:

Communicating moral values. Stories are an important means of building character and ensuring cohesion within the community. It is through stories that listeners begin to understand the cultural values and norms that are valued in their specific community. Without stories, how could one even begin to grasp the need for societal values and character traits such as honesty, integrity, morality, fairness and respect for elders?

Communicating information. Stories pass on the historical information that is necessary for a community to understand its heritage. Knowing where we have come from as a people is important when it comes to determining our future path. Other stories may communicate theological information or prophetic material, as in the following story told by the Gikuyu people. It uses symbolic language as it speaks of the building of the railway, the presence of airplanes, and the weapons of the colonialists:

> Muhang'u used to narrate to his son what the future held for the country as foretold by Mugo wa Kibiru, the great seer. "One day, a white man whose skin resembles that of a toad, will arrive in our land. He will bring with him a long snake which will embark on a long journey, starting from the great ocean in the east, and terminating at the great lake in the west. The snake will signify the advent of the white man. He will also bring with him butterflies which will fly high in the sky and disappear in the horizon, as the sun travels from east to west.

---
3. E. K. Taylor, *Using Folktales* (Cambridge: Cambridge University Press, 2000).

The white man will be armed with a stick which spits out fire and smoke and kills instantly." The great seer strongly advised against going to war with this man. "He is too strong for us to resist him, effectively. He will rule over us for many seasons, but eventually, when the fig tree (*Mugumo*) at Thika dries up, he will go, but not without a struggle."[4]

Passing on mythology. The myths and legends of a people are generally stories that explain their origins and the origins of natural phenomena.

Entertaining listeners. While the first three categories of stories all have a didactic or teaching purpose, the last category is merely intended for enjoyment.[5] Some stories are told simply for fun and entertainment.

While categorizations like these can be useful, it is important to remember that African stories are not rigid in function. They are flexible, and their function may vary depending on the teller and the occasion. Thus while the meaning of a story does not change, it may be used for several different functions.[6]

We must also remember that while stories from across Africa may seem to have similar plots, motifs and sometimes even characters, these superficial similarities should not lead us to ignore critical differences in tone and character. Finnegan gives us a good example of this. She retells the story of the misfortunes of the hen as told by storytellers from Kenya and from Sierra Leone. The story from Kenya explains why vultures prey on chickens. The story from Sierra Leone explains why eagles prey on chickens. While both stories have the same general framework, the plot unfolds in a different manner, and the story from Sierra Leone includes an additional character, a finch. In the story from Kenya, the hen is careless and fails to keep her promise to the eagle. In the one from Sierra Leone, the finch is the actual culprit but manages to put the blame on the hen. In both stories, while the "journey" is different, the outcome is the same – chickens become prey.[7]

---

4. As extracted from James M. Waiyaki, *The Story of Muhang'u: A Precolonial Look,* forthcoming.
5. Ruth Finnegan, *Oral Literature in Africa* (Oxford: Oxford University Press, 1976 (1994 printing), 321.
6. Finnegan, *Oral Literature in Africa,* 320.
7. Finnegan, 328–333.

At this point I should also point out that African stories include many kinds of characters. In some stories, the main characters are animals, whereas in others they are human beings (historical or otherwise). There are also stories that feature fantasy characters such as ogres. It is not unusual to find several different types of characters in one story, as well as a deity. Each type of character serves a specific purpose in the story. Fantasy characters, for example, often communicate certain values. For example, the ogre who frequently appears in Kalenjin stories symbolizes deception, destruction and the power of evil.[8]

While African stories must be read holistically, it is good to take the time to appreciate their beauty and artistry as well as how well they communicate. When we do this, we recognize how the details of the story and the narrator's technique provide us with an interpretive key. Once we have learned how to use this key on the African story that follows, we may also be able to use it to unlock the biblical story that follows.

Interpreting an African story

Immerse yourself in the short story below. Allow yourself to step into the world of the narrator, taking on first one character, then the other. Everything that should be viewed as narration has been italicized, while all direct speech is in regular font. In this story, as is common in folk stories from Africa, the hippopotamus is given the capacity to use language as a medium of communication.

> *The Gikuyu people believe that in the days of long, long ago, when the Good Lord N'gai made his plans for all the creatures upon his earth, he made the hippopotamus as an animal of the forests and plains. But the hippopotamus was greedy and, finding plenty of food all round him and no enemies to worry about, he grew fatter, and fatter and fatter. And the fatter he grew, the more he suffered from the heat of the equatorial midday sun.*
>
> *Day after day, when he waddled down to the river for his drink, he gazed with envy at the little fish that swam in the pool which was cooled by the melted snows from far-away Mount Kenya.* "Oh"

---

8. C. Chesaina, *Oral Literature of the Kalenjin* (Nairobi: East African Educational Publishers, 1991), 11.

he would sigh, "how wonderful it would be if I could live, like N'gai's little fish, in the clear, cool, refreshing water!"

The hippopotamus pondered over his trouble for many days, and eventually decided to approach the lord of all creation. "Please, Good Lord N'gai" *he cried loudly to the heavens upon one particularly hot day*, "allow me to leave the forests and the plains. Let me live instead in the clear, cool waters of your rivers and lakes, for the heat of the fiery sun is killing me!"

"No," *replied Lord N'gai*, "for my little fish are very dear to me, and if you were to live in the rivers and lakes, you might try a change of your eating habits, and begin to eat those little fish. That would never do. No, you must continue to live upon the dry land."

So the hippopotamus stayed sadly in his home in the forests and plains, where the sun continued to beat down mercilessly on his unprotected hide. "This is more that I can bear!" *moaned the poor creature.* "Please, please, Good Lord N'gai, let me leave the forests and plains, and become a creature of the rivers and lakes, I promise most faithfully that I will not eat your little fish."

The Great Lord N'gai thought the matter over, while he looked down upon the plains baking in the heat of the tropical sun, and eventually his heart softened. "Very well," *he agreed*, "I will allow you to live in my rivers and lakes, but how will you prove to me that you are not eating my little fish?"

"I will lie in the cool of the water by day, and at night time I will browse along the banks of the rivers and in the valleys," *replied the hippopotamus.* "I promise that I will not eat your little fish."

"But that will not be proof to me that you are keeping your promise!" *pointed out the Great Lord N'gai.* "Well then," *answered the hippopotamus*, "I will come out of the water every time that food passes through my body, and I will scatter my dung on the earth with my tail. All that I have eaten will be spread out in your sight, and you will see for yourself that there are no fish bones. Surely this will be proof enough!"

So this is why, to this very day, the hippopotamus comes out of the water to scatter its dung as it looks up to heaven

and says, "Look N'gai, no fish!" – and that is why hippos don't eat fish!

Even a simple story such as this communicates a great deal. We will become even more aware of this as we examine it, drawing on some of the elements referred to in the four-legged stool model we discussed in chapter 4.

Genre

This example is clearly a story told by a narrator. While we may not be able to identify the narrator in the written form of the story, the manner of telling shows evidence of a measure of authority. This storyteller is assumed to be a person of integrity because the story clearly supports aspects of the Gikuyu culture and worldview. The narrator's intention is also clear. He or she wants to explain why hippos are vegetarians, and specifically why they don't eat fish. There is no other hidden meaning to read between the lines, although we might draw out principles relating to self-control and gluttony and deduce certain things about the character of N'gai.

One can easily imagine a rapt audience taking in every word of the hippo's story, cheering or groaning as the story unfolds, sympathizing out loud with Hippo's torment, and even nodding in agreement as N'gai's judgement is pronounced.

The world of the story

The world of the story is concerned with what happens within the story itself, from the opening formula, "A long, long time ago" to the closing formula, "and that is why. . . ." A number of literary techniques work together to contribute to the world of the story and to the beauty and artistry with which it is presented. They also help to communicate its meaning.

Plot

The plot of many African stories can be described as cyclical linear. In other words, although the plot is constantly moving the story forward, there are times when things seem to be going backwards, particularly when a surprise element is introduced.

In the story above, the plot begins with Hippo's greed that leads to his becoming obese. His growing discomfort triggers his request to N'gai to allow him to live in the lake. This request will surprise African hearers who know that N'gai is transcendent and has only a distant relationship with this world. That is why Hippo does not take the decision to approach N'gai in person lightly but ponders his troubles for many days before doing so.

The plot continues to unfold with N'gai's refusal of Hippo's request. Knowing both his character and Hippo's, the hearers will not expect N'gai to change his mind. So the plot appears to move backwards to where it started, with Hippo enduring growing discomfort until he repeats his request. The listeners are again surprised that this time N'gai grants Hippo's request. However, Hippo is given permission to live in the water only on condition that he keep his promise not to eat fish. He will prove that he is obedient by scattering his dung so that its contents can be examined.

Clearly, every action in this story generates another action, moving the story forward (and sometimes seemingly backwards!) until we arrive at the conclusion.

Setting

The setting of a story is its context in terms of time, space and worldview. This is one key to understanding the historical/cultural context that is the fourth leg of our four-legged hermeneutical stool. Understanding the setting also allows us to visualize the story more vividly and locate the characters as the story moves forward.

1. *Time*: The time when this story takes place is identified as "in the days of long, long ago." It happens long before the time of the narrator and his or her listeners.
2. *Space*: We are not told exactly where the story takes place. However, it is clearly a hot region of equatorial Africa somewhere in the vicinity of Mount Kenya, which is mentioned as the source of the cool water. It is a region where there are rivers, lakes, forests, plains and valleys.
3. *Worldview*: The worldview of the characters in a story and of the one telling the story contribute to an accurate understanding of a story. In the story above, this worldview

is not explicitly identified, but given that this story is told by Gikuyu people, we can assume that the narrator and the original listeners shared the Gikuyu worldview. For the Gikuyu, religion was transactional in nature and involved a form of retribution theology. If you did good things, you could expect good from the deity, and if you did wrong, you would be punished. Understanding this worldview makes it even more surprising that Hippo would dare to approach N'gai, knowing full well that he had done wrong by gorging himself to obesity. Because this shared context would have been in the minds of the original listeners to this story, the interaction and dialogue between N'gai and Hippo would have been even more significant.

Repetition

Repetition is perhaps the most widespread and widely recognized stylistic feature of African narrative literature. This is because African stories generally tend to have a cyclical-linear structure and approach the core meaning of the story from many different angles. Repetition extends to words, sequences of words, themes, imagery, signs and scenes. In the story above, for example, there are numerous allusions to the scorching heat of the sun, Hippo's greed, and the sovereignty of N'gai. This repetition of words and themes adds to the impact of the story as it moves forward.

Narration and dialogue

The interplay of narration and dialogue is an essential feature of African stories. It is the narrator's voice that speaks to us, telling us the story. Dialogue occurs at crucial points, providing us with the characters' responses in their own words. Simply put, narration is the telling of the story and dialogue is the characters speaking in their own voices. A good story paces the two so that the narrative flows smoothly, either slowing down or heightening in tension where necessary.

This interplay is brought to the surface in the retelling of the story above where the narrative elements are in italic while the direct speech is in a regular font. The story begins with narration, which provides us with the setting and begins to develop the character of Hippo. Narrative is also used in brief formulaic introductions of speakers, using phrases such as "he would sigh," "he cried loudly," "replied Lord N'gai," "answered the hippopotamus," and so forth. Here the narration is playing a supportive role to what the characters actually say.

Note that almost half of the story is told in dialogue, all written in the first person, as is the norm with statements that reflect direct speech. Besides contributing to our understanding of the characters of the participants, the dialogue provides a sense of "real-ness" and immediacy to the narrative.

Finally, note the text in bold at the end of the story. It is neither narration nor dialogue but is an editorial comment provided by the narrator. It allows the narrator to provide details that are significant for our understanding of the story by posing the question that prompted the story – Why don't hippos eat fish?

Narrative time

In the story above, the slow passage of time is conveyed by elements such as "*day after day*, when he waddled down to the river . . . The hippopotamus pondered over his trouble *for many days* . . . the sun *continued to beat down* mercilessly on his unprotected hide." This skilful use of narrative time allows the listener to visualize the eternity of agony that Hippo is experiencing.

Dialogue, however, tends to imitate "real time," a technique that the narrator uses to signal to the listener that what the character is saying is important. It can also be used to slow down the time in a story. We experience the slower passage of time as N'gai makes a decision and Hippo begins to experience some relief.

Characterization

In African storytelling, animals often feature as main characters. These characters may not appear to be as well developed as characters in Western literature, but this is in part because stories like this are meant to be dramatized by the narrator.[9]

One thing is clear about Hippo's character – he is greedy! Indeed, his obesity can be directly blamed on his love for food. The other aspect of his character that shines through is that he is persistent and willing to do whatever it takes to find a solution for his problem.

---

9. Finnegan, *Oral Literature*, 373.

What about N'gai's character? Analysis of the story shows that he is sovereign (he created all things, including Hippo himself), he is fair to all his creation, compassionate and merciful, even when punishment seems justified. Moreover, he is intelligent and cannot be deceived by Hippo. His refusal of Hippo's initial request reveals the moral aspect of his character, addressing the question of right or wrong in the story. Preserving the lives of the fish is important to him.

The narrator of this story makes expert use of contrastive dialogue to bring out the characters of Hippo and N'gai. Their voices are distinct. Their different modes of expression serve as mirrors into their characters, dramatizing the profound difference between them. The pleading voice of Hippo is clearly distinguished from the authoritative voice of the deity.

Vividness

African stories tend to be very vivid, effortlessly drawing the listener into the action. There are constant references to nature, and almost all stories are told within a setting in which the images in the narrative are supported by earthy details. Understanding these details is crucial to understanding the story itself. For instance, in the story above there are references to the hot equatorial sun, the snow on Mount Kenya, the river and its banks, the forests and plains and valleys. These details create a vivid mental picture that allows the listener to experience the story almost first-hand. The image of Hippo sweeping his dung with his tail to show that there are no fish bones takes on such vividness in our minds that we can almost smell the effects of his action!

Other aspects that make for vividness include the narrator's implicit invitation to us, the listeners, to step behind the scenes. When we are allowed access to the conversation that takes place between Hippo and N'gai, the story suddenly begins to take on different colours, hues and shapes. The exaggeration in Hippo's plea "the heat of the fiery sun is killing me!" brings a vividness to the narrative that would not be possible if it were simply narrated. We are left with a picture of a desperate creature, unable to survive another day in this harsh, unyielding environment. The eloquence of his request is not lost on the listeners. We have no choice but to sympathize with his predicament, even though we are well aware that he himself is responsible for it. Through the desperate pleas of Hippo, the listener is encouraged to engage emotionally. If you recall, we said that narrative listening in Africa engages the listener at all levels. We are therefore not really surprised when N'gai eventually changes his mind. After all, who can turn away from such desperation? We certainly cannot! Most importantly, by the time the story is done, we have related so completely with Hippo that we too decide to practice the positive characteristics of behaviour emphasized in the story.

Figurative language

Figurative language such as metaphors, symbolism, imagery and idioms are commonly used in Africa.[10] Such language adds to the vividness of a story but can also serve other functions, including the communication of abstract ideas.[11] In the story above, personification is employed in that N'gai and Hippo have voices and speak. There is also hyperbole (exaggeration), particularly in Hippo's cry "the heat of the fiery sun is killing me!"

Non-direct approach

In closing, it is important to emphasize that in African storytelling, the whole story carries the message and every part of it has a role to play. In other words, there is no clear identification of the "moral" of the story. One cannot merely seek out the punchline to understand the message of the story. Storytelling is therefore not linear but cyclical linear; the story does progress forward but not in a straight line. It looks something like this:

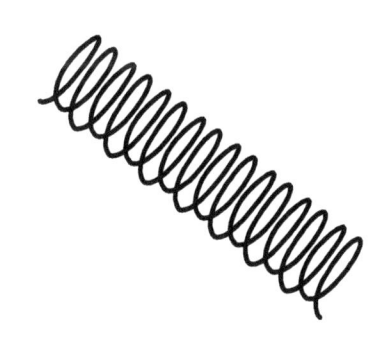

---

10. See, for example, the Maasai folk stories in Kipury, *Oral Literature of the Maasai*, 14.
11. Finnegan, *Oral Literature*, 61.

For instance, although the story above appears to have a punchline ("and that is why hippos don't eat fish!"), if you read closely, you will realize that the story in its entirety *is* the message! The meaning of the story is an explanation of Hippo's vegetarian nature. However, the "application" of the story goes beyond the simple fact that Hippos are vegetarian to reveal N'gai's character and nature and how we ought to respond to him. In many cases, such stories serve to enrich the worldview of African listeners as various aspects of the deity are revealed in the manner in which he relates to his creation.

Having looked at how stories function in Africa and how we are to interpret them, we now turn our attention to stories in the Bible. In this section, we will apply the four-legged stool model to a biblical story, while drawing on the specific principles that relate to African stories.

Stories in the Bible

As numerous scholars have pointed out, most of the Bible is written in the story genre. In the Old Testament this includes the Pentateuch, the historical books, and even large portions of the prophetic books. In the New Testament, this includes the gospels and Acts. The parables of Jesus are also stories, and so, in some respects, is the book of Revelation. That book includes letters, but it is essentially a story told with detailed symbolism and communicating a prophetic message – a style that is not unfamiliar because it is similar to the way prophetic messages were conveyed in Africa.

The function of stories in the Bible

Although the historical material in Scripture is often written in narrative mode, its function is not just informative or even aesthetic. These stories are also to be viewed as theological (giving us an understanding of God in our contexts), doxological (prompting us to worship God) and didactic (teaching us how to live).[12] They therefore demand a response from the reader in terms of a change in values, attitudes and behaviour. Bible stories give us insight into a world in which God is seen as acting in

---

12. Longman, *Literary Approaches*, 68–71.

history to shape events for his greater purpose. Stories transform our worldview, both individually as well as communally. The events related may be either descriptive (describing what happened) or prescriptive (prescribing what to do). A careful analysis of every story is necessary in order to distinguish in which mode it is operating. For example, in the book of Acts people often spoke in tongues after the apostles preached the gospel. Scholars continue to debate whether these accounts should be read as descriptive or prescriptive.

Studying a Bible story

The story of Ruth in the Old Testament is a familiar one. It is set in the time when the judges ruled and when famine had struck. This famine was the catalyst that caused some of the characters to migrate from Judah to Moab. These characters are Elimelech, his wife Naomi (who has an important role in the story), and their two sons, Mahlon and Kilion.

Elimelech dies in Moab, and Naomi's two sons marry Moabite women. A careful reader who knows the worldview of the Bible will note that this is actually an act of disobedience. God had commanded the Israelites not to marry foreign women. After about ten years, both Naomi's sons die, and she is left with two Moabite daughters-in-law, Orpah and Ruth.

The narrator does not give us any specific information about their state of affairs – whether positive or negative – while they were in Moab, but it is apparent that things are not going well. Naomi holds to the retribution theology that was prevalent at the time and she believes God has afflicted her by cruelly depriving her of both her sons (1:13, 20–21).

While in this despairing state of mind, she hears that God has changed the situation in Judah and proceeds to leave Moab with her two daughters-in-law. We are not told how far they travel together, but at some point she releases them from the obligation to go back home with her. It is not clear why she does this, for according to Jewish custom the two women were part of her household. It may be that she was testing them, or perhaps having felt the pain of living in a foreign land, she does not wish them to suffer the same pain. Whatever her reasons, she not only releases them but blesses them in any new marriage they may enter. After an emotional conversation, Orpah returns to her home. Ruth, however, pledges allegiance to Naomi. Most importantly, she promises to forsake her own gods and serve Naomi's God.

The story continues with their return to Bethlehem during the barley harvest. A careful reader will notice this apparently random piece of information. It is an indication of plenty after the famine, and it also sets the stage for Ruth to initiate contact with Boaz.

The narrator tells us that when they arrive in Bethlehem, the whole city took note of their arrival. It is likely that the women who met them on their return had witnessed the departure of Naomi and her husband and children more than ten years before. The fact that she is coming back without her family is a shock. Naomi is by this time a very bitter woman – so much so that she changes her name from Naomi, which means "pleasant," to Mara, which means "bitter."

Life back in Bethlehem soon picks up a steady rhythm. Ruth spends her days gleaning, an activity engaged in by the destitute. As "chance" would have it, she gleans in the fields of a man named Boaz, who happens to be a close relative of Naomi's late husband Elimelech. He is thus one of her kinsman-redeemers, that is, a close male relative who was responsible for acting on behalf of a female relative, to provide for her, and rescue her from any negative circumstances. The responsibilities of a kinsman-redeemer extended even to levirate marriage, which would preserve the name of the dead husband. Boaz notices Ruth and urges his harvesters not to harass her and to give her water when thirsty. Her kindness to her mother-in-law has been noted, and Boaz wishes to acknowledge it.

After a while, Naomi devises a plan to find a husband for Ruth. Closely following Naomi's instructions, Ruth dresses in her best clothes and puts on some perfume. Having identified where Boaz is to spend the night, she surprisingly (because it was against the norms of the day) lies down at his feet. Sometime in the night, Boaz awakens and is startled to feel someone lying there. The conversation that follows establishes that Ruth is requesting that he take her as his wife, since he is a kinsman-redeemer. Boaz accepts, but on condition that she allow a more closely related relative the first chance. This is a surprising twist to the plot. The introduction of a new character at this point leaves us with a sense of uncertainty. If there is a closer relative, why has he not shown himself? And why does Boaz have to prompt him to do his duty? And more importantly, will he honour the custom or not?

Things continue to unfold, with the closer kinsman-redeemer declining the opportunity to marry Ruth, and so Boaz takes Ruth as his wife. The previously barren Ruth soon conceives and gives birth to a son, whom they name Obed. The genealogy that follows reveals that he eventually becomes the father of Jesse, who in turn becomes the father of David, King of Israel.

Applying the four-legged stool model

As a reminder, the four-legged stool model recognizes the importance of basing all interpretation on the four "legs" that were explained in chapter four. These are parallels to the African context, the theological context of the story, its literary context, and its historical/cultural context. Only after these four legs are in place can we come to a firm application of the story.

Leg 1: Parallels to the African context

Biblical stories have many of the same features as African stories. They too involve narrators and listeners, and they too demand a response from their readers. Besides these generic similarities, there are other specific points of contact between the story of Ruth and our African realities.

Family relationships: Family, including the extended family, is very important in Africa. We admire the clear attachment of Naomi to her daughters-in-law (and vice versa), and Boaz's willingness to carry out his family responsibilities. In traditional Africa, any breakdown in these family relationships would incur the wrath of the god, the spirits and the community. Modern African readers are therefore not surprised to witness this closeness in a traditional family. In fact, in many societies in East Africa, a married woman is considered to have left her birth family and become a member of her husband's family. She remains so even after his death. It is not uncommon for disputes to arise if a widow wants to remarry because the children and property that her husband left her would pass to her new husband's family.

Levirate marriage: Naomi's attempt to organize a marriage between Ruth and a close relative of her dead son is not a strange idea to Africans. Among groups like the Luo of Kenya, there is a similar tradition of levirate marriage. When a woman loses her husband, her brother-in-law is expected to take on responsibility for his dead brother's family by marrying her. Although this trend is on the decline, the practice is still prevalent in some regions, particularly in rural areas.

Suffering: Africans understand the experience of suffering extremely well. Famine, hunger, poverty and wars are constant features of African life. We do not find it hard to relate to Naomi, and few would blame her for her growing bitterness. However, what really ties her experience of suffering to Africa is Naomi's belief that God is punishing her. As pointed out in the chapter on worldview, many Africans have a retribution theology that views suffering as punishment for wrongdoing.

Barrenness: In African culture, barrenness is a source of great embarrassment. It is considered shameful for a woman not to give her husband children – regardless of who is medically responsible for the problem. Barren wives are often discarded in favour of more fertile ones who will bring honour to the husband by bearing him children. We do not know how long Ruth had been married to Mahlon, but she had clearly borne him no children. In Jewish culture, she would have felt similar shame to that experienced by an African woman who remains childless.

While the elements identified above are not the only parallels to the African context, they provide a starting point from which to begin to relate to the biblical story. They can be used as bridges to promote understanding, internalization and application of the biblical text. As we pointed out in previous chapters, our goal is to move from our known world to the unknown one of the Bible by using bridges of communication.

Leg 2: Theological context

As pointed out in our discussion of the second leg of the hermeneutical stool, while Africans see things holistically, they do tend to give precedence to theological aspects of a story. In the case of the story of Ruth, we can identify some contrasting theological themes.

Apostasy vs. faithfulness: It is significant that right at the outset we are told that this story is set in the time of the judges, when "everyone did what was right in his own eyes" (Judg 17:6; 18:1; 19:1; 21:25). It was a time of great wickedness and apostasy, when the people of Israel had turned away from their covenant with God. Considering the apostate condition of Israel, it is likely that Elimelech himself had ceased to follow God's ways. He left Bethlehem in Judah during a time of famine, taking his family from a place of emptiness or barrenness in search of a place where their needs would be met. He chose to go to Moab, to live and eventually die there (1:2–3). Boaz, on the other hand, was a follower of Yahweh as is clear from his greeting to his reapers. The fact that he also adhered to the laws about gleaning (Lev 23:22) suggests that he, unlike many in the land, was a faithful follower of God (2:3–9).

Emptiness vs. fullness: There is a recurring theme of emptiness and loss. Naomi loses first her husband, and then her two sons, who die childless. Having come into the land of Moab full (at least in one sense), she loses everything. She sees things this way even though she has Ruth at her side, reminding us of how much Jewish culture devalued women, and especially barren ones. However, her circumstances are reversed by the end of the book, where she rejoices when Ruth gives birth to a son. Ruth's circumstances, too, are reversed. Her marriage to Mahlon had not produced any child and she would have endured the shame of barrenness. When she arrived in Bethlehem with Naomi, Naomi was greeted but Ruth was ignored. Yet by the end of the book, she is no longer a childless widow but the wife of a prominent man and the mother of a baby boy. She is also highly regarded by the townspeople, for the women testify that she is better than seven sons (4:15).

God's providence: It is only when we come to the end of the story and see Ruth's place in the lineage of King David that things become clearer and we recognize that this story, which begins in hopelessness but ends in joy, shows God's providence in providing for his people. The main theological theme of this story is thus God's providence. The story is a reminder that God's providence can come in very unexpected forms and that he often uses the lowly and the despised to accomplish his purposes.

Tentative application

The theme of God's providence leads to the conclusion that God is faithful in the midst of difficult circumstances and reverses negative situations in his own time. Taking this together with the other themes, we can begin to conclude that God rewards faithfulness and sometimes allows suffering for his own reasons.

Leg 3: Literary Context

Having delved into the parallels with the African context and the theological emphases of the text, the next step is to identify the type of literature we are dealing with, including its genre, the literary techniques and language used, and how this text fits in with the surrounding texts. The tentative points of application identified during leg 2 will be further clarified in leg 3.

Literary genre

The first thing we must identify in leg 3 is the genre of this text. In this case, there can be no doubt that the book of Ruth is story. We have already looked at elements of African stories, and now it is time to see how these elements are at work in the biblical text of Ruth.

Literary techniques

Plot: The plot revolves around first two and then three characters – Naomi, Ruth and Boaz. The development of the plot has two focal points. The first is divine providence, with God in the background ensuring that the story ends as he intends. The second is change and movement as Naomi and Ruth move physically from Moab to Bethlehem and move emotionally from despair to hope. Within Bethlehem itself, the narrator reports movement between the fields, the threshing floor, and the town where Ruth was living with Naomi. Movement is therefore a prominent aspect of this story.

The narrator is very skilful in taking the story in directions that we do not anticipate. For instance, he introduces another kinsman who has more rights over Ruth than Boaz does at the precise moment when we are not expecting any complications. The movement is therefore not purely linear. We find ourselves in a state of heightened suspense as the narrator raises, then dashes, then raises our hopes again.

Setting: The story of Ruth is set in the time between the judges and the establishment of the monarchy. The fact that the narrator begins with the phrase "In the days when the judges ruled" is a cue for us to position ourselves in that specific historical context. The spatial setting of the story begins in Judah, moves to Moab, and then ends in Bethlehem.

Narration and dialogue: As in the African story above, narration and dialogue play a very important role in the book of Ruth. The dialogue reveals important dimensions of the characters. For instance, note Ruth's words in 1:16–17.

> Don't urge me to leave you or to turn back from you. Where you go I will go, and where you stay I will stay. Your people will be my people and your God my God. Where you die I will die, and there I will be buried. May the LORD deal with me, be it ever so severely, if even death separates you and me.

Ruth's words reveal her emotional, religious and socio-political point of view.

In addition to narration and dialogue, the narrator also includes editorial comments such as in 4:7, where he explains how contracts were legalized in ancient Israel.

> Now in earlier times in Israel, for the redemption and transfer of property to become final, one party took off his sandal and gave it to the other. This was the method of legalizing transactions in Israel.

Figurative language: In 3:9 when the startled Boaz asks, "Who are you?" Ruth replies, "I am your servant Ruth. . . . Spread the corner of your garment over me, since you are a guardian-redeemer of our family." Asking him to spread his garment over her is a metaphor for extending his protection to her. This is only one example of the figurative language used in the story.

Repetition: There are at least six references to Ruth's being a Moabite (1:4, 22; 2:2, 7; 4:5, 10). The narrator does not want us to forget that the person God will use to produce a king who will reverse the circumstances of the nation of Israel is, in fact, a foreigner. The narrator also repeats the theme of emptiness vs. fullness in several ways throughout the story.

Narrative time: The narrator only gives explicit indications of time in 1:4, where he mentions that Naomi's family lived in Moab for about ten years, and in chapter 3 and 4, where Ruth's destiny is resolved when she goes to Boaz one night and a legal agreement is reached the following day. In other parts of the narrative, the narrator indicates the passage of time by referring to the beginning of the barley harvest (1:22), and the end of both the barley and the wheat harvest (2:23). The passage of time within the narrative also slows down as the narrative unfolds, creating an aura of suspense and tension. This slowing is particularly apparent in passages of dialogue and rises to a height in chapter 4 as the legal negotiations proceed. The slow pace of this section indicates that what is happening is very important. However, in the genealogies, time speeds up as the narrator covers many generations in a few lines.

Characterization: Although the book is named after Ruth, the character who is most developed in this story is Naomi. She is also the hero. She is present at every stage of the story and is responsible for initiating every action. Boaz and Ruth merely respond to her suggestions.

Naomi, Ruth and Boaz are all full-fledged characters who are portrayed in some depth and complexity. However, it is Naomi who speaks most, thus giving us greater insight into her character, with Boaz following. Ruth has the least dialogue, making it all the more surprising that the book is named after her. Orpah and the closest redeemer are as minor characters (agents), with the latter being even less defined than the former. Others such as Elimelech, Mahlon, Chilion and Obed are simply names without characters attached to them, while the overseer mentioned in chapter 2 lies in between these two categories.[13] As the events unfold, however, we are aware that there is another hero in the background – God. He is the real hero of this story. At the beginning of the story he provides food for the people of Judah (1:6) thus opening the door for the women to return. At the end, the narrator reveals that it is God who has reversed their circumstances and provided a son (4:16). The perspective of the characters also shows that God is present throughout the story (e.g. 1:21; 2:20; 4:14).

Non-direct approach

Some Bible stories are linear and clearly express the intended message, but many others, like the book of Ruth, are similar to African stories in that they have a non-direct approach. Ruth, for example, has what scholars refer to as a chiastic structure, which is also found in some African poetry.[14]

---

13. For more on this, see Adele Berlin, *Poetics and Interpretation of Biblical Narrative* (Sheffield: Almond Press, 1983), 85–86.
14. Finnegan, *Oral Literature*, 69.

The word *chiastic* comes from the Greek letter *chi*, which looks like the English letter X. It is used to refer to a pattern of writing that emphasizes themes or ideas by repeating them in the pattern A B C . . . C' B' A'. In the book of Ruth, the pattern looks something like this:[15]

Prologue 1:1–2 – The judges and the family of Elkanah
    A 1:3–22 – Naomi's loss, barrenness and bitterness
        B Ch. 2 – Reversals in the day
        B' Ch. 3 – Reversals in the night
    A' 4:1–17a – Naomi's joy and Ruth's fertility
Epilogue 4:17–22 – The genealogy of David, the coming king.

In other words, chapters 1 and 4 reflect the contrasting themes of barrenness and fullness, while chapters 2 and 3 show the different stages of Ruth's, and by implication Naomi's, reversal of circumstances. These chapters reflect both a sense of intensification of the improving circumstances and contrasting settings, with one taking place in the day with all the harvesters present, and the other taking place at night and involving an interaction between Boaz and Ruth.

Chapters 1 and 4 can also be referred to as an inclusio, that is, a structure in which the first and last chapters emphasize the same theme or message. Naomi is also very prominent at the beginning and at the end of the book.

Vividness: The vivid telling of the story of Ruth draws us so deeply into the narrative that we can almost imagine ourselves there. As Africans, we are familiar with the agony of famine, of separation from family and tribe, of suffering and death, of shame and despair. As the narrator tells his story, we are caught up with the characters in their various experiences. As the story draws to a close, we can almost hear the ululation of the women as they celebrate the birth of a much-desired child.

The narrator also supplies earthy details in his references to the barley and wheat harvests. These details enable us to appreciate Ruth's desperate condition. We can visualize her walking in the fields, picking up the few

---

15. See also J. P. Fokkelman, *Reading Biblical Narrative: An Introductory Guide* (Louisville: Westminster John Knox Press, 1999), 213.

stalks left behind by the harvesters. The reference to the harvest times also serves as a time marker in the story.

These techniques, as in African oral literature, are designed to encourage us to read the story holistically. Indeed, as we read it, it comes alive with its beauty and artistry. More than that, it demands that we, the readers, journey together with the main characters, suffering and rejoicing with them, until we arrive at the inevitable conclusion that God is indeed faithful.

Language

Because we are here looking at the entire book of Ruth, it is difficult to pick out particular words, sentences and paragraphs for attention. However, there are some words and phrases that we should take note of.

- The opening words in 1:1 – "In the days *when* the judges ruled." This phrase provides the historical/cultural/political context of the story. The time marker *when* is significant as it indicates that the events that follow happened during the time of the judges.
- The term "kinsman-redeemer" (also translated as "guardian-redeemer"). The significance of this term is explained in the historical/cultural section below.
- The repetition of the word "Moabite" in conjunction with the name "Ruth." This has been mentioned above and will be further explained in the historical/cultural context section below.
- The emphasis on the word "bitter." It is used in 1:13 ("It is more *bitter* for me than for you, because the LORD's hand has turned against me!") and again in 1:20 ("Don't call me Naomi," she told them. "Call me Mara, because the Almighty has made my life very *bitter*"). The emphasis placed on this word adds to our appreciation of her changed circumstances by the end of the book.

Literary flow

The book of Ruth has long enjoyed canonical status. In the ancient Septuagint translation of the Old Testament, it appears in the same position as it does in our modern Bibles.[16] It should therefore be read in this context of the books of Judges and Samuel, which immediately precede and follow it.

The narrator refers to the era of the judges in the prologue (Ruth 1:1–2), so giving us essential information about the book's historical setting. Then in 1 Samuel we see Israel beginning to move away from theocracy (rule by God as king) and establish a monarchy (rule by a human king). Ruth thus marks a transitional point between the period of the judges and that of the monarchy. It prepares us for the arrival of King David, whose genealogy ends the story of Ruth (4:18–22).

Yet although set in the same time period as the book of Judges, the book of Ruth offers a different perspective on faithfulness and obedience to God. Rather than focusing on the nation of Israel as a whole, it focuses on a few individual players.

Tentative application

The literary context confirms that God, who is active in the history of Israel, is in fact the main character in this story. This serves to confirm the tentative applications arrived at above. God's providence is revealed in his faithfulness to his people, even in the midst of suffering. He reverses negative situations in his own time, and in this case, in very unexpected ways. He also rewards faithfulness and sometimes allows suffering for his own reasons. An additional application point revealed through the various features of the literary context is that one should have hope in the midst of seemingly hopeless situations.

Leg 4: Historical/Cultural context

One of the surprising things about this story is that the book has been named after Ruth. As we observed above, she is not the main character. More than that, she is not even an Israelite; we are frequently reminded that she is a Moabite. In fact, Ruth is the only book in the Old Testament named after a non-Israelite. It is thus important that we understand something about the Moabites and their relationship with the Israelites.

The Moabites were descended from Moab, who was the son of Lot through an incestuous union with his eldest daughter (Gen 19:30–38).

---

16. Daniel I. Block, "Ruth," in *The New American Commentary*, vol. 6, gen. ed. E. Ray Clendenen (Nashville: Broadman & Holman, 1999), 588–589.

The relationship between the Israelites and the Moabites was extremely negative. They had opposed the Israelites on their journey through the wilderness to the promised land, going so far as to hire Balaam to curse Israel (Deut 23:3–4). Because of these actions, the Moabites and their descendants were prohibited from entering the assembly of the Lord. The Israelites were instructed, "Do not seek a treaty of friendship with them as long as you live" (Deut 23:6). It is thus all the more amazing that a Moabite woman is among David's ancestors.

Who wrote the book of Ruth? The book itself gives no indication of an author, but many believe it was written by Samuel. However, others argue that since internal evidence indicates that the book was written when David was king (4:17–22), Samuel cannot be the author since he died before David came to the throne.[17] However, it is possible that the genealogy was added at a later date.

It is also almost impossible to say when the book was written. Remember that a book may be written long after the events described in it took place. If you recall, most of the stories of the Old Testament were passed down from generation to generation through an oral tradition. Several scholars suggest that this book was written centuries later, during the period after the exile. They argue that this explains features of the language of the book, the need to explain legal customs such as the use of a sandal, the interest in genealogies, the favourable portrait of a Moabite woman, and the allusion to the work of the judges and the book's canonical placement. However, none of these arguments are conclusive.[18] Moreover, the lack of hostility towards Moab is compatible with the early years of David, but not with the later period of the monarchy.[19]

There are some cultural practices in this story that need explaining if we are to understand the perspective and mindset of the narrator and thus fully appreciate the story. As we noted in chapter four, these are rarely made explicit since the author assumes that his readers are familiar with them as he and they share a common cultural context.

The first custom that needs explanation is levirate marriage. According to the levirate law, if a man died without leaving a male heir, his brother had to marry the widow. The first son of this union would take the name

---

17. A. E. Cundall, "Ruth, Book of," *The Zondervan Pictorial Encyclopaedia of the Bible*, vol. 5, gen ed. Merrill C. Tenney (Grand Rapids: Zondervan, 1977), 176.
18. Block, "Ruth," 591.
19. Cundall, *Zondervan*, 178.

of the brother who had died, so ensuring that his name was preserved in the genealogies of Israel (Deut 25:5–6). This custom is mentioned in Genesis 38:24–30 with reference to Judah and Tamar, who are linked to Ruth and Boaz by the narrator in Ruth 4:12.

The second custom is the removal of a sandal. This reveals the mindset of the narrator, who steps in to explain that this was customary when handling matters concerning the redemption and exchange of property (cf. 4:7). According to levirate law, if a brother refused to marry the widow, he was refusing to build up his brother's house. The widow would then bring him before the elders of the city, remove a sandal from his foot and spit in his face (Deut 25:7–10). The man would be exposed to public shame. It may be that the narrator included the information about the custom of the sandal to serve two purposes. First, it implied that the deal having been sealed, Boaz was now free to marry Ruth. Second, the close relative, having failed to act honourably towards Ruth, would be regarded as having been shamed.

Tentative application

The historical/cultural context further sharpens the theme of God's providence by showing that God can use whomever he desires in order to accomplish his purpose. In its original context, the readers would have understood that God's providence sometimes comes in very unexpected forms. God can use even the lowly and the despised to accomplish his purposes. In this case, a foreign woman, from a people hated by the Israelites, becomes an ancestor of a future king. God's use of an unexpected "hero" is thus clarified through the historical/cultural context.

Seat: Application

As we have worked through the various legs of the four-legged stool model, we have examined the story of Ruth from many different angles and have come up with tentative application points that have been strengthened through the process. This last step allows us to examine and confirm our conclusions so far.

When discussing the seat of the stool in chapter 4, we distinguished between meaning and significance. The meaning of the story is what it meant to the original readers. We have considered this as we worked on the four legs of the stool. Now, however, we have to establish its significance for us, that is, its application for us as African readers.

The story of Ruth, which begins in hopelessness but ends on a joyful note, serves to focus us, the readers, on God's providence in redeeming his people. It has a number of possible application points:

1. God's providence is revealed in his faithfulness to his people, even in the midst of suffering.
2. God can choose to use whomever he desires to accomplish his purpose.
3. God is able to reverse negative situations – however, he does this in his own time and sometimes in very unexpected ways.
4. God rewards faithfulness.
5. God sometimes allows suffering for his own reasons.
6. We need to have hope in the midst of seemingly hopeless situations.

These application points offer encouragement to those in contexts where there is famine, internal conflict, economic depression and so forth. They also offer hope to those facing personal challenges. Thus the story of Ruth, while entertaining, offers far more than merely entertainment. It is a story that reveals how God relates to his chosen people. The lessons that it teaches have far-reaching implications for how we live our day-to-day lives.

A BRIEF LOOK AT PARABLES

A parable is a short, true-to-life or realistic story designed to teach a spiritual or moral lesson. However, we cannot interpret them simply as stories because they are also rooted in the wisdom tradition of Israel. In fact the Hebrew word from which the word "parable" is derived is also used for "saying," "proverb," "wisdom saying," or "mocking song."[20] Parables must therefore be interpreted both as stories and as wisdom literature (the topic of the next chapter).

Features that parables share with stories include earthiness, conciseness, major and minor points, repetition, a conclusion, listener-relatedness, and reversal of expectations. Jesus's parables also focus on a kingdom-centred eschatology, kingdom ethics, God and salvation.[21] Identifying these characteristics and understanding what role they play in a particular parable is crucial for correct interpretation.

At least one-third of Jesus's teaching was presented in the form of parables. Some of these were stories like the parables of the sower (Mark 4:1–9, 13–20; Matt 13:1–9, 18–23; Luke 8:4–8, 11–15), the mustard seed (Mark 4:30–32; Matt 13:31–32; Luke 13:18–19), the wedding feast (Matt 22:1–14; Luke 14:15–24) and the talents (Matt 25:14–30; Luke 19:11–27). However, he also used other types of parables like extended similes (e.g. Matt 13:33), short parables (e.g. Luke 17:7–10) and allegorical parables (e.g. Mark 12:1–12). It is not always easy to draw exact lines between these categories.

Parables serve at least two functions. The first is didactic. Since parables are not based on historical fact, the characters and the story are created to teach a particular spiritual or moral lesson. The second is to demand a response from the hearer. The parables of Jesus are not merely word pictures to illustrate Jesus's teaching and they are not just vehicles to reveal truth. His parables are intended to elicit a response from the hearers. Hence, they do not only convey the message; they are themselves the message. The content of parables and the way in which they are told is meant to engage listeners at all levels and force them to confront their ideas about life and change them in light of the kingdom of God. The following statement summarizes the nature and function of parables:

> It seems clear that Jesus did indeed have a larger purpose in using the parable form. Parables are an "encounter mechanism" and

---

20. Gerald Wilson, "לשמ," *NIDOTTE* 2:1134–36.
21. Osborne, *Hermeneutical Spiral*, 239–44. What follows is based largely on Osborne's work.

function differently depending on the audience. . . . The parables encounter, interpret and invite the listener/reader to participate in Jesus's new world vision of the kingdom. They are a "speech-event" . . . that never allows us to remain neutral; they grasp our attention and force us to interact with the presence of the kingdom in Jesus, either positively (those "around" Jesus in Mark 4:10–12) or negatively (those "outside").[22]

While the Gospel of John does not have any parables, the three Synoptic Gospels, Matthew, Mark and Luke, include numerous parables. When we read them, we note that the literary context before and after similar parables is not necessarily the same in each gospel. Consider the parable of the wicked tenants, which is found in all three Synoptic Gospels. Whereas Mark and Luke place this parable in the context of Jesus's authority, Matthew places it in the context of Israel's rejection of him.

Mark 11:27–33 The authority of Jesus questioned	Matthew 21:28–32 The parable of the two sons	Luke 20:1–18 The authority of Jesus questioned
Mark 12:1–12	Matthew 21:33–46	Luke 20:9–19
The parable of the wicked tenants		
Mark 12:13–17 Paying taxes to Caesar	Matthew 22:1–14 The parable of the wedding banquet	Luke 20:20–26 Paying taxes to Caesar

The different order may be because Jesus retold some of his parables on different occasions. However, it is also likely that the gospel writers arranged the parables thematically to highlight the particular theological point each wished to make.[23]

Parables generally make more than one point, and so we should not confine a parable to one point if it is evident that more than one truth is being conveyed. Recent parable studies have come to the conclusion that approximately two-thirds of Jesus's parables have three main characters, who each reflect different parts of the overall meaning of the parable.[24] So, for instance, the parable of the Good Samaritan conveys three truths:

---

22. Osborne, *Hermeneutical Spiral*, 238.
23. See Klyne R. Snodgrass, "Parable," *Dictionary of Jesus and the Gospels*, 596–598, for the distribution of parables in the Synoptics.
24. Klein et al., *Biblical Interpretation*, 413; Craig L. Blomberg, *Interpreting the Parables* (Downers Grove: InterVarsity Press, 2006), 171.

From the example of the priest and Levite comes the principle that religious status or legalistic casuistry does not excuse lovelessness. From the Samaritan one learns that one must show compassion to those in dire need regardless of the religious or ethnic barriers that divide people. From the man in the ditch emerges the lesson that even one's enemy is one's neighbor.[25]

---

25. Blomberg, *Interpreting the Parables*, 414.

7

INTERPRETING WISDOM

If I were to ask you to give me an example of a story, you would be able to do so. However, you might have more difficulty if I were to ask you for an example of wisdom literature. Yet all cultures have elements of wisdom literature, even if we often fail to notice them because we take them for granted.

The Wisdom Genre

Like stories, wisdom literature is found in both oral and written forms. In this chapter, we will be focusing primarily on wisdom as it manifests itself in the proverbs we use, hear or read.

A proverb can be defined as "a saying in more or less fixed form marked by 'shortness, sense, and salt' and distinguished by the popular acceptance of the truth tersely expressed in it."[1] Another definition is that proverbs are aphorisms (i.e. wise sayings) that are generally concise and metaphorical in nature.[2] This definition expands on the previous one by including figurative language. Proverbs can therefore be understood as short, colourful, memorable statements that communicate truth for wise living in a community. The fact that they are short and memorable means that they are widely used for socializing the young and encouraging everyone to live up to the standards of the community.

---

1. Finnegan, *Oral Literature*, 383.
2. Chesaina, *Oral Literature*, 13. Although this book focuses on the Kalenjin peoples of Kenya, the general categories, nature and function of wisdom literature are very similar throughout Africa.

The choice to focus on proverbs in this chapter is also a reminder that wisdom literature leans more towards practical than philosophical wisdom. While philosophical wisdom focuses on abstract questions about the meaning of life, practical wisdom deals with day-to-day matters. Proverbs can be used to admonish, encourage, warn, praise, curse or bless. They also communicate information about the worldview, culture and theological beliefs of the community.

When looking at proverbs, it is important to remember that they are neither promises nor commands. Rather, they convey a general truth, something that is usually true. However, as we all know, "circumstances alter cases," and so a particular generalization may not always apply. Thus we sometimes encounter two contrasting wisdom sayings within the same wisdom tradition. This happens both in African wisdom literature and in biblical wisdom literature. For an African example we can quote two Swahili proverbs:

> The patient one eats the ripe fruit
> The patient one eats the rotten fruit.[3]

While patience is a good character trait, sometimes waiting too long can be disadvantageous or harmful!

Because wisdom is practical knowledge and is not limited to any one group of people, we sometimes find common elements between biblical wisdom sayings and the wisdom sayings of other peoples and cultures. For instance, some biblical proverbs sound very much like African proverbs, as shown in the examples below.

- Proverbs 10:1b "A wise son brings joy to his father, but a foolish son brings grief to his mother" is very similar to the African proverb, "A bad son gives a bad name to his mother."
- Jesus said, "No good tree bears bad fruit, nor does a bad tree bear good fruit. Each tree is recognized by its own fruit. People do not pick figs from thornbushes, or grapes from briers." (Luke 6:43–44). An African proverb says, "A tree is known by its fruit." Although these two proverbs sound similar, their meanings are different. The African proverb means that success is shown by

---

3. Leonidas Kalugila, *More Swahili Proverbs from East Africa* (Uppsala: Scandinavian Institute of African Studies, 1980), 7.

one's deeds, whereas the proverb from Luke teaches that what we are on the inside is revealed by our outward actions.
- Job 1:21 "The LORD gave and the LORD has taken away" is very similar to the Swahili proverb *Muumba ndiye muumbua* (loosely translated as "The creator is the one who gives life and he is the only one who can take it").
- Jesus's words, "the mouth speaks what the heart is full of" (Matt 12:34; Luke 6:45), sound very much like the African proverb, "When the heart overflows, it comes out through the mouth."
- Proverbs 21:26 ("All day long he craves for more, but the righteous give without sparing") can be compared to the African proverb "The greedy man grabs out for water," although the biblical proverb goes beyond the African one by adding a corrective to the attitude of the greedy. Rather than allowing greed to consume us, we should learn to give.

Africa and Wisdom

If you close your eyes, you can almost hear the voice of a storyteller effortlessly weaving in proverb after proverb, riddle after riddle, as she tells a story of courage, wisdom and honesty; as she warns against immoral behaviour, theft and lies; as she encourages the discouraged and praises those who have brought honour to the community. The power of the African wisdom genre to communicate all this is unquestionable.

Sources of the wisdom tradition in Africa

The wisdom tradition in Africa has several sources.[4] The first is oral tradition. Like stories, wisdom was originally passed on orally. Even though there are now numerous literary works that have put this wisdom in writing, much of it is still known in oral form in myths, legends, stories, liturgies, songs, proverbs, riddles and wise sayings. Frequently, nuggets of wisdom are inserted into the stories told around the fire and the songs sung at community gatherings.

---
4. Kunhiyop, *African Christian*, 9–25.

The second source of the African wisdom tradition is liturgy, that is, the form or order of public religious worship. Wisdom was passed on to the community through invocations, prayers, rituals and sacrifices to the ancestors, divinities and the Supreme Being.

Third, the wisdom tradition is rooted in customs that emphasized ethical principles and rules of conduct. Each tribe or community had certain rules governing how people were to live and relate to one another. As these were passed down from generation to generation, they formed part of the oral wisdom tradition.

Finally, wisdom is derived from observation of community life. As people went about their day-to-day lives, certain patterns would emerge. Some attitudes and behaviours were seen to have negative consequences, while others had positive ones. These observations would eventually be embedded in proverbs and riddles.

It is important to note that wisdom was available to everyone in the community. However, because the elders were responsible for passing it on, they were regarded as the wise men or women in the community.

The function of the wisdom tradition in Africa

As discussed above, wisdom literature provides practical guidance on how we should conduct ourselves in relation to the Supreme Being (and other deities), spiritual entities, ancestors, and others in the community. It thus serves a didactic (teaching) function and is crucial for communicating important life lessons and a worldview. Given that the African worldview emphasizes the community rather than the individual, African wisdom sought to inculcate values that would contribute to unity and harmony in the community.

Studying African wisdom

While there are several types of wisdom literature in Africa, I will limit the discussion here to the two most common types, proverbs and riddles. It must, however, be pointed out that in some contexts there is an overlap between the different types of wisdom, so that one cannot always distinguish between a proverb, a riddle and a tale.[5]

---

5. Finnegan, *Oral Literature*, 380–81.

Proverbs

Proverbs have played a crucial role in traditional African societies and are still common in Africa today.

Purpose

While proverbs have several functions, their major ones are to warn, advise, inform, and clarify.[6] Because of their flexible nature, they are used "in settling disputes, general discussions, conversations and in cases where an older person advises a younger."[7] They are therefore important elements in informal education. However, they are also common in everyday conversation where they may be used merely to illustrate a point or to make statements more colourful and thus more enjoyable.[8]

Proverbs also feature prominently in storytelling, marriage ceremonies, religious rites, and, more recently, in the written works of African authors. When inserted into a story, a proverb generally appears at the end as a summary or conclusion. Its function is to clarify the point being communicated throughout the story.[9]

Literary techniques

African proverbs often have a poetic or rhythmic quality, so that sometimes it is not easy to tell whether one is reciting poetry or quoting a proverb. Kalugila even states that "proverbs cannot be compared to anything but poetry."[10] That is why some proverbs are classified as lyrical proverbs, combining both genres. Unfortunately, their poetic qualities tend to get lost in translation.

In general, proverbs are quite straightforward and can be readily understood by the members of the community. However, in some cases, proverbs have a deeper meaning that is not immediately obvious.[11] Metaphors, for instance, may use some non-human activity to comment on the way people behave. Thus if someone has an exaggerated sense of their own importance, the Sotho of Southern Africa may quote the

---

6. Wanjiku Mukabi Kabira and Karegi wa Mutahi, *Gikuyu Oral Literature* (Nairobi: East African Educational Publishers, 1993, 2011).
7. Chesaina, *Oral Literature*, 13.
8. Chesaina, 27.
9. Chesaina, 28.
10. Kalugila, *More Swahili Proverbs*, 85.
11. Finnegan, *Oral Literature*, 380.

proverb, "'I and my rhinoceros,' said the tickbird."[12] The tiny tickbird assumes that it is the one directing a huge rhinoceros!

Another literary technique that is common in proverbs is some kind of parallelism. In other words, the proverb involves two statements, the second of which either explains the first by providing a contrast or emphasizes the first through repeating some words or phrases.[13] (Note once again the importance of repetition in African literature.) Sometimes, the parallelism even provides contradictory viewpoints.

Historical context

The historical context of proverbs is very difficult to determine since they are versatile and have been used in many situations. So it is almost impossible to establish what prompted the creation of a particular proverb. Additionally, similar proverbs may be found in several African cultures, reflecting the truth that life experiences have many commonalities.

Examples of proverbs

The examples below, taken from different African countries, demonstrate the power of this type of wisdom. As you read each proverb, pay careful attention to its conciseness, its use of figurative language, and the truth that is being communicated. Think about whether there are similar proverbs in your own cultural context that communicate the same truths. Later, you may want to consider whether there are biblical proverbs that express similar sentiments.

- "When the heart overflows, it comes out through the mouth" (Ethiopia) reflects the truth that our words are an expression of what is really going on in our hearts.
- "Women have no upright words but only crooked ones" (Kenya) is an indication of the low social standing of women in many African communities.
- "I have been bitten by a tsetse fly" (Tanzania) means that someone will continually bother you until you pay off your debt.
- "A bad son gives a bad name to his mother" (Ivory Coast) is self-explanatory!

---

12. Finnegan, 385–386.
13. Finnegan, 389.

- "God says ask and I will give you" (Kenya) reminds us that God is our provider.
- "An eyewitness is better than a hearer of tales" (Tanzania) emphasizes the truth that an eyewitness is able to give a more faithful account of an event than one who merely hears about it second or even third hand.
- "A tree is known by its fruit" (South Africa) states that success is shown by one's deeds.
- "People of the same blood despise one another" (Kenya) reflects the truth that all too often those closest to us do not see our gifts or abilities and discourage rather than encourage us.
- "Hit the head; this animal is not one of us – he comes from a strange place" (Kenya) reveals that people from other tribes were often viewed in a dehumanizing way.
- "One who beats one child beats all children" (East Africa) emphasizes that if you give something to one child, you must be fair and give something to the other children as well. This proverb is generally a request, as the one quoting it also wants a present!
- "The greedy man grabs out for water" (Kenya) evokes a vivid image of someone greedily grasping water, even though it will inevitably trickle through their fingers. Their greed is never satisfied.
- "The water you fetch from far, you use sparingly" (East Africa) means that when something has been difficult to get, it is treated with care.
- "The word of a friend makes you cry; the word of an enemy makes you laugh" warns against listening to the advice of an enemy as it will mislead you. On the other hand, the advice of a friend, while it may sometimes hurt, will be the truth and therefore preferable. This is a common proverb among the peoples of Algeria, Burkina Faso, Mali, Mauritania, and Niger.

Riddles

A second major type of wisdom literature found in Africa is the riddle. Riddles are very like proverbs. As Finnegan points out, "they are expressed briefly and concisely; they involve analogy, whether of meaning, sound, rhythm, or tone; and the two forms are sometimes even combined in the 'proverb-riddle.'"[14] Like all wisdom literature, riddles are drawn from community life and are therefore in a sense limited to the community in which they arose. In most cases, the listener is expected to recognize an analogy between the question and the answer.[15] Riddles can therefore be defined as concise statements in which a problem is set through the comparison of two "similar" things familiar to the audience. In general, riddles are directed only to children; however, in some cases they are used for the entire community, both young and old.[16]

A more complex explanation of the nature of riddles is provided by Scheub and Gunner:

> In the riddle, two unlike, and sometimes unlikely, things are compared. The obvious thing that happens during this comparison is that a problem is set, then solved. But there is something more important here, involving the riddle as a figurative form: the riddle is composed of two sets, and, during the process of riddling, the aspects of each of the sets are transferred to the other. On the surface it appears that the riddle is largely an intellectual rather than a poetic activity. But through its imagery and the tension between the two sets, the imagination of the audience is also engaged. As they seek the solution to the riddle, the audience itself becomes a part of the images and therefore – and most significantly – of the metaphorical transformation.[17]

Purpose

One major function of riddles is to encourage active participation in a story, song or poem. Indeed, they are often used at the beginning

---

14. Finnegan, 413.
15. Finnegan, 417.
16. Finnegan, 413.
17. Scheub and Gunner, *African Literature*, retrieved from http://www.britannica.com/art/African-literature#toc57038.

of stories to initiate audience participation. They can also be found strategically placed within a story for the same reason. As noted earlier, listening in Africa involves holistic listening and active participation. Riddles encourage this because of the way in which they are set up.

A second major function of riddles is to encourage creativity. Chesaina states, "At the beginning of storytelling sessions, they make a significant contribution by stimulating the audience and sharpening their imagination."[18] This creativity is also reflected in another function of riddles, which is to help individuals, particularly children, develop their skills in oratory.[19]

Finally, riddles are also used in traditional African communities to build healthy relationships between individuals in the community. Riddles communicate social values and expectations that members are meant to emulate in order to promote harmony within the community.

Literary features

We have already mentioned the use of comparisons and imagery in riddles. Riddles are also always structured in a specific way that is familiar to the community in which the riddle is told. For instance, in certain parts of East Africa, a riddle is introduced with the word, *kitendawili*. The listener then knows that a riddle is coming and responds by saying "*tega*" ["set it"].[20] Both the narrator and the listener understand the rules of riddling and faithfully follow them. If the listener fails to solve the riddle, he or she would then have to respond to other phrases from the narrator until the narrator felt it was okay to continue. For instance, the narrator might say, "Give me a head" several times, to which the listener would respond by saying "head." After a few such exchanges, the narrator would then ask for the name of a village, and if the listener satisfied the narrator with his/her answer, the riddling would continue.[21] These additional questions were a way of simplifying things so that the respondent could move forward.

---

18. Scheub and Gunner.
19. Chesaina, *Oral Literature*, 27.
20. Kalugila, *More Swahili Proverbs*, 62.
21. Kalugila, 62.

Examples of riddles

Below are some examples of riddles, with the answers supplied in parentheses.[22] See if you can solve each riddle before looking at the answer. Try to identify the similarities in the things compared:

- I have a child who washes herself all the time (Answer: A fly)
- Thin, thin legs that are about to break (Answer: A crested crane)
- My sister's home is long but you cannot reach there (Answer: The spinal cord)
- A big knife that does not cut anything (Answer: A road)
- A grandmother is beating the bedding (Answer: Thunder)
- It cuts like a sharp knife (Answer: The tongue)
- Our mother is one (Answer: A cooking pot)
- I have my large blanket but you cannot fold it (Answer: Heaven)

Interpreting African wisdom literature

Wisdom literature focuses on the practical dimensions of life. Therefore, in interpreting it readers should look for lessons that will improve their lives and their relationships with others in community. It is not enough merely to intellectually grasp the meaning of a proverb or riddle. One has not truly grasped the meaning until one identifies the change that is expected in one's own character and behaviour and begun to apply what one has learned.

In interpreting this genre, we must consider several things:

Figurative language

The first step in interpreting an African wisdom saying is to come to grips with the figurative language used. Such sayings make extensive use of figurative and poetic language such as metaphors, similes, hyperboles

---

22. Taken from Chesaina, *Oral Literature*, 160–166, and Kalugila, *More Swahili Proverbs*, 63–74.

and paradoxes[23] that communicate information clearly but indirectly, so avoiding direct offence to the person at whom a saying is directed. Thus one of the first steps in interpreting a wisdom saying is to identity the literal meaning behind the figurative language.

Let us look at an example where the imagery, as often in Africa, is drawn from the animal world: "A hyena cannot smell its own stench."[24] What is the literal reality behind this image? It is that hyenas are widely regarded as ugly, cowardly, foul-smelling animals that spend their time scavenging for rotting flesh. The imagery thus evokes the idea of an animal that is so unaware of its foul habits that it does not notice its own body odour.

Note that the person to whom this proverb is said understands that the person quoting it is not wanting to have a conversation about hyenas as such but is commenting on some aspect of human behaviour.

General context

The second step is to identify the situational nature of the wisdom saying. In what context is it likely to be used? The interpretation of this genre is almost impossible without some understanding of the cultural cues embedded within it. These cues guide one in determining when a wisdom saying is to be used, what type of saying is appropriate for the situation, and which specific saying or sayings would best accomplish the purpose. To return to the hyena: The hyena itself is not bothered by its own foul smell; it is so used to it that it is no longer aware of it. It is others who find it offensive. So we can say that this proverb does not seem to focus on personal insight but on interpersonal relationships.

Didactic purpose

The third step is to identify what lesson the wisdom saying intends to communicate. You will remember that one function of wisdom is to educate the listeners and encourage them to choose the right path in life – the path that will lead to joy, peace, prosperity and good relationships. What lesson is the proverb of the hyena teaching? All too often people are not aware of their negative behaviour and its effect on others. Because of this lack of self-awareness, they may say or do things that

---

23. Finnegan, *Oral Literature*, 388.
24. Proverb from Chesaina, *Oral Literature*, 14.

offend those around them. So this proverb is used to alert listeners to some questionable behaviour that is likely to disrupt their relationships with others.

Embedded nature

Wisdom sayings are often found embedded in some other genre like the stories we looked at in the previous chapter. The narrator may choose to insert a wisdom saying into a story to vary the style, to draw attention to an aspect of the story, or even to encourage greater audience participation. In such cases, the wisdom saying must be interpreted in light of the larger context of the story. For instance, if the proverb above were quoted in the context of a story about the need for good relationships in the community, it would be quite straightforward to arrive at its meaning since the entire story would build up to this conclusion. The proverb would therefore work with the story to complement or emphasize the message.

We must be careful not to overlook wisdom sayings embedded in other genres. Too often, we focus only on the message of the larger story or song in which it is embedded. Or we regard the wisdom saying as no more than additional "colour" designed to enhance the telling of the story. However, a good interpreter will be observant and ensure that all aspects of the text are dealt with, including any wisdom sayings used within it.

Wisdom Literature in the Bible

Almost all the wisdom literature of the Bible is found in the Old Testament. However, it is not completely absent from the New Testament. There are wisdom themes in some of Jesus's sayings and parables, and the book of James has many similarities to Old Testament wisdom literature. Some even refer to James as "the Proverbs of the New Testament" because it is full of practical wisdom and advice for day-to-day living.

We sometimes find this wisdom literature puzzling because it does not fit neatly into the chronological narrative framework that characterizes much of the Old Testament. We are all familiar with that story, which begins with Adam and Eve and the introduction of sin into the world and moves on through the appearance of a people of God through

Abraham, their enslavement by Pharaoh and deliverance through Moses, the exodus, the change from a theocracy to a monarchy beginning with King Saul, and the consistent disobedience of the people of Israel and the prophets that God used to bring them back – this story is familiar to a student of the Old Testament.

But how are we to read wisdom books like Proverbs, Ecclesiastes and Job? Or even wisdom psalms like Psalms 1, 37, 49, and 73? It is important to recognize that these books continue to tell the story of the people of Israel and the events that define them, but from a different perspective. These books teach us about Israel's wisdom tradition and provide valuable guidelines for daily living.

Sources of biblical wisdom literature

Biblical wisdom literature has much in common with African wisdom literature. It too was rooted in the experiences of daily life and was used as part of the everyday life. It too originated in families or tribes and was first passed on in oral forms. And biblical wisdom too makes good use of poetry as the medium of expression.[25] It too majors on moral and spiritual matters, dealing with themes such as the fear of God, wise and foolish choices, the use of the tongue, friendships, pride and so forth. Wisdom literature was one way the worldview of the hearers could be shaped to be more pleasing to God. Those responsible for passing on this wisdom were regarded as wise.

We also know that Israel's wisdom literature was part of a larger pool of wisdom literature in the Ancient Near East and has much in common with it. For instance, an ancient Egyptian text known as *The Instruction of Amen-em-opet*, written in about 1200 BC, contains thirty chapters of instruction that are very similar to Proverbs 22:17–24:22. Many scholars believe that it influenced the book of Proverbs, and that this influence may have found its way to Israel through Solomon, who had an Egyptian wife. The theme of the righteous sufferer, which permeates the books of Job and Ecclesiastes, was also well known in the region long before the book of Job was written. A Babylonian work known as *The Dialogue*

---

25. John H. Tullock and Mark McEntire, *The Old Testament Story*, 8th ed. (Upper Saddle River, NJ: Pearson Prentice Hall, 2009), 330.

about Human Misery (c.1000 BC) echoes ideas found in both Job and Ecclesiastes.[26]

While it is not surprising that there are similarities between biblical and other wisdom, it is important to be aware that there are also significant differences. What sets biblical wisdom apart from all other wisdom is its monotheistic perspective and its repeated emphasis on the fear of the Lord. The wisdom found in the Bible is more than just what can be gleaned by natural intelligence or common sense; it looks to God as its ultimate authority. Wisdom was thus viewed as a divine gift of moral discernment, of the kind given to Solomon (1 Kgs 3:9, 12).

The theological dimension in biblical wisdom determines how it is to be interpreted. For instance, an African proverb might emphasize the preservation of community values because these are deeply respected in the African worldview. A biblical proverb, however, will go beyond the community and focus on the relationship with God that is expressed in obedience.

The Bible asserts that wise living is the natural outcome for those who take the fear of the Lord seriously. They will have a wisdom that results in blessings, rather than the foolishness that brings suffering.

Subgenres of wisdom literature in the Bible

Biblical wisdom literature can take the form of concise sayings such as proverbs and riddles, as well as the longer forms that are embedded in stories, songs and poetry. As with African wisdom literature, there is considerable overlap between the categories. The Hebrew term *mašal*, usually translated "proverb," can also be translated as "saying," "wisdom saying," or "mocking song."[27]

Riddles are not very common in the Bible. However, one example that stands out is in Judges 14:14, where Samson poses a riddle to the men of Timnah after he had found honey in the carcass of a lion he had killed: "Out of the eater, something to eat; out of the strong, something sweet" (Answer: Honey).

In general, biblical wisdom is categorized in three subgenres, namely instruction, example stories and reflection, and disputation speeches.[28]

---

26. For sample excerpts see Arnold and Beyer, *Encountering the Old Testament*, 291–92, 319.
27. Gerald Wilson, "לשמ," *NIDOTTE* 2:1134–36.
28. Klein et al., *Biblical Interpretation*, 316–318.

Instruction

The instruction subgenre is the one that is most directly comparable to the proverbs or riddles in African wisdom. Instruction is generally proverbial in nature and may include brief exhortations or may take a longer form as in Proverbs 1–9. The wisdom speech (Prov 1:20–33; 8:1–36; 9:1–6) is also found in this category. The goal of the instruction is to persuade the listener to adopt or abandon certain conduct or attitudes. It presents absolute demands for obedience.

Example stories and reflections

Example stories tend to be more autobiographical in nature. The narrator tells of some personal experience or offers an illustration from which they have leant truths they want to pass on (e.g. Prov 24:30–34). In the reflection subgenre, the writer presents his reflections on some truth, often with first-hand observations, example stories and lengthy thought (e.g. the book of Ecclesiastes).

Disputation speeches

In the disputation subgenre, the writer seeks to persuade the reader of some truth, and often uses poetry to do so. This genre dominates the book of Job. Both the reflection genre and disputation speeches may be equated with the embedding of wisdom literature within the story or poetic genre.

Applying the four-legged stool model

The three subgenres of wisdom listed above can all be approached in the same way, and so we will apply the four-legged stool model to only one of them, namely the subgenre of instruction, which consists mainly of proverbs. The longer examples of wisdom literature such as Ecclesiastes and Job integrate both the story and the wisdom genre (and in some instances, poetry) and therefore a combination of all the approaches relevant to these genres is needed to come to an understanding of those texts. A brief overview of these books is provided at the end of this chapter.

The proverbs we will study are found in Proverbs 11:18–21. Because they are very similar, they can be interpreted together.

The wicked man earns deceptive wages, but he who sows righteousness reaps a sure reward.

The truly righteous man attains life, but he who pursues evil goes to his death.

The LORD detests men of perverse heart but he delights in those whose ways are blameless.

Be sure of this: The wicked will not go unpunished, but those who are righteous will go free.

Leg 1: Parallels to the African context

The first leg of the hermeneutical stool is to establish whether these proverbs have any parallels with African wisdom sayings that we can use as a bridge to understanding the biblical proverb. We also need to see whether there is any conflict between these sayings and African sayings. If there is, it may indicate a wrong assumption we need to confront.

Form: Like the African proverb "The word of a friend makes you cry; the word of an enemy makes you laugh," these proverbs are presented in a contrastive manner. Each of the quoted proverbs contrasts the outcome of two opposing ways of life, one of which leads to punishment and the other to reward. The contrasted lifestyles are opposite sides of the same coin.

Worldview: The traditional African worldview sees life in terms of retribution and reward. Those who do what is right can expect a reward. Those who live without regard for what the community or the deity think will be punished. This worldview is still present in modern Africa, and it is also present in the biblical proverbs quoted above.

A second aspect of the African worldview that displays similarities to these proverbs is their focus on relationships. In traditional African communities, it was assumed that any breakdown of relationships, whether with the deity, spirits, ancestors or living members of the community, would result in punishment. The preservation of good relationships is still important in Africa today. Thus the worldview of the biblical proverbs, with their focus on a good and bad relationship between God and an individual, is not strange to us.

Content: The third parallel relates to the content of the proverbs. There are African proverbs that could almost be used to summarize these biblical proverbs. For example, a Kiswahili proverb says *Mungu hamfichi mnafiki* ["God will expose wrongdoers"].

Leg 2: Theological context

The next leg of the hermeneutical stool involves considering the theological context of the quoted proverbs. What are the main theological themes expressed?

God's justice: The first major theological theme is God's justice. These proverbs clearly demonstrate that God is aware of both righteousness and wickedness in society and is ready to reward or punish as the context deserves. This is a key theme in the entire book of Proverbs. It also reflects the general thrust of retribution theology in various Old Testament texts. For instance, Deuteronomy 28 contrasts living in obedience and so choosing blessing and life with living in disobedience and so choosing cursing and death.

Righteousness vs. wickedness: Given the contrastive nature of the proverbs, it is not surprising that the second theme is the contrast between righteousness and wickedness. Theologically, these categories define people as either aligned with God or opposed to him. This theme is not unique to these particular proverbs. The book of Proverbs, and indeed the entire Bible, reveals that righteousness is an attribute of God that reflects his very nature. The Bible also portrays the origin and increase of wickedness and evil in the world as drawing people away from God. There is an ongoing battle between righteousness and wickedness that will end only with the defeat of Satan.

Tentative application

These major theological themes lead to the conclusion that it matters how we live our lives. God is just, and those who live a righteous life can expect a reward, while those who practice wickedness or unrighteousness can expect punishment.

Leg 3: Literary context

The third leg of the hermeneutical stool involves identifying the type of literature we are dealing with (its genre), any literary techniques used, details of language usage, and the relation of this text to the surrounding texts. As noted in earlier chapters, this will throw more light on the tentative points of application derived while working on leg 2.

Literary genre

We have already noted that each genre has particular features that must be taken into account when interpreting it. This whole chapter is devoted to the genre of wisdom literature, and within that genre we are looking at the subgenre of proverbs. Within that category we are looking at instructional proverbs (see above). Proverbs of this type serve a didactic purpose and are intended to teach that how one lives matters.

Although wisdom literature is sometimes embedded in other genres, this is not the case with the proverbs we are looking at here.

Literary techniques

The biblical proverbs being discussed make use of some of the same literary techniques we noted in African proverbs.

Figurative language: Identifying the use of figurative and poetic language is key to understanding wisdom literature, as we saw in the discussion of African proverbs. The biblical proverbs being studied here also use some metaphorical language, although not quite as much as one sees in most African proverbs. Note the following examples:

- 11:18 – the phrase "sows righteousness" evokes an image of a farmer sowing seed in a field. It implies a deliberate action with an expectation that a good harvest will be the result.
- 11:19 – the phrase "pursues evil" makes it clear that the person being referred to does not accidentally stumble into an evil way of life but actively seeks to do harm.
- 11:20 – a "perverse heart" is not a reference to the physical heart in someone's body but to the motivation for their wicked actions.

Parallelism: Parallelism is a common feature of African wisdom and is also present in the biblical proverbs. In those we are looking at, it takes the form of contrast conveyed through antonyms (words that have opposite meanings). You can see this in the table below:

Verse	Word	Contrast
18	wicked	righteousness
	deceptive	sure
19	righteousness	evil
	life	death
20	detests	delights
	perverse	blameless
21	wicked	righteous

The antithetical parallelism used here communicates that wickedness/evil and righteousness are completely opposed to each other – they cannot operate in harmony. Thus the parallelism brings out God's absolute demand for righteous living while encouraging the righteous and warning the wicked.

Repetition and intensification: The four proverbs we are looking at all make the same point, which intensifies its impact. The ideas of verses 18 and 19 are repeated in verses 20 and 21 using different words. However, the narrator also used parallelism to drive home the point, as we can see when we compare verses 18 and 19:

v. 18	**earns** deceptive wages	**sows** righteousness
v. 19	goes to his own **death**	attains **life**

The metaphors of "earning" and "sowing" in verse 18 suddenly take on a much darker hue when they are replaced with "life" and "death" in verse 19.

We see the same process of intensification at work when we compare verses 20 and 21:

v. 20	**detests** those whose hearts are perverse	**Delights** in those whose ways are blameless
v. 21	will **not go unpunished**	will go **free**

We may regard the detesting and delighting in verse 20 as merely emotions; but we sit up and take notice when they are set parallel to punishment and freedom. The consequences of two contrasting ways of life are thrown into stark relief. This type of repetition and intensification is common in African literature of all kinds and serves to reinforce important ideas.

Language

Regarding the grammar and syntax, the use of the contrastive conjunction "but" emphasizes the contrast between the two ways of life and their consequences. The word "but" is used in all the proverbs under study to introduce an opposing idea. The narrator also makes extensive use of antonyms to communicate contrast.

Tense also plays a major role in communicating the message of these proverbs. The contrast between present tense verbs (e.g. "purses evil," "attains life") and future tense verbs ("will not go unpunished," "will go free") clarifies that how one chooses to live in the present has future consequences. Whether this consequence comes in this life or in the life to come is not clear from these proverbs alone. The present tense in this context also points out the habitual nature of the action or state being described.

Literary flow

It is sometimes difficult to determine exactly how biblical proverbs fit together since most were originally in separate collections that were then compiled into the format we know today. Moreover, the proverbs in chapters 10 to 22 of the book of Proverbs are all short sayings that address many different subjects, making it difficult to determine literary flow.

The proverb immediately preceding those we are studying is "Those who are kind benefit themselves, but the cruel bring ruin on themselves" (Prov 11:17). The one immediately following them is "Like a gold ring in a pig's snout is a beautiful woman who shows no discretion" (Prov 11:22). The proverbs are somewhat similar to those we are looking at in that they also present antithetical ideas.

If we look at the whole of chapter 11, we see that almost all the proverbs included in it deal with the contrast between a righteous way of life and a wicked way of life and with the consequences of these lifestyles. This wider context also confirms that these consequences are not merely rewards and punishment in the life to come but are also experienced in this life: "If the righteous receive their due on earth, how much more the ungodly and the sinner!" (Prov 11:31).

Finally, the literary context of the entire book of Proverbs emphasizes two paths, those of wisdom and folly. This point is made clear in the purpose statement at the start of the book: "The fear of the LORD is the beginning of knowledge, but fools despise wisdom and instruction" (Prov 1:7).

Tentative application

The various aspects of the literary context confirm and clarify the tentative application arrived at in legs 1 and 2. Not only is God just but he does indeed reward righteousness and punish wickedness. The certainty of this reward or punishment is unquestionable. An additional application point revealed by our examination of the literary context is that these rewards are to be expected in this present life and not just in the life to come.

Leg 4: Historical/Cultural context

It is difficult to reconstruct the specific historical and cultural context of the proverbs we are looking at. Therefore, the first step is to recognize that their general context is the wisdom literature of the Old Testament and, in particular, the book of Proverbs. This is a book that has hardly any references to the salvation history of Israel, and many of the sayings in the book do not refer directly to God. Nevertheless, he is mentioned in the introduction that states the purpose of the whole book (1:1–7) and the references to Solomon (1:1; 10:1; 25:1) and Hezekiah (25:1) place these texts squarely within Israel's history. Although at least three contributors are named (Solomon –1 :1; 10:1; 25:1; Agur – 30:1; Lemuel – 31:1), the whole book is associated with Solomon as the exemplary wise man. Most scholars agree that he is responsible for the proverbs between 10:1 and 22:16, which must therefore predate his death in 930 BC.[29] They should therefore be understood within the framework of 1 Kings 3–10, which documents the reign of Solomon. What we know of this period is that Solomon made many foreign alliances and compromised his faith because of this failure. Beyond this, it is difficult to give a more specific historical/cultural context.

Tentative application

The historical and cultural context does not add much detail to the analysis of these proverbs since it cannot be clearly isolated. However, given that the general historical context of these proverbs is wisdom

---

29. Musa Gotom, "1 and 2 Kings," in *Africa Bible Commentary* (Nairobi: WordAlive Publishers, 2006), 411.

literature, we can expect these proverbs to deal with wise living as a choice. In their original contexts, these proverbs must have been used to emphasize the contrast between righteousness and wickedness and to challenge the original listeners to live morally upright lives.

Seat: Application

Finally, how do we apply these proverbs to modern African readers, some of whom have either rejected biblical values altogether or have begun to move away from them? Consequently, they live without any regard for righteousness. Many embrace the misguided idea that they can do what they wish without any fear of negative consequences. Moreover, the digital era has made alternative views of life extremely accessible. For instance, postmodernism, which argues that there is no certainty about anything, has greatly compromised belief in the authority of the Bible. Indeed, the argument, "If it feels right to me or benefits me, it is right. It doesn't matter if anyone else gets hurt," continues to grow in many African circles. These proverbs tell us otherwise. God has standards that must be upheld, and the Bible is the final authority for faith and practice. We must be careful to live our lives in a godly and upright way because God's justice means that there are always consequences for our failure to do so. Bribery, corruption, sexual immorality, hostility to those of a different ethnicity (to name a few issues) are not acceptable. These proverbs show us what the right attitude in life ought to be. They also encourage us by reminding us that there is a reward for those who live uprightly.

JOB AND ECCLESIASTES

Both Job and Ecclesiastes are examples of wisdom literature. While we cannot discuss them in depth here, it is hoped that the following brief comments will whet your interest in further study of these books.

Ecclesiastes

The book of Ecclesiastes falls in the subgenre of example story because it records one man's search for the meaning of life. This theme places it squarely in the category of wisdom literature.

The main character is Qoheleth, a Hebrew word that the NIV translates as "the Teacher." Like many of us, he is a man struggling to understand his world and to come to terms with what he poetically describes as "life under the sun." In his search for the meaning of life Qoheleth deliberately engages in a range of activities, both wise and foolish. His two characteristic phrases, "meaningless, meaningless" (or "utterly futile") and "a chasing after the wind" vividly capture his struggle to come to terms with a difficult world. He does not arrive at his conclusions lightly, but only after intense soul-searching and careful observation of life around him (Eccl 12:9).

How are we to understand this book? Are we to assume that life is utterly meaningless as the opening words suggest? No, for there is more to the book of Ecclesiastes than this. Qoheleth himself implies that the possibility of a meaningful life exists when he advocates seeking to enjoy life and find satisfaction in our toil (e.g. 2:24–25; 3:12–13, 22; 5:18–20; 8:15; 9:7). However, while trying to enjoy what God has provided, we must always be aware that our lives are temporary while God is permanent. It is folly to try and live well without giving God his proper place. To do so is a hopeless endeavour.

Qoheleth recommends wisdom as a solution to many of life's problems (2:13; 4:13; 7:11–12, 19; 9:13–18).[30] However, he notes that it too offers only temporary fixes. He wants the listeners to understand that it is only when one recognizes the centrality of God that life begins to take on any real meaning and significance. This can be seen in such key texts as 2:24–25; 3:12–13, 22; 5:18–20; 8:15; 9:7; 12:13 (this last verse summarizes the entire message of the book).

Qoheleth's message resonates with Africans who have long recognized that God (or the Supreme Being) is at the centre of all of life and that nothing happens without his knowledge or his involvement in some

---

30. Robert V. McCabe, "The Message of Ecclesiastes," *DBSJ* 1 (1996): 93.

way. All relationships ultimately come back to him – if there is no peace with those with whom we live and interact, then there can be no peace with him. Consequently, attempting to live life without giving God his proper place is indeed a hopeless endeavour. The book of Ecclesiastes not only affirms this basic African belief but goes beyond it, because the God described in it is the sovereign God of the Bible. If the deity in the African worldview is seen as the only one who can give true significance and meaning to human life, how much more the Christian God who is the creator of all things?

Job

The book of Job uses several genres to communicate its message. The first two chapters, which are in the story genre, introduce the main characters and the setting. They also initiate the plot by raising the problem that needs resolution: Why is Job suffering despite his apparent innocence? It is this focus on trying to understand a fundamental human problem that puts this book in the category of wisdom literature.

Job's dialogues with his friends, found in chapters 3 to 31, are in the subgenre of wisdom literature known as disputation speeches. There are three cycles of highly poetic dialogue in which each of Job's friends addresses him, with Job responding to each in turn. The order of the speakers is always first Eliphaz, then Bildad, then Zophar. A new character, Elihu, is introduced towards the end of the book.

Finally, the last eleven verses of the book (Job 42:7–17) revert to the story genre.

How is the book of Job to be understood? Throughout this book, we see the thread of philosophical wisdom that forces readers to confront the issue of suffering. Even more importantly, it forces us to ask the question "Is God just?"

Job's friends insist that God is indeed just. Therefore, even though they have witnessed Job's righteous living, they argue that he must have sinned. It is the only way to explain his suffering. Consequently, the only solution is for Job to repent. They insist that repentance will ensure healing and restoration of blessings (Job 5:8–27).

Their understanding of life was that all human actions result either in God's reward for obedience or punishment for disobedience. Their worldview assumed that a good person prospers while a wicked person fails. Sickness was thus a sign that a person had sinned and was enduring God's judgement. If the narrator had not already given us a glimpse of the events happening behind the scenes, especially the conversation between God and Satan that leads to Job's woes, we might be carried along by the retribution theology of Job's friends. However, throughout his entire ordeal, Job is confident that God will vindicate him. He says, "I know that my redeemer lives, and that in the end he will stand on the earth" (Job 19:25).

The true message of the book emerges in God's speeches in Job 38:1–42:6. These speeches make it crystal clear that God alone is the source of wisdom and that he distributes wisdom as he sees fit. They also stress that suffering cannot be attributed only to sin. The wrong theology of Job's friends is demolished and Job begins a new phase of his life, with greater blessings than he had before.

In Africa, many are like Job's friends in believing that suffering must be the result of sin, that is, of offending God in some way. This belief is rooted in the traditional African worldview. The traditional gods are harsh, inflicting punishment on those who offend them. People's relationship with them is transactional: Good deeds earn you favour, bad deeds earn you punishment. However, the book of Job gives us a very different picture of God, presenting him as one who recognizes the integrity and righteous living of his own (Job 1:8) and yet allows Satan to test them.

This understanding means that we must not assume that plagues such as HIV/AIDS, Ebola, cancer, disabilities, famine, conflict and war are always a punishment for sin. God is sovereign and does what he wishes, as the example of Job demonstrates. A Christian worldview recognizes that sin is not the only explanation for suffering. Job was suffering as a test of his faithfulness to God. Consequently, our response when confronted with suffering ought to be to trust in God. Even though we may not understand the reasons behind our suffering, we can be sure that ultimately it is bringing glory to God.

8

INTERPRETING SONGS

It is now time to turn our attention to the genre of song, which includes both songs that are sung and songs that are recited (poetry) and see how the hermeneutical model can be applied here.

The Song Genre

It can sometimes be difficult to distinguish between poetry and prose because they represent the ends of a literary continuum, with poetry being dominated by the poetic line and prose by the grammatical sentence or paragraph.

| Poetry (poetic line) | Prose (grammatical sentence, paragraph) |

⟵──────────────────────────────⟶

Literary works may exist at different points along this continuum, with some prose being very poetic, and some poetry having narrative features. We can, however, use the following two characteristics to distinguish between them: (1) A poem does not usually have a chronological order or plot; (2) The clauses in a poem follow rules of quantity and metre and the author makes considerable use of stylistic devices including repetition.[1]

Poems are generally more compact than prose, for

---

1. Fokkelman, *Reading Biblical Narrative*, 171–73.

the ultimate purpose of lyric poetry is not simply to communicate information to the mind. If that were the case, poetry would be an unnecessarily inefficient means. Poetry does convey cognitive data, but that is only a part of its purpose. The poet uses language to reconstruct in the reader an experience comparable to what the poet felt. The poet broadens and deepens the reader's experience by guiding him into participation with the author's experience.[2]

All that is said above about poetry could also apply to songs, with the principle difference being that songs are generally accompanied by musical instruments, and even when these are absent, the words are usually sung.

Song in Africa

Song is the genre that best represents the heartbeat of African peoples. Whether in our traditional or modern contexts, songs are never far from our lips. What is a wedding without songs of rejoicing? Or a funeral without songs to express our sorrow? How else would politicians express their political agenda except through songs and poetry? And what is a religious ceremony without songs, accompanied by music and dancing? This feature of life has not changed in modern Africa. African poets and musicians continue to compose songs and poems that reflect modern Africa.

African song is a means of recreating experiences for the listener. It is how hope and disappointment, sorrow and joy, pain and pleasure are expressed. Song is consequently the most flexible genre in oral literature as it adapts readily to everyday life and ever-changing circumstances. It is therefore not surprising that songs and poems are heard in almost all contexts, be it social, political or religious.

Sources of African songs

Many African songs are rooted in oral tradition, passed on from generation to generation. Because communities have had unique experiences, each

---

2. D. J. Estes, "The Hermeneutics of Biblical Lyric Poetry," *Bibliotheca Sacra* 152 (1995): 419.

community has its own unique songs and poems. At the same time, because of the commonalities of life, many of the themes expressed in songs tend to be similar.

African songs have also been created by specialists, some associated with royal courts and others with religion. The songs and poems from these sources are very sophisticated and elaborate in their composition and performance.[3] There are also some freelance professionals who compose similarly elaborate songs.

The third source of African songs is the general public, that is, non-professionals and "ordinary" people in the community.[4] Because song encourages participation, everyone has a certain degree of expertise in making music. This can be seen in the responsive songs or poems found in stories, the songs sung while working, the lullabies sung to children, and the spontaneous outbursts of song when children are playing.

Many traditional and modern songs and poems have now been written down or recorded. Technology enables us to preserve them and has given us access to a far wider repertoire of songs. The Internet has also opened affordable ways for many to practice their skills in the composition and performance of songs and poetry. The result is a borrowing of styles and themes from within the continent and outside it, resulting in new subgenres of African song. African fusion is one such subgenre. It combines rap music with African rhythms to produce a new kind of music.

The function of African songs

Songs serve many functions in Africa, but before looking at these, it is good to consider three factors affecting these functions:

- *The time or season when a song is composed or performed.* A song composed to celebrate the birth of a baby is very different from one composed to mourn a death or one sung during harvest time.
- *The context or situation in the community.* A song or poem may be written during a good political era, during a drought, or during a time of spiritual renewal in the community. If we do not know that context, we may be puzzled by the content of the song.

---

3. Estes, "Hermeneutics of Biblical Lyric Poetry," 90.
4. Finnegan, *Oral Literature*, 99–100.

- *The song's content.* The content of a song or poem determines its function. For instance, a song celebrating the union of two people cannot be used to celebrate a good harvest.

To illustrate these points, read the song below, which is sung by Maasai women in East Africa.[5] The content sounds startling until we identify its function: It is a prayer that God will grant children to the women of the tribe. This particular song is mediated through the elders of the community.

> I plead and pray to thee, my father of the heavens
> I pray to thee through the Iltuati and Iltareto
> Grant me the many things that I ask of you
> Grant me the cloak with the corners
> Grant me the rolled up skirt with urine
> Of the beloved one that I suckle
> Grant me the smelly gourd of the infant
> Grant me the waist belt that I shall not unfasten
> The producers of children say we want maternity
> The children say we want maternity

Note the difference between that song and the song below, whose contents reflect that it is a song sung by children at play.[6]

> Shekagondo (a lizard) bring us sun
> It is shining in Maghamba
> Swee sounding Swee
> The father is taking out the gourd and smoking tobacco

This song is sung by children from the Shambaa tribe of Tanzania when they are tired of cold and sunless days and crave sunshine. They sing to the lizard to bring them sun so that they can enjoy life and feel good.

Like all oral literature in Africa, song generally serves a teaching function. And, again like other genres of African literature, song encourages holistic listening. This is because "it is easy to take new

---

5. Kipury, *Oral Literature of the Maasai*, 212.
6. As presented by Seth Mesiaki Ole Sululu, *Tanzanian Traditional Children's Songs, Games and Dances*, School of Music, Northern Illinois University DeKalb, IL from http://www.ilmea.org/site_media/filer_public/2012/04/17/sululu_seth.pdf.

ideas or words and tie them into song without altering the structure, the rhythm or the body movements involved."[7] Because of this, song is an effective teaching tool, instrumental in socializing the young and in passing on the culture, worldview and values of the community. Song is also crucial for teaching doctrine and theology through liturgy.

A second function of the song genre is to communicate messages. For instance, song is a crucial vehicle in modern Africa for sensitizing communities to societal injustices and health crises such as HIV/AIDS.

A third function of song is to communicate the philosophy and aesthetics of a community. Although there are many commonalities, communities differ across Africa. Through the vehicle of song, the distinctive aspects of a community can be communicated and preserved.

The fourth function of song is a social one. Songs communicate a community's attitude to groups within the community such as women, children, the disabled, etc. Songs also communicated what a community thought of other tribes. They are also used to correct wrongdoing and encourage positive behaviour.

The fifth function of song is to preserve the history of a community. Through songs and poetry, kings, warriors, and battles won and lost can be remembered.

A sixth function of song is that it plays a key role in various rites of passage. Finnegan notes the following:

> The various crucial points in the human life cycle also provide contexts for festivity and thus for artistic performance. Occasions such as initiations, weddings, or funerals provide fertile stimuli for poetic exhibition. Here again the range is wide – from occasions when those most intimately involved sing just as part of their general social obligations in the ceremony, to special appearances of famous artists or bands. Even within one society, different rituals may have different degrees of expertise considered appropriate to them.[8]

Finally, song, generally accompanied by performance, also serves to entertain. Even in modern Africa, political, social, religious and even

---

7. Kabira and Mutahi, *Gikuyu Oral Literature*, 18.
8. Finnegan, *Oral Literature*, 102.

cultural functions are incomplete without the entertainment provided by song and dance.

The song below is a good example of one sung for entertainment.[9] The singer is singing about dance partners – praising one and ridiculing another. The man who lets his wife attend dances while he stays at home also does not escape the singer's mockery.

1. To dance with Magenda (x2)
   People of Aceera clan
   It is like eating sweets (x2)

2. To dance with Mariiyũ (x2)
   People of Aceera clan
   It is like drinking sugarless tea from a calabash

3. I shall dance with this one (x2)
   People of Aceera clan
   This one, a wife of the foolish man at home.

One of the key qualities of song is that while it can stand alone, it is often inserted into other genres such as story and wisdom. Narrators do this for several reasons. Thus, in addition to the general functions described above, a song or poem can also take on any one of the following functions when we encounter it in another genre.

1. It positions the listeners to hear what is coming. A change in genre often signals that what the narrator is about to say is very important.
2. It communicates or emphasizes a lesson or a point.
3. It communicates emotion. If the narrator wants to communicate an emotion, he or she may introduce a song.
4. It adds more "colour" as the language of song and poetry generally uses more imagery.
5. It enriches the style by creating variety and adding rhythm.
6. It encourages the listeners to participate by singing or reciting a poem along with the narrator.

---

9. Song from Kabira and Mutahi, *Gikuyu Oral Literature*, 24.

Subgenres of African songs

Earlier we said that poetry and prose are the two endpoints of a continuum and that it can sometimes be difficult to distinguish them. The same is true of poems and songs. For example, the Swahili peoples of East Africa are well known for their *mashairi*, which are poems recited in a characteristically rhythmic fashion, somewhat like songs. Rather than trying to impose a distinction, the discussion in this section will collapse the two categories. In addition, as mentioned in the previous chapter, there is sometimes an overlap between recited songs and other genres such as proverbs.

The many different functions of song make it almost impossible to classify poems and songs in specific categories. However, as a basic guideline, we will use Finnegan's categories. She identifies two main categories of songs:

1. Topical and political songs. Topical songs encompass all aspects of community life, including songs sung during rites of passage.
2. Children's songs and rhymes.

She also identifies at least four types of poetry:

1. Praise poetry generally directed towards a king, chief or leader in the community.
2. Dirge or funeral poetry.
3. Religious poetry, which includes hymns, prayers and incantations.
4. Special purpose poetry, which relates to war, hunting and work.

However, even with this kind of categorization, it is generally understood that content is the best indication of the function of a song or poem.

Literary techniques in African songs

A typical African song or poem may have just a few of the characteristics listed below or it may have all of them.

Rhythm: As in many other cultures, African song is organized around rhythm. The symmetry that is achieved through rhythm adds a depth and richness to the work that makes it distinct. In the song of the women quoted above, the repetition of the phrase "grant me" produces a rhythmic effect.

Quantity: Although most African languages do not have vowel quantity (i.e. long and short vowels), some poetry and songs do include syllable counts in addition to rhythm. This makes it possible to have stanzas or verses.

Tone: The term "tone" as used here is not the same as literary tone, which refers to the attitude of a narrator towards his subject matter. In regard to African songs, tone refers to a sound of a specific quality. A song or poem may be structurally organized around tonal patterns ranging from high, to mid, to low. However, it is difficult to identify this element unless the song or poem is performed.

Stress: Certain syllables may be stressed to achieve a rhythmic pattern in the song or poem. This is especially true of *mashairi*.

Alliteration and assonance: These effects may be achieved informally through parallelism or more formally by having a structure in which all the initial words in the poem must have the same sound.

Ideophones: African song is greatly enriched by its use of ideophones, that is, words that imitate the sounds of actions in the song or poem. For instance, the sound of knocking is represented by *ku ku ku* in many East African languages. *Swee Swee* in the children's song above is an ideophone that represents the sound of the lizard. This vivid capturing of actions through words is one of the features of oral literature in Africa that effectively draws the listener into the singer's or poet's world.

Interpreting an African song

Having understood the general function and nature of African song, we now move on to interpreting an example of this genre that is embedded in a story. Read the song below, noting the introductory words of the narrator and listening carefully to the voice of the singer.[10]

---

10. Extracted from "The Story of Wanjiru" in Kabira and Mutahi, *Gikuyu Oral Literature*, 16–17. The story is also available at http://www.bluegecko.org/kenya/tribes/kikuyu/stories-rugano.htm.

> She [Wanjiru] was brought to a place where there was a very
> big river. She sang,
> Rain fall and make this ridge green
> Make this ridge green
> My father said I should be lost I should be lost
> My mother said I should be lost I should be lost
> Rain fall and make this ridge green
> Make this ridge green

Genre

As with all interpretation, it is important to identify the genre to determine what rules will apply. The rhythm and symmetry of the words quoted above suggest that it is poetry, and the introductory words reveal that it was sung, not recited. Hence, this is a song and not a poem.

Song is participatory. It is meant to be experienced – not just listened to. It is an emotional engagement, with the singer or poet controlling the emotions of the audience through various means. It is therefore important to recognize that the sound of the singer or poet's voice, the varying tones, the rhythm, and their body movements are an integral part of any song or poem. Clearly, it is not possible to assess these when analysing a song or poem in written form.

Context

A key to interpreting a song is situating it in its context, which includes the historical context that gave rise to the song and the literary context if the song is embedded in another genre such as a story or wisdom literature. In identifying the context, the content can provide a clue. For instance, a song with content that points to a political message can be placed in a general political context even though the specific political era may not be known.

What is the context of the song above? It is embedded in a traditional story about a girl named Wanjiru who lived in the land of the Gikuyu people of Kenya at a time when there was a severe drought. Faced with death, the people decided that the only way to break the drought and end their suffering was to offer a human sacrifice. Moreover, not just any sacrifice would do. It would have to be Wanjiru, the most beautiful girl in the land, who would have to wade into a river and drown. Wanjiru sings this song four times in the story: as she stands on the banks of the river, as the water reaches her knees, as it reaches her waist, and finally as it reaches her neck.

Having looked at the content and context of the song we can categorize it as a topical song about death.

Function

Next, we must identify the function of the song or poem under analysis. As was pointed out earlier, songs and poems can have several different functions depending on the season, the time, the context and the contents. One must therefore determine whether the song is meant to teach a lesson, communicate a value, promote an agenda, provide historical data, entertain, emphasize a point in a story and so forth. If the song or poem is found in a story, the reader must determine why the song or poem has been inserted there and then determine its function in light of the larger context of the story.

Wanjiru's song has been inserted into the story of a community's efforts to appease God so that a drought will end. We must understand the song within the context of this story. It does not merely communicate information; it re-creates Wanjiru's experience so that we are encouraged to participate in her pain as she goes to her death. Its function is to teach the culture, worldview and values of the people as regards their relationship to the Supreme Being. In this case, the people have sinned in some way, and the only way to appease him is through sacrifice.[11] The worldview presented through the story and the song is that the Supreme Being rewards good and punishes wrongdoing in a transactional relationship.

Mood

Identifying the mood of a song or poem is very important in grasping its meaning. This is the third step in the interpretation process. The mood may be amused, optimistic, cheerful, sorrowful, romantic, calm and so forth. As a general definition, mood is how the song or poem makes the listeners feel. The narrator creates this feeling or atmosphere by using the setting, tone and theme of the song or poem.

---

11. For a deeper analysis of this story with particular reference to worldview, see Elizabeth Mburu, "Is God a God of Retribution?" in *Christianity and Suffering: African Perspectives*, ed. Rodney L. Reed, ASET series (Carlisle: Langham Global Library, 2017), 201–222. The model used in this book is a development of that earlier model.

In the song of Wanjiru above, the mood is clearly sorrowful. The narrator of the story in which the song is embedded slows down narrative time as he allows Wanjiru herself to speak as she wades into the water, singing this same song four times. The most important people in her life have forsaken her and her death is certain. This sadness colours the entire song such that it draws us in, changing our mood to one of sorrow and mourning.

Repetition

Repetition features in many of the songs and poems of Africa. As in the story genre, it serves to emphasize a point. But it also provides symmetry and rhythm to the words of a song or poem. Listeners must pay careful attention to the repeated words and phrases as they provide clues to understanding.

Notice the repetition in the song above. As we have said before, the song in its entirety is repeated four times in the story. This repetition draws the listeners deeper into Wanjiru's sadness, encourages them to participate actively in the story, and allows them to experience catharsis or release.[12]

Each time the song is sung, it begins and ends with the refrain, "Rain fall and make this ridge green, make this ridge green." Here the repetition adds to the symmetry and rhythm of the song. It also emphasizes Wanjiru's faith in the outcome. She is aware that her sacrifice is not an empty one. She expects that God will hear and will send the much-needed rain.

Figurative language

African song generally makes extensive use of imagery and metaphorical language, which are in constant interaction.[13] They are tools that the singer or poet uses to communicate emotion and to encourage the listeners to get emotionally involved. Thus when analysing a song or poem we need to understand how this language is being used and the message that is being communicated. The images often provide a clue to the meaning of a song or poem.

---

12. Kabira and Mutahi, *Gikuyu Oral Literature*, 18.
13. Scheub and Gunner, *African Literature*.

Metaphors, similes, hyperbole and euphemism are common features of African song, but are sparsely represented in this example. However, Wanjiru's song does use euphemism when she speaks of being "lost" rather than of dying.

Song in the Bible

When one thinks about song in the Bible, what comes to mind are generally the Old Testament books of Psalms and Song of Solomon. However, even a brief look at the Old Testament reveals that there are many songs and poems in the narrative and prophetic books. For instance, 2 Samuel 22 and 23:1–7 contain what are known as orphan psalms – that is, psalms found outside the book of Psalms. Both are said to have come from David, and both are hymns of praise. Miriam's song in Exodus 15:21 is another example of song embedded in narrative. Both the prophetic books of Isaiah and Jeremiah also have extensive sections of poetry. So do the wisdom books of Job and Ecclesiastes. There is also poetry in the New Testament. We see it in the doxologies of Paul as well as in the hymns that he includes in his letters (e.g. Phil 2:6–11; Col 1:15–20).

Sources of biblical song

Most of the songs in the Bible began their life as oral literature even though we now have them in written form.

Sources of Old Testament songs

The book of Psalms represents the Israelites' personal and communal worship of God. It has been compared to a modern hymnbook. The name most associated with this collection is that of David, the most famous king of Israel. Many psalms have the title "A Psalm of David," thus acknowledging him as the author. Other authors mentioned in the titles of psalms include Asaph (Pss 73–83), the sons of Korah (Pss 84; 85; 87), Heman and Ethan, the Ezrahites (Pss 88 and 89, respectively), and Moses (Ps 90). However, many psalms are anonymous, for we do not know who wrote them. Nor do we know when they were written, for they found their way into Israel's worship over many years and thus reflect different periods in Israel's history.

The other familiar source of songs in the Old Testament is the Song of Solomon, which is a collection of love songs between a man and a woman. Many acknowledge Solomon as the source, and the book itself begins with the title: "Solomon's Song of Songs."

Lamentations has at least five dirges or funeral songs that are traditionally believed to have been composed and sung by Jeremiah (although this can be debated).

Among the oldest songs in the Bible is the song of Moses and Miriam, which they sang after crossing the Red Sea (Exod 15). The contents of the song reveal that it was an original composition based on the events that had just happened. Deuteronomy 31:22 also records that when Moses was commissioning Joshua, he wrote down the song recorded in Deuteronomy 32 and taught it to the Israelites. Numbers 21:17–18 records that the Israelites sang a song together. While the specific source of that song is not identified, it was clearly composed by the Israelites.

Later, Hannah sang the song recorded in 1 Samuel 2:1–10 that is based on her specific circumstances. Finally, prophetic books such as Ezekiel, Isaiah, and Habakkuk include songs that one assumes were composed by the authors.

Sources of New Testament songs

The Magnificat in Luke 1 is a song sung by Mary, the mother of Jesus. Although scholars acknowledge that the song of Hannah served as a source for this song, certain aspects of the Magnificat are unique to Mary.

The New Testament also sometimes mentions singing without telling us the words being sung. For example, Matthew 15 records that Jesus and his disciples sang a hymn in the upper room, and Acts records that Paul and Silas were singing a hymn when God delivered them from the Philippian jail.

Scholars have long recognized that the doxologies in Paul's letters resemble poetry, both in their rhythmic presentation and rich language (e.g. Rom 11:36; Phil 4:20; 1 Tim 1:17). We do not know whether he composed these hymns and poems himself or whether he was quoting songs that were already being sung by Christian believers.

Finally, the book of Revelation shows us the throne room of God where the elders and the four living creatures sing a new song (Rev

5:9–10). Then in Revelation 15:3–4 the vast company of the redeemed sing a song that is identified as "the song of God's servant Moses and of the Lamb."

Functions of biblical song

As with the other genres examined so far, the functions of biblical song are almost identical with those of song in Africa. For example, the first function of biblical song was to encourage participation through the recreation of experiences. A second function of song was to teach. The oral tradition of the Israelites meant that they were dependent on memory for preserving and passing on traditions. Just as the short, colourful statements found in the wisdom tradition were easy to memorize, so the rhythmic pattern found in songs and poems made it easy to memorize what was sung or recited. Closely related to this is a third function of song, which was to preserve history. It provided a convenient device for preserving key memories regarding Israelite history and religion.[14] Fourth, songs were sung during times of worship, celebration and mourning in the community.

Like African songs, many biblical songs and poems are embedded in other genres. When embedded in a narrative, a song can serve at least four major functions, which overlap with the functions noted above for African song:[15]

1. It may further explain the material, contain a lesson, or highlight a point that has been made in the surrounding genre.
2. It may focus attention on the message by emphasizing the meaning of the narrative.
3. It may add a point to the narrative by providing a conclusion. In such cases, the song generally serves a theological purpose.
4. It may be used as a literary device to add variety to the style of the narrative or even to structure and define the surrounding material.

---

14. Fee and Stuart, *How to Read the Bible*, 198.
15. Fokkelman, *Reading Biblical Narrative*, 178–9.

At this point the function of the book of Psalms deserves special mention. The poems in this book (which were all set to music and are thus songs) are unique in their portrayal of deep emotions addressed to God by individuals and by the community. As such, they are intended to be used by individuals and by the community for the worship of God. They represent different voices, viewpoints, contexts, and a wide range of emotions ranging from joy to anger.

> The psalter . . . operates with a whole range of selves, voices, viewpoints, personae, and situational contexts of utterance. Some psalms are attributed, or even anchored in space and time, and others emerge from nowhere. Some are soliloquies, others appeals, still others dialogues; some speak with one voice, others with many voices; some in the voice of the individual, others of the collective.[16]

Literary techniques of biblical song

Figurative language

Because it strives to recreate an experience for the listeners, biblical song is filled with figurative language such as metaphors, similes, personification (where inanimate objects or abstract ideas are portrayed as human), anthropomorphism (where God is given human attributes) and so forth. Biblical song also frequently uses merism, that is, referring to two extremes to communicate the scope of something.[17] For instance, the psalmist uses merism in Psalm 103:11–12 to communicate the totality of the love and forgiveness of God: "For as high as the heavens are above the earth, so great is his love for those who fear him; as far as the east is from the west, so far has he removed our transgressions from us."

Rhyme, alliteration, assonance and onomatopoeia

Besides imagery that connects with the listeners at the emotional level, Hebrew poetry also makes use of the resources supplied by the sound of words. Sometimes it makes use of rhyming sounds, either at the end of

---

16. Meir Sternberg, *The Poetics of Biblical Narrative: Ideological Literature and the Drama of Reading* (Bloomington: Indiana University Press, 1987), 72.
17. Klein et al., *Biblical Interpretation*, 302.

successive lines or poetry or in word-pair rhymes, in which two or more words in a row rhyme.[18]

Closely related to rhyme are the literary devices of alliteration and assonance. They involve the use of similar sounding vowels (assonance) or consonants (alliteration) to create a poetic effect of wholeness and emphasis. These too are useful aids to memory.

Hebrew poetry also uses what is known as onomatopoeia. This is the use of words that imitate the actual sounds of the words they portray. An English example would be a reference to the buzzing of a bee.[19]

Repetition and parallelism

Earlier we noted that wisdom literature tends to use parallelism as a literary device. This is also the case with the genre of biblical song. There are three main kinds of parallelism – synonymous, antithetic and synthetic parallelism.[20]

- *Synonymous parallelism*: In synonymous parallelism, the second line echoes the first line. We can see an example of this in Psalm 19:1 "The heavens declare the glory of God; the skies proclaim the work of his hands." In this verse, the second line is merely another way of restating the first by repeating the same basic idea.

- *Antithetic parallelism*: In antithetic parallelism, the second line contrasts with the idea in the first line. We can see this in Psalm 1:1–2:

> Blessed is the one
> > who does not walk in step with the wicked
> or stand in the way that sinners take
> > or sit in the company of mockers,
> but whose delight is in the law of the LORD,
> > and who meditates on his law day and night.

The use of the adversative conjunction "but" provides a contrast between

---

18. Klein et al., 276.
19. Klein et al., 276–277.
20. Note that different authors may use different categorizations. The one adopted here is the simplest. For this categorization and the explanations following, see Bill T. Arnold and Bryan E. Beyer, *Encountering the Old Testament: A Christian Survey*, 2nd ed. (Grand Rapids: Baker Academic, 2008), 282–284.

the righteous and the wicked man. In some instances, this conjunction is left out, but the idea of contrast is still communicated.

- *Synthetic parallelism*: In synthetic parallelism, the first line states the introductory idea and the second complements or completes it by continuing the idea, comparing it with something else, making it more specific, or even intensifying it. We see this in Ecclesiastes 11:1: "Ship your grain across the sea; after many days you may receive a return." The second line continues the idea of the first by giving the reason for the command.

Chiasm

Another structural device that is common in biblical song is chiasm. As noted in the chapter on the story genre, this is a particular writing pattern that uses structured repetition of themes or ideas to emphasize or highlight the message of the text. The word order of poetic lines may be exactly the same, or reversed, or some combination of the two, as in the following illustration from Psalm 8:[21]

A (Verse 1a: God's excellent name)
    B (Verse 1b–3: God's rule)
        C (Verse 4: Humanity's smallness)
        C' (Verse 5: Humanity's greatness)
    B' (Verse 6–8: Humanity's rule)
A' (Verse 9: God's excellent name)

In this case, the ideas in lines A and A' are restated exactly while those in B and C are "restated" in reverse in lines C' and B'. When chiasm is used, the central lines contain the main idea of the song.[22] The verses that stand at the beginning and at the end form an inclusio or envelope that encompasses and highlights the message of the middle verses.

Subgenres of biblical songs

There are several subgenres of song in the Bible.[23]

---

21. Adapted from Arnold and Beyer, *Encountering the Old Testament*, 285. They, in turn, adapted it from Robert L. Alden, *Psalms: Songs of Devotion* (Chicago: Moody, 1974), 24.
22. Klein et al., *Biblical Interpretation*, 298.
23. Tullock, *The Old Testament Story*, 353–359.

Love songs: These are found primarily in the Song of Solomon.

Hymns of praise: These usually have three parts: A call to praise God, the reason for praising God, and a renewed call to praise God. The key word in these hymns is "Hallelujah." A sizeable number of the psalms, as well as songs sung by individuals and the community, fall into this category.

Songs of thanksgiving: These are similar to hymns of praise except that they were more specifically used by the community or individuals to praise God for deliverance from a particular situation.

Laments: These include both communal and individual laments. They are cries to God to bring deliverance from a specific communal or personal disaster.

Royal psalms: These were special occasion psalms used in religious services in the presence of the king.

Other smaller genres of psalms include songs of pilgrimage, wisdom poems, liturgies (this includes Torah liturgies, which are focused on the law, and prophetic liturgies, which are focused more on God's judgement on the wicked) as well as mixed poems which combine the subgenres.

Applying the four-legged hermeneutical stool model

Read the psalm below in its entirety. As you read it, experience its message, the beauty of the figurative language, and the rhythm and symmetry of the words.

> Blessed is the one
>   who does not walk in step with the wicked
> or stand in the way that sinners take
>   or sit in the company of mockers,
> but whose delight is in the law of the LORD,
>   and who meditates on his law day and night.
> That person is like a tree planted by streams of water,
>   which yields its fruit in season
> and whose leaf does not wither –
>   whatever they do prospers.
>
> Not so the wicked!
>   They are like chaff

that the wind blows away.
Therefore the wicked will not stand in the judgement,
   nor sinners in the assembly of the righteous.
For the LORD watches over the way of the righteous,
   but the way of the wicked leads to destruction. (Ps 1)

Leg 1: Parallels to the African context

The first step is to establish whether this psalm has any parallels with the traditional or modern African context that can help shed light on its meaning. As with the other genres studied so far, this may be with regard to worldview, theology, practice, or form. If there are similarities, these can be used as a bridge to understand the biblical psalm. If there is a conflicting message, then this can be used to correct any wrong assumptions we might have.

Worldview

The first parallel that we observe relates to worldview. The worldview presented in this psalm recognizes two opposing ways of life, one wise and the other foolish. This has similarities with the African worldview. Themes of wisdom and folly feature prominently in African oral literature, and the purpose of African wisdom literature is to teach individuals how to live wisely and preserve social relationships. Foolish choices leading to negative consequences are discouraged, often through punishment.

This worldview is closely connected with reward and retribution. The psalm appears to present a retribution theology similar to that seen in traditional African religions and passed down to modern African society. We have seen examples of this in previous chapters. However, in looking at the book of Job, we noted biblical evidence that retribution theology is an oversimplification of the relationship of the biblical God with those who believe in him. Nevertheless, a failure to believe in Christ and obey God will lead to negative consequences.

This psalm does not therefore present a strange worldview, although we need to note the corrective with regards to retribution.

Form

The psalm under study is in a familiar form. The use of figurative language and the indirect way of referring to foolish living is very common in

Africa. In addition, this psalm has rhythm and symmetry, which are also part of the African song genre.

While these are not the only parallels to the African context, they are enough to provide a common starting point from which to begin to relate to the psalm.

Leg 2: Theological context

What are the key theological emphases in this psalm? The broad topic is clearly the righteous person, while the more specific theme is the contrasting of two ways of life, the one righteous and the other wicked. Numerous other psalms, as well as the wisdom literature, reveal that those who follow these ways are either for God or against him. This psalm draws a vivid contrast between the lives of the righteous and the wicked, pointing out the characteristics of each lifestyle and their different fates. As Craigie comments, "the prosperity of the righteous reflects the wisdom of a life lived according to the plan of the Giver of all life."[24]

Tentative application

The general theme of righteous versus wicked living reminds us that God requires us to make choices in life. These choices have consequences that affect us either positively or negatively.

Leg 3: Literary context

The next leg of the hermeneutical stool involves identifying the type of literature we are dealing with here, including its genre, literary techniques, language use and the progression of the text in relation to surrounding texts. The tentative points of application derived in leg 2 will be further sharpened and clarified during this step.

Literary genre

As noted in earlier chapters, each genre has specific and sometimes unique guidelines for interpretation that enrich one's understanding. Those that relate particularly to song will now be applied to Psalm 1.

The rhythm and symmetry of this psalm, combined with its extensive use of figurative language, place it in the general genre of song. Since its

---

24. Peter C. Craigie, "Psalms 1–50," in *Word Biblical Commentary*, vol. 19, eds. David A. Hubbard and Glenn W. Barker (Waco, TX: Word Books, 1983), 61.

theme (the contrast between a righteous and a wicked life) is shared with much Old Testament wisdom literature, this psalm can be categorized in the subgenre of wisdom poetry.

Function: What is the function of Psalm 1? The subgenre of wisdom poetry is meditative in mood and didactic in intention.[25] It sets out to address ethical issues. Psalm 1 was therefore intended as a teaching tool for instructing individuals and the community about the right perspective on life. The psalmist begins with what righteous people ought not to do, before moving on to what they should do. Specifically, the function of this psalm was to teach individuals the value of righteous living and to warn against wicked lifestyles. However, it is worth noting that the placement of this psalm at the start of the psalter suggests that it also serves as an introduction or prologue to the whole book of Psalms.

Mood: The mood of this psalm is mixed. In the first part of the psalm, it is generally positive and happy. In verse 3, the psalmist equates the righteous with fruitful, well-watered trees. Whatever they do prospers. As we listen to this part of the psalm, we feel uplifted and joyful. However, the mood in the second part of the psalm changes drastically. It becomes gloomy and depressing as the psalmist speaks about the fate of the wicked, who are compared to "chaff that the wind blows away" (v. 4).

Literary techniques

Repetition: As in Africa, song and poetry in the Bible are characterized by repetition that creates symmetry and rhythm. In the case of this psalm, one form of repetition is present in the chiastic structure in verse 2, as illustrated below:

A But his delight
    B is in the law of the LORD,
    B' and on his law
A' he meditates day and night

This structure emphasizes the positive characteristics of the righteous man and puts the law of the Lord in a central position, thus emphasizing its importance in directing our attitudes and behaviour.

---

25. Klein et al., *Biblical Interpretation*, 290.

Parallelism: Parallel structures are very common in African song. As we noted above, Hebrew poetry uses three main kinds of parallelism. In this psalm, the psalmist uses all three. There is synthetic parallelism in the description of what a righteous person does not do, with three clauses that intensify in meaning: "*Walk* in step with the wicked, or *stand* in the way that sinners take or *sit* in the company of mockers." The parallelism conveys a picture of a person who progressively falls deeper and deeper into sin. In verse 3, the poet again uses synthetic parallelism. The second thought ("which yields its fruit in season and whose leaf does not wither – whatever they do prospers") explains the first thought ("That person is like a tree planted by streams of water").

In verse 5, the psalmist uses synonymous parallelism: "Therefore the wicked will not stand in the judgement, nor sinners in the assembly of the righteous." Both lines express the same idea – because of their rejection of godly choices, wicked people cannot expect the reward of the righteous.

In verse 6, the psalmist uses antithetical parallelism to contrast two ways of life – that of the righteous and the wicked – and their consequences.

Figurative language: The psalmist uses a significant amount of figurative language in this psalm, including metaphors and similes. The behaviour of a righteous person is described in three metaphorical clauses phrased in negative terms. The blessed or happy person is one who "does not walk in step with the wicked." This symbolizes someone who does not engage in and is not influenced by the lifestyle of the ungodly. Such a person also does not "stand in the way that sinners take," a metaphor for participation in ungodly activities. The third metaphor refers to one who does not "sit in the company of mockers," or in other words, does not align himself or herself with ungodly people. These metaphors add emotional depth to the psalm as they guide us in visualizing what a righteous person does not do.

Then in verse 3 the psalmist turns to simile, describing one who delights in the law of the Lord as being "*like* a tree planted firmly by streams of water." The key features of such a tree are that it "yields its fruit in season" and that its leaves do "not wither." This is a sure sign of prosperity. By contrast, in verse 4, he describes those who are wicked with a very different simile: "the wicked . . . are *like* chaff that the wind blows away." These similes vividly portray the contrast between the wicked who lack stability and substance and the righteous who are firmly planted. Because this psalm was written to a people who understood agriculture, these similes are appropriate for deepening their understanding.

Merism: Merism uses two extremes to express the totality of an idea, as in the reference to the righteous person meditating on God's law "day and night." Because righteous people understand the importance of the law of the Lord, they give it priority in their life. They have the discipline to "slow down" and allow the word of God to take root in their lives as they meditate on it.

Hyperbole: Verse 3 also uses hyperbole in the statement "Whatever they do prospers." There are examples of righteous people in the Bible who were not successful in everything they attempted. The hyperbole here is meant to demonstrate the positive benefits of a life dependent on the law of the Lord. Such a person will indeed have a successful life as defined by God's standards.

Language

Grammar and syntax: The grammar and syntax used in this psalm also provide us with clues to its meaning. The psalmist explains in verse 2 that the righteous delight in the law of the Lord. The adversative conjunction "but" that begins this verse points readers to the contrast between the negatives (what righteous people do *not do*) and the positives (what they *do*).

In verses 1 to 4, the psalmist uses present tense verbs to describe the activities that define the righteous and the wicked. The use of this tense shows that this is their habitual lifestyle, not something that only happens occasionally. In verses 5 and 6, verbs in the future tense point to the certain future doom of the wicked. However, the verbs that refer to the righteous are in the present tense, reminding us that the benefits of a righteous life are experienced in the present, and not only in the future.

Understanding the meanings of some of the key words in this psalm sheds light on how we are to interpret it.

Blessed: The word that begins this psalm has been translated as "blessed" (NIV, KJV, NASB) or "happy" (CSB, GNT, NRSV). While modern English would tend to make a distinction between these two words, seeing "blessed" as being more religious and "happy" as secular, the Hebrew makes no such distinction. The most accurate rendering of this word is "truly happy." It places "decided emphasis on a life in right relationship with God" (see also Deut 33:29; Pss 2:12; 65:4; 84:4).[26]

The wicked (1:1, 4–5): This word, which is also translated as "the ungodly," occurs more often in wisdom literature than in any other genre. An ungodly person (1:1, 5) is one who is opposed to righteousness (1:6) and is characterized by "negative behavior or evil thoughts, words, and deeds that are not only contrary to God's character but are also hostile to the surrounding community."[27]

Sinners (1:1, 5): In the Old Testament, this word is generally understood to refer to those who are opposed to or disobedient to God's word.

Mockers (1:1): In the Bible, the word translated "scornful" (KJV), "scoffers" (NASB) or "mockers" (NIV) appears most frequently in the wisdom literature. It refers to people whose attitudes and actions are corrupt and sow discord. They are gluttonous and proud and lack wisdom. They walk alongside the wicked and the fool and share their fate (see Prov 9:12; 19:29; Isa 29:20).[28]

Meditate: The word translated "meditate" has a number of meanings, many of them related to low vocalizations like murmurs and muttering. Thus it can be used to describe the cooing of a dove, the growling of a lion, and wailing and moaning in sorrow. When used with regard to the wicked, the word means to plot, plan, devise or scheme (see Pss 2:1; 38:12; Prov 24:2). However, when used of the righteous, the word can refer to praising God, making plans, and engaging in deep reflective thought. The purpose of such meditation is to help them conform their life to that on which they are meditating (see Josh 1:8).[29]

Literary flow

Like the proverbs analysed in the previous chapter, psalms stand in isolation. Psalm 1 is not embedded in any story and therefore it is almost impossible to identify its literary and specific historical context. However,

---

26. Michael L. Brown, "רשא," *NIDOTTE* 1:570–71.
27. Eugene Carpenter and Michael A. Grisanti, "עשר," *NIDOTTE* 3:1201–2.
28. Tim Powell, "ליץ," *NIDOTTE* 2:798.
29. M. V. Van Pelt and Walter C. Kaiser, Jr., "הגה," *NIDOTTE* 1:1006–8.

the fact that it is the first psalm in the psalter may be significant in that it serves as the introduction or prologue to the whole book of Psalms.

Psalm 1 is also the first psalm in the first book of psalms, which covers Psalms 1–41. However, it is difficult to know what conclusion to draw from this as we do not know how the different collections that make up the five books of the Psalms were compiled.

Some scholars suggest that Psalm 1 was originally fused with Psalm 2 as a single unit.[30] That would fit with the theme of judgement that is evident in both psalms. However, in Psalm 2 this judgement is set far in the future with the coming of a future king and a Son who will rule the nations forever. As far as literary flow is concerned, this would give the theme of wise and foolish living both a present and a future thrust.

Tentative application

The various aspects of the literary context confirm that the righteous live righteous lives because they rely on all God's instructions. One who does this will have a successful life as defined by God's standards. Thoughtful, ongoing reflection on God's law is a source of pleasure to those who are righteous. By contrast, those who choose to immerse themselves in wickedness will experience God's punishment.

Leg 4: Historical context

Psalm 1 does not provide significant clues that can help us discover its specific historical context. Unlike many of the other psalms, it has no inscription and is therefore anonymous. However, the mention of "the law of the LORD" indicates that it was composed after the Mosaic law had been given. We find another clue to its dating in the use of the word "mockers" in verse 1. This is the only occasion on which this word is used in the entire book of Psalms. However, the same word occurs several times in the book of Proverbs, suggesting that it came to be used to describe unbelievers from Solomon's time on.[31] Finally, if Jeremiah is quoting this psalm in Jeremiah 17:5–8, as seems likely, then the psalm must have been written before his time. So we can say that it was probably written sometime during the period of the monarchy. Beyond this, it can only be placed in the larger context of Israel's history and the nation's life

---

30. Craigie, "Psalms 1–50," *Word Biblical Commentary*, 59.
31. C. F. Keil and F. Delitzsch, "Psalms," *Commentary on the Old Testament*, trans. Francis Bolton (Peabody, MA: Hendrickson, 1866–91, 2006), 48.

and worship of God. Any reconstruction of its specific historical context beyond this point would be speculative.

Tentative application

The biblical history of Israel records that there were times during the monarchy when the law of God was virtually forgotten and the people experienced much suffering because of their sin. This suggests the further application that the psalmist was concerned to warn the Israelites against compromising their worship of God.

Seat: Application

In the world of the listeners to this psalm, wisdom was highly valued. The teaching in this psalm was intended to motivate them to consider a lifestyle dependent on God through obedience to his law. In our modern African context, this psalm teaches us that a righteous lifestyle is the result of constant and consistent reflection on God's word. This is the only way that we can learn and apply godly values.

In today's fast-paced world, information is accessed at extremely high speeds through the Internet and media. Not many have the patience and the discipline to spend time studying the Bible. Sadly, this is the only key to the lifestyle described in this psalm.

It is no wonder that there are so many nominal Christians who have chosen to live as they please, with no regard for God's word and godly values. One evidence of the neglect of the counsel described in this psalm is lowered morality. Practices such as corruption, drug and alcohol abuse, lowered standards of sexuality, alternative lifestyles (including homosexuality and transgenderism) and so forth have flooded the continent. Beyond this, there are numerous false teachings that undercut biblical truth and encourage these wrong practices. An application of this psalm in the life of a believer today should result in an attitude change, an inner transformation of values, and a renewed commitment to live life righteously as required by God. Without this change, we can only expect punishment.

9

INTERPRETING LETTERS

Today letters have largely been replaced by emails, text messages and messages sent via different social media platforms. However, letters are an important part of the Bible, and that is why we need to study this genre. As with the other chapters, we will begin with a definition of the letter genre and consider two sample letters from Africa. Thereafter we will apply the four-legged hermeneutical stool model to a sampling of biblical letters.

The Letter Genre

Although a relatively new genre in Africa, letters have a long history in the rest of the world, where they have been used whenever people wanted to stay in contact over a long distance. We could possibly even classify the oral messages that were carried long distances in Africa as oral letter.

The functions of letters are related to the well-being of a community and of individuals. Thus their primary function is to convey information and messages between two or more parties. Sometimes this information concerns external events, and sometimes it concerns the well-being of the sender or the recipient and those connected to them. Moreover, when a question is asked by an individual or a community and an oral response is not possible, a letter is the appropriate way to respond. Finally, if a problem needs to be resolved and it cannot be done in person, a letter is the appropriate way to address the issue. Thus when interpreting a letter, it is important to understand the situation in and for which it was written.

Letters can be either formal or informal, depending on the relationship between the sender and the recipient and the situation being addressed.

Africa and Letters

The written letter is a relatively new genre in sub-Saharan Africa. This is understandable, given the oral nature of communication in traditional Africa. Consequently, most examples of letters date from the colonial and post-colonial periods.

Prior to the colonial era, information in Africa was generally communicated orally. If a chief or leader wanted to convey information or respond to chiefs or leaders in surrounding villages, he would summon a messenger and entrust the message to him. The messenger would then pass on the message exactly as it had been given to him. Thus messengers were required to be trustworthy and to have a good memory. They also needed to know the terrain that they would need to travel through. Sometimes people within the community also asked travellers to carry oral messages to family members.

Some cultures, especially in West Africa, also used drums to communicate messages over long distances. This was done on religious or ceremonial occasions. The beats and rhythms of the drums mimicked the speech of the community, thus making communication possible.

During and after the colonial era, there was rapid growth in literacy. As more and more people moved from their traditional homes into the cities, and even to other countries, the need for communication across long distances grew, and so did the popularity of the letter genre.

The style of African letters

The style used of African letters is related to colonial systems of education. Thus in Kenya letter writers use a British format, while in Francophone Africa, French models predominate. However, in general, we would expect to see the following elements in an African letter (although some of them may be omitted).

- *Address of Sender*: This is usually written at the top of the letter. It serves to let the recipient know where the letter was written.

- *Date*: The date follows immediately after the sender's address. It is often an important clue to the general historical context of the letter.
- *Salutation and Addressee*: The letter proper begins with an identification of the recipient.
- *Greetings*: All letters begin with greetings from the sender and sometimes other individuals who know the recipient.
- *Body*: The body of the letter follows the greetings. This is generally the longest section of the letter and includes the main information that the sender wants to convey.
- *Closing greetings*: Most letters conclude with further greetings. These tend to reiterate the greetings already given by members of the family and friends, but may include greetings from others too.
- *Blessing and sender*: The letter concludes with a blessing and identification of the sender.

Interpreting African letters

Look at the following sample letter from a parent in East Africa to his adult son who is working away from home.[1] Can you identify the elements mentioned above?

Munyaka Village
P.O. Box 1432
Mamburuki

23rd September 1942

To my Child,
My child whom I love, Njaramba, receive my warm greetings from the time we were last together. Your mother and I, your sisters Mwicigia and Nyambura are well and they also send their greetings. All is well here as God Almighty has taken care of us and we praise Him.
 This is land preparation season as we wait for the rains so we can plant. We trust God for the rains since He controls the heavens and the earth. For this season, we are planning to plant fast growing maize variety because it is short rain season. We also plan to plant some potatoes.

---

1. Sample provided by Dr Kariba J. C. Munio.

The calf that was born during your last visit is now pretty big but it is still suckling. The boundary case between us and our neighbours was resolved amicably and boundary lilies were planted to clearly demarcate the land. The elders held a traditional ceremony to mark the event and make sure we all stick to the boundary agreement. This is our custom.

Mine, as your father, is to continue with advice so you can make something with your life. Please know that not all the people, in the place where you are working, mean well. So be very careful with the company you keep and put all effort to lay firm foundation for yourself. Work hard and remember there is a tomorrow to be taken care of. I am happy because you informed us that you are taking evening classes after work. It is wise to go further with your formal education.

My age mate, Elder Kigutha, has informed me that there is a piece of land for sale and I want us to acquire it. I will advise you the details after we finalize the negotiations. Acquiring more land, as I have constantly told you, is to our advantage for future prosperity.

I also want you to know that your aunt, Wanyora, had visited us. The good news is that her offspring who had been lost for around three months has been found. He had been taken by a childless couple who are now in court. We had a thanksgiving ceremony and thanked God for his protection and returning him.

All the members of the family send you greetings and are reminding you to make a visit. Some clothes for the Christmas Holiday are much welcome. Come and let us celebrate together.

All peace and grace to you.

From your father,

Joe Kamanya

This is an informal letter from a father to his son, intended to inform the son about what is happening in the family. It includes greetings from family members, and information about livestock and land issues. This kind of information is expected, given the significance of these issues in African communities. The father is also keen to give his son advice. It seems that the son has found a job in the city, and the father is afraid that he will fall into bad company. The status given to education also comes through clearly in the letter, for the son is commended for continuing with his education. The last paragraph is a hint that the son should buy clothing for other members of the family. After all, he does have a job in the city! The importance of family and community is very evident throughout this letter.

Now let us take a closer look at another African letter.[2]

Wangige Market
P.O. Box 122,
Kikuyu
KENYA

3–9–1952

To my sweetheart,
First, I give thanks to our Almighty Creator Jehovah. Secondly, receive and accept my warm greetings. My love for you is as much as the leaves canopy under the forest tree cover and as much as the sands on the sea shore.

After that, you are now ready for my news update. My return trip from my aunt's home was safe and pleasant and I am now safely home. I can hardly sleep and my heart is unsettled because of your absence. How am I going to survive all these days without you and without seeing you? My heart is as heavy as a heap of steel. I can hardly eat because of lack of appetite, all because of missing you.

I am kindly requesting you to come and visit me. Let me know when you will be coming in your reply to this letter. For your information, my relative, Karanu is always crying to be brought over to visit you. He has, as well, lost his appetite over you. As for me, my heart continues to miss some heart beats when I think of you.

Let me stop there since too much is poison and a little is as sweet as sugar.

Your loving sweetheart,

Kienjeku Wa Horo

As before, we first identify the genre of a text in order to know what rules will apply when we read it. The format and contents identify the text above as a letter. So we can apply the following guidelines for interpreting this genre:

Elements

The first step in interpreting a letter is to identify whether it has all of the seven elements of a letter. Not all of them are present in the above letter. It does include the address of the sender and the date. It also identifies the recipient and conveys greetings from the sender. The body of the letter contains a declaration of love. However, there is no closing greeting or blessing in this letter. Instead, it ends with an intimate identification of the sender.

---

2. Sample provided by Dr Kariba J. C. Munio.

Function

The second step is to identify the function of the letter. The language used shows that this is an informal letter. The contents reveal that it is a young man's declaration of love to his sweetheart. The function of this letter is thus to convey information of an intimate nature. Like many love letters, it makes much use of figurative language.

Context

Can we identify a specific historical context for this letter? In other words, what were the circumstances that led to its being written? Are there any significant social, economic, political, or religious details of the context that we should note?

All we can say in response to those questions is that the date of the letter shows that it was written during the colonial era. Beyond that, the letter offers no clues to its historical context. All we can tell is that the writer of the letter is a lovesick young man who is writing to express his affection for his loved one. He misses her and longs to see her.

Letters in the Bible

There are few letters in the Old Testament, although the subgenre of report does offer some examples that may be somewhat comparable to letters, for reports generally convey information about a situation. Examples of reports include battle reports (Gen 14:1–12; Josh 10:1–15), census reports (Num 1:17–46; 26:1–62), and building reports (1 Kgs 6–7). However, in general, the letter genre is found only in the New Testament, where the letters are sometimes referred to as epistles. Of the twenty-seven books of the New Testament, twenty-one are letters. These are divided into three major groups – Pauline letters, Johannine letters, and general letters.

Most of the letters in the New Testament were written by the apostle Paul to various churches and individuals. Of the thirteen Pauline letters, four are known as the prison letters (Ephesians, Philippians, Colossians and Philemon) because they were written while Paul was in prison. Three others (1 and 2 Timothy and Titus) are known as the pastoral letters because they were written to various individuals involved in pastoral leadership.

Other New Testament letters were written by the apostle Peter (two letters: 1 and 2 Peter), James and Jude the half-brothers of Jesus (one letter each: James and Jude) and John, the beloved disciple (three letters: 1, 2 and 3 John). We do not know who wrote the letter to the Hebrews.

Revelation is unique among the Bible books in that it is a letter, a prophecy and an apocalypse at the same time. Although in previous chapters we identified it as story, those sections that can be interpreted as letters should be treated as such. These sections include the letters to the seven churches found in Revelation 2 and 3.

Understanding letters in the Bible

The New Testament letters were generally written to address specific situations in churches. They were sent to resolve a problem, encourage a church or an individual, confront false teaching, correct wrong attitudes and behaviour or respond to an issue raised by the church. A letter represented the writer in his physical absence and constituted adequate communication.

Because of their occasional nature (i.e. because they were written in response to specific situations), letters were not meant to address every theological or ethical concern that a reader might have. This means that one should not read a letter like, say, Romans as if it is merely a theological treatise. Nor should we even expect a letter to be organized systematically so as to answer all our theological questions.

An important implication of this is that we must try to understand the letters of the New Testament within the specific historical and cultural contexts that led to their being written. We must always look beyond the small section we are studying in order to understand the larger context of the communication.

The style of biblical letters

Just as the authors of Kenyan letters follow the style conventions of British letters, so the authors of biblical letters generally followed the letter-writing conventions of their day.[3] We can see this in Paul's letters,

---

3. Witherington, *New Testament Story*, 51.

which generally have the following structure:[4]

- *Salutation* – identification of author, recipients, some kind of greeting
- *Prayer or expression of thanks* for the well-being of the recipients
- *Body* setting out the major reasons for writing
- *Advice or exhortation*
- *Closing farewell*

It should be noted that while some letters have all the characteristics identified above, others have only a few. For instance, the beginning of the letter to the Hebrews does not resemble a letter.

> In the past God spoke to our forefathers through the prophets at many times and in various ways, but in these last days he has spoken to us by his Son, whom he appointed heir of all things, and through whom also he made the universe. (Heb 1:1–2)

Another example of a letter lacking the characteristics noted above is the ending of James:

> My brothers and sisters, if one of you should wander from the truth and someone should bring that person back, remember this: Whoever turns a sinner from the error of their way will save them from death and cover over a multitude of sins. (Jas 5:19–20)

In fact, both Hebrews and James resemble sermons more than letters. Scholars have suggested that they should be regarded as a series of written sermons or homilies.

Other letters that do not have all the characteristics include 1 John, which does not have a salutation or a closing, and Galatians, which has no thanksgiving.[5]

Applying the four-legged stool hermeneutical

---

4. Klein et al., *Biblical Interpretation*, 355.
5. Klein et al., 353, 359.

model to a biblical letter

Before reading the passage below, read the letter to the Galatians in its entirety. It is important to read the entire letter first in order to understand the context of the specific verses we will be analyzing. As you read it, put yourself in the shoes of an individual in the Galatians church.

> [1] Paul, an apostle – sent not from men nor by a man, but by Jesus Christ and God the Father, who raised him from the dead – [2] and all the brothers and sisters with me,
>
> To the churches in Galatia:
> [3] Grace and peace to you from God our Father and the Lord Jesus Christ, [4] who gave himself for our sins to rescue us from the present evil age, according to the will of our God and Father, [5] to whom be glory for ever and ever. Amen.
> [6] I am astonished that you are so quickly deserting the one who called you to live in the grace of Christ and are turning to a different gospel – [7] which is really no gospel at all. Evidently some people are throwing you into confusion and are trying to pervert the gospel of Christ. [8] But even if we or an angel from heaven should preach a gospel other than the one we preached to you, let them be under God's curse! [9] As we have already said, so now I say again: If anybody is preaching to you a gospel other than what you accepted, let them be under God's curse!
> [10] Am I now trying to win the approval of human beings, or of God? Or am I trying to please people? If I were still trying to please people, I would not be a servant of Christ. (Gal 1:1–10)

The context of the letter to the Galatians

As pointed out above, it is important to place this text in the context of the entire letter. Without that context, it is difficult to understand the message being communicated since we end up seeing only a brief portion of the whole communication. So before presenting a detailed analysis of Galatians 1:1–10, we will look at the overall literary, historical, and theological context of the letter as a whole.

Literary context

In terms of genre, this letter uses the literary style and conventions common in that period. However, in Galatians, Paul omits the usual thanksgiving. We will look at this in more detail when we analyse the passage.

Historical context

The author of this letter identifies himself as the apostle Paul (Gal 1:1; 6:11). We first met Paul (then known as Saul) in Acts 7:38 during the stoning of Stephen. He was a Hellenistic Jew with a deep knowledge of Judaism, the Septuagint, and Greek style of writing. He became known as the apostle to the Gentiles (Gal 2:8; Eph 3:8).

The recipients of this letter were Galatian Christians (1:2; 3:1). However, we are not sure whether Paul was writing to the ethnic group known as Galatians who lived in the north of the Roman province called Galatia, or whether he was writing to the churches he had established in the southern part of that province. This question is important because it affects the dating of the letter. If the recipients were the South Galatians, then the letter was written either before or just after the Jerusalem Council (Acts 15:1–35), that is, in around AD 48 to AD 50. However, if the recipients were North Galatians, the letter was probably written at a later date, sometime between AD 50 and AD 57.[6] However, scholarly arguments about the specific recipients and the dating of this letter do not affect its core message to the original readers or its significance for us today.

Theological context

The letter to the Galatians was written to confront and counteract false teaching being propagated by a group known as Judaizers. The main issue was whether people are saved by grace or by obeying the Old Testament law. Paul recognized that any perversion of the gospel of grace would lead to legalism, and so wrote this letter.

Four major theological themes emerge from the letter as a whole.[7]

---

6. Thomas Schreiner, *Galatians*, Zondervan Exegetical Commentary on the New Testament (Grand Rapids: Zondervan, 2010), 31.
7. Themes from Andreas J. Kostenberger, L. Scott Kellum and Charles L. Quarles, eds., *The Cradle, the Crown and the Cross: An Introduction to the New Testament* (Nashville: Broadman & Holman Academic, 2009), 425–427.

Justification by faith. Our response of faith to Christ is all that is needed for salvation. We are not saved by obedience to the Old Testament law.

Atonement. Galatians emphasizes the substitutionary nature of Christ's death. In other words, Christ paid the penalty for sin by dying a cursed death on the cross in order that sinners might be made right with God (1:4; 3:10–14; see also Deut 27:26). Relying on obedience to the law for salvation leads to a divine curse.

Transformation of the believer. The Judaizers not only argued that obedience to the law is necessary for salvation but also insisted that the law on its own is able to restrain sinful conduct. Meanwhile, others in the Galatian church said that it does not matter if believers sin because they are saved by faith alone. Paul opposes both groups, teaching that personal righteousness is very important but can only be attained with the help of the Holy Spirit (5:5, 22).

Identity of Jesus. The letter stresses Jesus's unique identity. On four occasions he is referred to as God's Son (1:16; 2:20; 4:4, 6), and he is also repeatedly referred to as "Lord," a title that reflects his deity.

Following this brief overview of the general context of the letter, we will now turn our attention to the specific text of 1:1–10.

Leg 1: Parallels to the African context

Does this text have any parallels with the traditional or modern African context that can shed light on its meaning? As with the other genres studied so far, this may be with respect to worldview, theology, practice, form and so on. If there are similarities, this information can be used as a bridge to help us understand the passage. If there is a conflicting message, then this information can be used to confront our wrong assumptions.

False teaching

Paul was writing to people who were confused because they were hearing two different gospels. One was the true gospel and the other was a corrupted version of it. This situation is not unfamiliar in Africa, where there are many teachings that pervert and corrupt the gospel. The most prominent is the prosperity gospel, which teaches that the blessings that come from faith in Christ are material in nature, and that if we are not receiving abundant material blessings, there is something wrong with our faith. There are also many syncretistic beliefs and practices that confuse Christians about what is truly biblical faith and practice. While the issues we face in Africa are not identical to the issues Paul addresses in this text, the idea that the gospel may be perverted is not strange to an African reader.

The language of curse

In traditional Africa, curses were pronounced on members of the community who had offended the spiritual realm or the physical community. It was believed that these curses would have both spiritual and physical consequences. Even today, it is not unusual to hear someone explain that a misfortune in their life is due to a curse. Some East African churches conduct deliverance services to free members from ancestral curses. While the type of curse being discussed in Galatians is very different from the African understanding of a curse, Paul's statement that anyone who perverts the gospel is cursed is familiar language for an African reader.

Form

Paul's letter has a familiar format. He begins by identifying whom he is writing to, namely the churches in Galatia. While his identification of himself as the writer of the letter comes at the beginning of the letter (rather than at the end as in African letters), nevertheless he does identify himself. The letter also includes greetings and an expression of praise (a doxology). His purpose is to address some problems in the church, and this he does in the body of the letter. Hence, while the form does not match up exactly with African letters, nevertheless there are enough familiar features to create a sense of familiarity.

These parallels to the African context provide a starting point from which to begin to relate to the passage being studied.

Leg 2: Theological context

What are the key theological emphases in Galatians 1:1–10? The major theological emphasis is the superiority of the gospel of grace. Paul insists that faith in Christ is all that is needed for salvation, which is accomplished through Christ's substitutionary death (1:4). Anyone who teaches anything else must be rejected.

Tentative application

The tentative application that suggests itself is that we need to examine our doctrine and practice carefully to ensure that they align with the biblical truth presented here. Christ is the cornerstone of our faith and adding anything else is a perversion of the gospel.

Leg 3: Literary context

The next leg is to identify the type of literature we are dealing with here, including its genre, literary techniques, language used and the progression of the text in relation to surrounding texts. The tentative application derived in leg 2 will be further sharpened and clarified during this step.

Genre

The genre of Galatians is a letter to specific recipients, namely believers who belong to the churches in Galatia (1:2). The letter is clearly occasional in its content. Its structure is that of a typical first-century letter. In our examination of the genre of the letter, we will first identify the elements present in the letter as a whole before analysing the specific verses under review.

Address of sender and date: The letter is not dated, and the writer gives no indication of his address. This is usual for letters of that period.

Salutation and Addressee: Paul begins by identifying himself, mentioning his co-workers and naming the addressees as "the churches in Galatia" (1:1–2).

Greetings: He continues with a salutation or greeting (1:3) as well as an expression of praise to God (1:5). He also makes an extended comment on the work of Christ in this opening section, something he does not do in his other letters (1:4). What is noticeably absent is any expression of thanksgiving for the welfare of his readers.

Body: The body of the letter follows the doxology. It begins at 1:6 and ends at 6:15. As in the letters discussed so far, this is the longest section of the letter and includes the main information that Paul wanted to convey.

Closing greetings: At the end of his letter, Paul includes closing greetings and signs the letter himself, reminding his readers of his apostolic position in Christ (6:11, 16, 17).

Blessing and sender: Paul ends the letter with a final blessing (6:18).

Analysis of 1:1–10

The passage we are studying begins with the words "Paul, an apostle" and continues with Paul's strong assertion that he has been sent by Jesus Christ and God, not by any man or group of men (v. 1). Given that the word "apostle" means "one who has been sent," Paul is saying that he has been specifically appointed as an apostle by God. This calling took place when he met the risen Lord on his way to Damascus (1:1; see also Acts 9:4–6).

This opening statement sets the tone for the entire letter. Paul insists that the gospel he proclaims is authoritative and true because it comes from Christ and from God. His mention of the fellow believers who are with him strengthens his authority, for they are additional witnesses to his apostleship and his message (v. 2).

Galatians is the only letter in which Paul devotes so many of his opening words to emphasizing his apostolic calling. This suggests that his apostleship was being called into question by his opponents, who doubted "the credibility of his apostleship, arguing that Paul's gospel had a human origin."[8] As we shall see as we continue reading the letter, this is the beginning of his defence against his challengers.

Paul addresses his letter to multiple churches in Galatia, not just one (v. 2). The salutation, which is one he commonly uses, wishes them grace and peace (v. 3). He stresses that these blessings came from "God our Father and the Lord Jesus Christ." By referring to God as "our Father," he reminds his readers of the relationship they have with God. The other source of this grace and peace is Jesus Christ. In contrast to the brevity of his description of God ("our Father"), Paul follows his mention of Christ with a long description of the work of Christ, which could even be said to summarize the core of the gospel. This makes sense in light of the letter as a whole, because, as we noted when we read the letter, Paul in concerned that the Galatians have forgotten the significance of Christ's work, and so are reverting to Old Testament practices like circumcision (2:20–21; 3:1, 13; 4:4–5; 5:11, 24; 6:12, 14, 17).

---

8. Schreiner, *Galatians*, 74.

Paul stresses that Christ gave himself "for our sins" and that Christ's purpose was to rescue believers "from the present evil age" (v. 4). Background reading reveals that the Jews at that time distinguished the present age, which was evil, from the future age when God would reign. So when Paul says that Christ has rescued believers from this age, he is implying that his readers can already consider themselves to be citizens of God's future age.[9]

From our reading of the rest of the letter, we also know that this implicit reference to a new age is matched by Paul's reference to "the new creation" at the close of the letter (6:15). Together, these two verses form what is known as an inclusio (envelope structure) which emphasizes the theme of the ushering in of this new age through Christ.

In the opening verses of this letter, Paul has thus introduced the two main themes that he wishes to address in the body of the letter, namely the nature of his apostleship and the nature of the gospel.

Paul concludes this introductory section of the letter with a doxology, a song of praise (v. 5). In most of his other letters, Paul's praise of God is accompanied by thanksgiving for God's blessings on the recipients of the letter. Alert readers will note that this letter is different. There is no sign of this thanksgiving in Paul's letter to the Galatians. Instead, he begins verse 6 with the words "I am astonished." Clearly, these words are intended to introduce a rebuke.

What is it that astonishes Paul? It is the fact that the Galatians have so quickly deserted Christ to turn to "a different gospel" (v. 6). This is the core of the problem. But what does Paul mean when he says they are "deserting?" In this context, he means that they are turning away from Christ and from the gospel that had been presented to them.

The words "so quickly" may indicate that only a short time has elapsed since Paul's last visit to Galatia (see 1:9) or they may reflect the contrast between the Galatians beginning and their present state. In other words, it may mean that Paul is surprised at how quickly the Galatians have turned away from Christ after their conversion.

To make matters worse, the Galatians were not turning to something better but to a different gospel "which is really no gospel at all" (v. 7).

---

9. Craig Keener, *The IVP Bible Background Commentary*, 2nd ed. (Downers Grove: InterVarsity Press, 2014), 525.

As we see later in the letter, the purpose of the troublemakers was to intentionally bring about division by advocating a different foundation for salvation, namely circumcision (2:3–5; 5:2–6; 5:22; 6:12–13).

In ancient times, those who misrepresented a message with which they had been entrusted were likely to face legal penalties.[10] But what these Judaizers were doing was far more serious than anything that could be settled in a human court. It is so serious that Paul declares that anyone (including himself or even an angel) who perverts the gospel deserves to be under God's curse (v. 8). God's curse implies final destruction and condemnation, the eschatological punishment administered by God himself![11]

The strong language Paul uses implies that he does not consider his opponents to be believers, for they preach a different gospel. Paul repeats this statement in verse 9 thus reaffirming the curse pronounced in verse 8, but this time he applies it to the Galatians own situation. Before doing so, however, he reminds his readers that he is not saying anything new. He has explained this before, which may be part of why he finds the Galatian behaviour so astonishing.

Paul then asks two rhetorical questions: "Am I now trying to win the approval of human beings, or of God? Or am I trying to please people?" The function of this verse in the argument is disputed, but it is most likely a transitional verse, completing the thought of verses 6–9 and introducing his defence of his apostolic authority in the following verses. These questions also remind us of the occasional nature of the letter, for Paul seems to be responding to accusations made about him that we do not have access to.

Paul ends this section with two questions of his own, forcing his readers to come to the logical conclusion that it is impossible to please human beings and God at the same time. The two are incompatible. One cannot have two gospels – there is only one. The true gospel recognizes the finished work of Jesus Christ on the cross and puts the law where it belongs – in the past.

---

10. Keener, *IVP Bible Background Commentary*, 525.
11. Longenecker, *Galatians*, 17.

Function

The next step is to identify the function of this passage. This function must be understood within the context of the function of the letter as a whole, which was to correct a false teaching that was promoting the addition of aspects of the law to the gospel. We can say that the function of Galatians 1:1–10 is to start the letter in the usual style and then to offer a rebuke that leads into Paul's indictment of the false teachers.

Literary techniques

One of the techniques Paul uses in this text is figurative language. He uses hyperbole or exaggeration in verse 8 when he mentions himself in the same breath as "an angel from heaven" and instructs them to reject any new version of the gospel that comes to them from any source, no matter how exalted. He also uses repetition, with verse 8 repeating much of what is said in verse 9, and he ends both verses with the same powerful injunction, "Let them be under God's curse!" This technique is very effective in impressing on the readers the importance of what he is saying and the great danger they face if they listen to false teachers. The gospel being proclaimed by those who are under God's curse can only lead to separation from God.

Finally, in verse 10 he uses two rhetorical questions. The power of rhetorical questions lies in their ability to focus the reader on the issues without requiring a verbal response. Since the original readers were aware of the underlying issues that prompted these questions, Paul's use of this technique here would have been very effective.

Language

In verse 3, Paul combines the words "grace" and "peace" in his greeting. In so doing, he combines two common Greek and Hebrew greetings. Paul frequently uses this formulaic combination in his letters.[12] However, for Paul, this greeting is not just a commonplace but reflects the essence of the gospel, with particular emphasis on its cause ("grace") and effect ("peace").[13] It is significant that he identifies both God and Christ as the source of this grace and peace, thus emphasizing the core of the gospel right at the start of a letter in which the message of the gospel is being

---

12. Werner Foerster, "εἰρήνη," *TDNT* 2:411.
13. Longenecker, *Galatians*, 7.

challenged.

The verb translated "deserting" in verse 6 may also mean to turn from, to fall away or to become apostate.[14] Elsewhere in Jewish literature the same verb is used to describe a departure from the Jewish way of life, or apostasy (e.g. 2 Macc 7:24).[15] In the text under study, it means "to turn away from" in the sense of apostasy. It is in the present tense signifying that this is an ongoing action rather than merely a one-time occurrence.

In verse 7, Paul accuses his opponents of perverting the gospel. The word translated "pervert" also meant to change or to turn. This verb only occurs twice in the entire New Testament (the other use is in Acts 2:20).[16] For Paul, the "gospel" that was being actively promoted by his opponents did not resemble the true gospel.

Literary flow

This text comes at the beginning of the letter and so there is no prior literary context. The verses that follow in 1:11–17 are a continuation of Paul's argument as he defends the authenticity of the gospel and his own apostolic calling. He asserts that the gospel he preached was a law-free gospel given to him by revelation, and that what he preached was in line with what was preached by other apostles.

Tentative application

The tentative application arrived at from the theological context is further strengthened by the examination of the literary context. Christ and his finished work on the cross must always be central to our faith and practice. There are eternal consequences for preaching wrong doctrine and leading others astray. Those called to lead must aim to please God rather than others.

We must never be afraid to confront doctrinal error when we recognize it in our churches. This means that Christian leaders must be prepared to take a stand against false ideas even if this leads to conflict or other negative consequences. This is especially pertinent for Christian leaders in an African cultural context where status and position are held in such high regard.

---

14. Christian Maurer, "μετατίθημι," *TDNT* 8:161.
15. Schreiner, *Galatians*, 84.
16. Georg Bertram, "μεταστρέφω," *TDNT* 7:729.

Leg 4: Historical context

We can deduce something about the historical context from the contents of the letter as a whole. Clearly, there was conflict because some people were sowing confusion in the Galatian churches by asserting that Paul was preaching a defective or inadequate gospel. These troublemakers were probably a group of Jewish Christians who argued that keeping the law of Moses (and in particular the rite of circumcision) was essential for salvation.[17] A similar group of Judaizers had caused trouble in Antioch, telling the believers there, "Unless you are circumcised according to the custom prescribed by Moses, you cannot be saved" (Acts 15:1). Paul's apostleship was being challenged and he was being accused of having removed some essential features of the gospel in order to make it more attractive to Gentiles.

Tentative application

The historical context confirms the tentative application points arrived at above and adds detail about the specific situation being addressed. While we in Africa do not face controversies about Old Testament law, we do encounter controversies when people try to corrupt the gospel of truth by encouraging churches to adopt doctrines and practices rooted in African traditional religions. It is easy for this to happen, especially since we want to express our faith in ways that reflect our African context. But we need to be careful not to lapse into the kind of syncretism that is present in some African Initiated Churches that encourage consulting witchdoctors, healers and spirits and the performance of some traditional rituals. As this passage emphasizes, all doctrine and practice must be related to the person and work of Christ, in full recognition that we can add nothing to the work of Christ since salvation is a response of faith to the grace of God.

Seat: Application

The main application point that suggests itself from this text is that we must confront the false teaching and syncretistic practices that have taken root in the African church. Paul did not look away when people's demands that believers be circumcised invaded the Galatian churches,

---

17. Keener, *Bible Background Commentary*, 523–524.

and we should not look away when the gospel is corrupted by prosperity teachings and syncretistic practices. While it is true that we must worship God as the Africans we are and contextualize our teaching and church practices, we must not do so casually. We must weigh every doctrine and practice in the African church against Scripture and retain only that which does not compromise God's truth. We must not be afraid to confront doctrinal error when we recognize it in our churches, and we must never allow the true gospel to be challenged or corrupted. As pointed out above, error has eternal consequences.

A second application point is that recognition of the centrality of Christ in our salvation should lead us to praise. The African church is known for its exuberant worship. However, the choruses that are sung in our churches sometimes lack theological depth and are sometimes more focused on the feelings of the worshippers than on the God being worshipped. Paul provides us with an example of what true praise should look like.

A final application is that those who consider themselves to have a calling to serve God must always keep in mind that it is God who calls us to serve; we should not appoint ourselves. Self-called ministers, bishops, or even apostles have no place in the ministry. Those called by God to be teachers and leaders must be careful to remain faithful to the true message of the gospel.

10
CONCLUSION

A Backward Look

Our journey together began with the question: Why do African Christians live dichotomized lives? I observed that this leads to the phenomenon of "Sunday Christians" – believers who live according to the values of the world during the week, but "put on" Christ on Sundays. This has weakened the African church, causing it to lose its moral voice in the world. Why has this happened? I argue that part of the problem lies in our failure to interpret the Bible accurately and allow it to guide our everyday lives.

Where did we go wrong? There is a Somali proverb that says, "Don't start out on a journey using someone else's donkey." Our problem can be understood in light of this proverb. In the early days of Christianity, Africans were among the leading Bible interpreters and teachers. However, we have now inherited from the missionaries a Western approach to the biblical text that fails to consider our African culture and worldview. The dichotomy that we see today can partially be attributed to "foreign" ways of interpreting the biblical text. We, as Africans, have started off on our journey of Bible interpretation with our neighbour's donkey!

I am proposing that we correct this problem by considering a contextualized approach. As we have seen throughout this book, our culture and worldview are important in interpreting and communicating the biblical message. The parallels between our African material and non-material culture and that of the Bible form useful bridges for interpretation. We need to take our cue from the apostle Paul, who used this strategy in his Areopagus speech (Acts 17) to introduce his hearers to the true God. Rather than bombard them with a strange gospel, he built bridges to the gospel from the Athenian culture. He was able to seamlessly expand their old context with new ideas.

Since hermeneutics is a science as well as an art, it must have a theoretical framework as well as specific rules. In this book I have introduced a four-legged hermeneutical model to help us apply the rules accurately. This model starts in our familiar world and moves directly into the more unfamiliar world of the Bible, without taking a detour into "foreign" methods.

As we apply this model, we see that genre dictates how one approaches the text and influences how one understands the message being communicated. This is because one knows what to expect (and not expect) of writing in a particular genre. In fact, I compared the rules of a genre to the rules that determine how games are played. This understanding helps us interpret the sampled texts in the way that the author intended. The four main genres of the Bible are identified as story, poetry, wisdom and letter. However, these are broad genres and there are several subgenres that fall within them.

On every step of our journey, I have provided examples of how specific genres can be interpreted, drawing on existing African literature, both traditional and post-colonial. This gives the text an air of familiarity because it speaks to us in our heart language. At the same time, we must take care not to fall into the trap of syncretism. I identified this error as the mixing of religious and cultural forms with the biblical message without considering whether they contradict biblical truth. Since there is no such thing as a neutral reading of the text, the method proposed provides a way of assessing our assumptions as readers. Those assumptions that agree with biblical truth can be used positively, and those that contradict biblical truth are confronted and corrected.

What Next?

As he was coming to the end of his life, the apostle Paul wrote a letter to Timothy, a young man whom he referred to affectionately as "my true son in the faith." In this very personal letter, he wrote, "Do your best to present yourself to God as one approved, a worker who does not need to be ashamed and who correctly handles the word of truth" (2 Tim 2:15). This admonition still holds true for us today, whether we are preparing a sermon, or a lesson, or studying the Bible for personal growth.

Our journey together is now complete. You now have the knowledge and skills you need to "correctly handle the word of truth" within your familiar African context. However, this should not be viewed as the end of *your* journey. It is merely a foundation to help you get started on the road to accurate biblical interpretation. Beyond the knowledge and the skills that you have acquired through the chapters of this book, there are other tools that are beneficial for this task.

As a student of the Bible, it is important to invest in theologically sound Bible commentaries that help to clarify our understanding of the biblical text. Commentaries come in all shapes and sizes, and some are more useful than others. Try to find a commentary that is understandable, but not so simple that it does not address key issues or problems in the text. If available, invest in a commentary that not only handles the biblical context, but also provides insight into African culture.

You should also invest in other theological tools such as Bible atlases, Bible dictionaries and encyclopaedias. These tools will help you learn more about the historical/cultural contexts of Bible passages. As we have seen throughout this book, biblical authors wrote from and to specific historical and cultural contexts. Failure to understand these contexts is likely to lead to a misinterpretation of what the author intended to communicate.

The most useful Bible dictionaries are those that provide an explanation of what a word or phrase meant in the language in which it was originally written, whether Hebrew, Greek or Aramaic. This is sometimes critical for understanding since there is no such thing as a word-for-word correspondence between two languages. The impact of a word in its original is sometimes lost in translation.

We have also seen how important it is to understand the context in which we live. Traditional Africa and the Africa in which we live today are worlds apart. Globalization and the digital revolution have magnified this distance. Invest in resources that will help you understand our culture and the contextual realities that affect us as Africans. Become a student of people, ask questions, watch the news, read books that address African issues and so forth. Remember that a sound interpretation of the Bible requires that you understand your culture and worldview so as not to impose it on the biblical text.

Finally, invest in yourself. The process of Bible interpretation requires that we rely on the Holy Spirit. We are handling the word of God and not just any ordinary book. To truly understand what the Bible says, we need the Holy Spirit to help us. Prayer, fasting, and meditation are all necessary for our spiritual growth. The more we grow in our faith, the fewer hindrances we will encounter in our understanding of God's word.

I hope that this book has motivated you to study the Bible in depth as you apply the principles contained in it. However, study of the Bible is futile if it remains just that. We must move from understanding to internalization and application. Our goal in studying the Bible is to grow in Christlikeness, to develop deep roots in the word so that we might be able to bear fruit that lasts. In this way, we will overcome the dichotomy that is so deeply entrenched in our African Christianity.

FURTHER READING

Fee, Gordon D., and Douglas Stuart. *How to Read the Bible for All Its Worth*. Grand Rapids: Zondervan, 1993.

Hirsch, E. D. *The Aims of Interpretation*. Chicago: University of Chicago Press, 1978.

———. *Validity in Interpretation*. New Haven: Yale University Press, 1967.

Keener, Craig. *The IVP Bible Background Commentary*, 2nd edition. Downers Grove: InterVarsity Press, 2014.

Kunhiyop, Samuel Waje. *African Christian Theology*. Nairobi: HippoBooks, 2012.

Loba-Mkole, Jean-Claude, and Ernst R. Wendland, eds. *Interacting with Scriptures in Africa*. Nairobi: Acton Publishers, 2005.

Osborne, Grant. *The Hermeneutical Spiral: A Comprehensive Introduction to Biblical Interpretation*. Downers Grove: InterVarsity Press, 2010.

Plantinga, Cornelius. *Engaging God's World: A Christian Vision of Faith, Learning, and Living*. Grand Rapids: Eerdmans, 2002.

Sire, James W. *Naming the Elephant*. Downers Grove: InterVarsity Press, 2004.

Turaki, Yusufu. *Foundations of African Traditional Religion and Worldview*. Nairobi: WordAlive, 2006.

Ukachukwu, Chris Manus. *Intercultural Hermeneutics in Africa: Methods and Approaches*. Nairobi: Acton Publishers, 2003.

West, Gerald. "African Biblical Hermeneutics and Bible Translation." In *Interacting with Scriptures in Africa*, edited by Jean-Claude Loba-Mkole and Ernst R. Wendland, 3–29. Nairobi: Acton Publishers, 2005.

William, Klein W., Craig L. Blomberg, and Robert L. Hubbard Jr. *Introduction to Biblical Interpretation.* Revised edition. Nashville: Thomas Nelson, 2005.

BIBLIOGRAPHY

Anderson, Keith B. *Introductory Course on African Traditional Religion*. Nairobi: Provincial Board of Theological Education, Church of the Province of Kenya, 1986.

Arnold, Bill T., and Arnold Beyer. *Encountering the Old Testament*. Grand Rapids: Baker Academic, 1999, 2008.

Bansikiza, Constance. *Restoring Moral Formation in Africa*. Nairobi: AMECEA Gate Publications, n.d.

Berlin, Adele. *Poetics and Interpretation of Biblical Narrative*. Sheffield: Almond Press, 1983.

Bitrus, Daniel. *The Extended Family: An African Christian Perspective*. Nairobi: Christian Learning Materials Centre, 2000.

Block, Daniel I. *Judges, Ruth*. The New American Commentary, vol. 6. Nashville: Broadman & Holman, 1999.

Bruce, F. F. *The Book of the Acts*. The New International Commentary on the New Testament, revised edition. Grand Rapids: Eerdmans, 1988.

Bujo, Benezet. *African Christian Morality at the Age of Inculturation*. Nairobi: St. Paul Publications, 1990.

Buswell, James O. III. "Contextualization: Theory, Tradition and Method." In *Theology and Mission*, edited by David J. Hesselgrave, 87–111. Grand Rapids: Baker, 1978.

Chesaina, C. *Oral Literature of the Kalenjin*. Nairobi: East African Educational Publishers, 1991.

Craigie, Peter C. *Psalms 1–50*. Word Biblical Commentary, vol. 19. Waco, TX: Word Books, 1983.

Croy, N. Clayton. "Hellenistic Philosophies and the Preaching of the Resurrection (Acts 17:18, 32)." *Novum Testamentum* 39 (1997): 32–36.

Cundall, A. E. "Ruth, Book of." *The Zondervan Pictorial Encyclopedia of the Bible*, vol. 5. Grand Rapids: Zondervan, 1977.

Davies, Margaret. *Rhetoric and Reference in the Fourth Gospel.* JSNTSup 63. Sheffield: JSOT, 1992.

Evans, Craig A., and Stanley E. Porter, eds. *Dictionary of New Testament Background*. Downers Grove: InterVarsity Press, 2000.

Estes, D. J. "The Hermeneutics of Biblical Lyric Poetry." *Bibliotheca Sacra* 152 (October–December 1995): 413–430.

Faber, Riemer. http://spindleworks.com/library/rfaber/aratus.htm retrieved 26/7/2016. Last updated: March 12, 2001. Taken with permission from *Clarion* 42 (1993): 13.

Fee, Gordon D., and Douglas Stuart. *How to Read the Bible for All Its Worth.* Grand Rapids: Zondervan, 1993.

Finnegan, Ruth. *Oral Literature in Africa.* World Oral Literature Series, vol. 1. http://www.oralliterature.org/collections/rfinnegan001.

———. *Oral Literature in Africa.* Oxford: Oxford University Press, 1976 (1994 printing).

Fokkelman, J. P. *Reading Biblical Narrative: An Introductory Guide.* Louisville: Westminster John Knox Press, 1999.

Gehman, Richard J. *African Traditional Religion in Biblical Perspective.* Kijabe, Kenya: Kesho Publication, 1989.

Gotom, Musa. "1 and 2 Kings." In *Africa Bible Commentary*, edited by Tokunboh Adeyemo, 409–466. Nairobi: WordAlive Publishers, 2006.

Green, Joel B., and Scot McKnight, eds. *Dictionary of Jesus and the Gospels.* Downers Grove: InterVarsity Press, 1992.

Green, Joel B., Scot McKnight, and I. Howard Marshall, eds. *Dictionary of Jesus and the Gospels.* Downers Grove: InterVarsity Press, 1992.

Hillman, Eugene. *Toward an African Christianity: Inculturation Applied.* New York: Paulist Press, 1993.

Hirsch, E. D. *The Aims of Interpretation.* Chicago: University of Chicago Press, 1978.

———. *Validity in Interpretation.* New Haven: Yale University Press, 1967.

Kabira, Wanjiku Mukabi, and Karegi wa Mutahi. *Gikuyu Oral Literature*. Nairobi: East African Educational Publishers, 1993, 2011.

Kalugila, Leonidas. *More Swahili Proverbs from East Africa*. Uppsala: Scandinavian Institute of African Studies, 1980.

Kato, Byang H. "Contextualization and Religious Syncretism in Africa." In *Biblical Christianity in Africa: A Collection of Papers and Addresses*, edited by Tite Tienou, 23–31. Theological Perspectives in Africa 2. Accra: Africa Christian Press, 1985.

———."Theological Anemia in Africa." In *Biblical Christianity in Africa: A Collection of Papers and Addresses*, edited by Tite Tienou, 11–14. Theological Perspectives in Africa 2. Accra: Africa Christian Press, 1985.

Keener, Craig. *The IVP Bible Background Commentary*, 2nd edition. Downers Grove: InterVarsity Press, 2014.

Keil, C. F., and F. Delitzsch. "Psalms." In *Commentary on the Old Testament*, translated by Francis Bolton, 1866–1891. Peabody, MA: Hendrickson, 2006.

Kenny, Anthony. *An Illustrated Brief History of Western Philosophy*. Malden, MA: Blackwell, 2006.

Kenyatta, Jomo. *Facing Mount Kenya*. Nairobi: Kenway Publication, 1938, repr. 2002.

Kipury, Naomi. *Oral Literature of the Maasai*. Nairobi: East African Educational Publishers, 1983.

Kittel, Gerhard, and Gerhard Friedrich, eds. *Theological Dictionary of the New Testament*. Translated by Geoffrey W. Bromiley. 10 vols. Grand Rapids: Eerdmans, 1964–1976.

Köstenberger, Andreas J. *John*. Baker Exegetical Commentary on the New Testament, vol. 4. Grand Rapids: Baker Academic, 2004.

Kostenberger, Andreas J., L. Scott Kellum, and Charles L. Quarles, eds. *The Cradle, the Crown and the Cross: An Introduction to the New Testament*. Nashville: Broadman & Holman Academic, 2009.

Kunhiyop, Samuel Waje. *African Christian Theology*. Nairobi: HippoBooks, 2012.

———. *Foundations of African Christian Ethics*. Nairobi: HippoBooks, 2008.

Laertius, Diogenes. *Lives of Eminent Philosophers,* vol. 10, 1925. Translated by R. D. Hicks. LCL. Harvard University Press.

Leeming, David Adams. *Creation Myths of the World: An Encyclopedia.* Santa Barbara, CA: ABC-CLIO LLC, 2010.

Loba Mkole, Jean-Claude. "Beyond Just Wages: An Intercultural Analysis of Mt. 20:1–16." *Journal of Early Christian History* 4, no. 1 (2014): 112–134.

———. "From Inculturation Theology to Intercultural Exegesis." In *Cultural Readings of the Bible,* edited by A. Kabasele Mukenge, J. C. Loba-Mkole and D. Aroga Bessong, 39–68. Clé: Yaoundé, 2007.

———. "Intercultural Construction of the New Testament Canons." *The Bible Translator* 67, no. 2 (2016): 240–261.

———. "An Intercultural Criticism of New Testament Translations." *Translation* 3 (2013): 96–119.

———. "The New Testament and Intercultural Exegesis in Africa." In *New Testament Interpretations in Africa* (Special Issue of the Journal for the Study of the New Testament 30, no. 1 (2007): 7–28. Sheffield: SAGE, 2007.

———. "Paul and Africa?" *HTS Teologiese Studies/Theological Studies* 67, no. 1 (2011): 1–11.

———. *Triple Heritage: Gospels in Intercultural Mediations.* Nairobi: WordAlive, 2012.

Loba-Mkole, Jean-Claude, and Ernst R. Wendland, eds. *Interacting with Scriptures in Africa.* Nairobi: Acton Publishers, 2005.

Longenecker, Richard N. *Galatians.* Word Bible Commentary, vol. 41. Nashville: Thomas Nelson, 1990.

Longman, Tremper III. *Literary Approaches to Biblical Interpretation.* Foundations of Contemporary Interpretation. Grand Rapids: Zondervan, 1987.

Magesa, Laurenti. *African Religion: The Moral Traditions of Abundant Life.* Maryknoll, NY: Orbis Books, 1997.

Martin, Francis, ed. *Acts.* Ancient Christian Commentary on Scripture: New Testament, vol. 5. Downers Grove: InterVarsity Press, 2006.

Mbiti, John S. *African Religions and Philosophy*. Nairobi: East African Educational Publishers, 1969, repr. 1992.

———. *Introduction to African Religion*. New York: Praeger, 1975.

Mburu, Elizabeth. "From the Classroom to the Pulpit: Navigating the Challenges." In *African Contextual Realities*, edited by Rodney Reed, 227–248. ASET Series. Carlisle: Langham Global Library, 2018.

———. "Is God a God of Retribution?" In *Christianity and Suffering: African Perspectives*, edited by Rodney L. Reed, 201–226. ASET Series. Carlisle: Langham Global Library, 2017.

———. "Leadership – Isolation, Absorption or Engagement: Paul, the Paradigmatic Role Model." *Africa Journal of Evangelical Theology* 32, no. 1 (2013): 3–19.

McCabe, Robert V. "The Message of Ecclesiastes." *DBSJ* 1 (1996): 85–112.

Mugambi, J. N. K. *African Christian Theology: An Introduction*. Nairobi: East African Educational Publishers, 1989.

———. *African Heritage and Contemporary Christianity*. Nairobi: Longman Kenya, 1989.

Mulholland, Robert. "Sociological Criticism." In *New Testament Criticism & Interpretation*, edited by David Alan Black and David S. Dockery, 297–316. Grand Rapids: Zondervan, 1991.

Nash, Ronald N. *Worldviews in Conflict: Choosing Christianity in a World of Ideas*. Grand Rapids: Zondervan, 1992.

Ndereba, Kevin Murithii. "Youth Worldviews among the De-Churched in Nairobi and Implications for Ministry." Thesis, International Leadership University, Nairobi, Kenya, 2015.

O'Donovan, Wilbur. *Biblical Christianity in Modern Africa*. Carlisle: Paternoster, 2000.

Ole Sululu, Seth Mesiaki. *Tanzanian Traditional Children's Songs, Games and Dances*. School of Music, Northern Illinois University DeKalb, IL. http://www.ilmea.org/site_media/filer_public/2012/04/17/sululu_seth.pdf.

Onwu, N. "The Hermeneutical Model: The Dilemma of the African Theologian." *Africa Theological Journal* 14, no. 3 (1985):145–160.

Osborne, Grant. *The Hermeneutical Spiral: A Comprehensive Introduction to Biblical Interpretation*. Downers Grove: InterVarsity Press, 2010.

Parrinder, Geoffrey. *Religion in Africa*. Harmondsworth, UK: Penguin, 1969.

Parsons, Mikeal C., and Martin M. Culy. *Acts: A Handbook on the Greek Text*. Waco, TX: Baylor University Press, 2003.

Plantinga, Cornelius. *Engaging God's World: A Christian Vision of Faith, Learning, and Living*. Grand Rapids: Eerdmans, 2002.

Porter, S. E. "Literary Approaches to the New Testament: From Formalism to Deconstruction and Back." In *Approaches to New Testament Study*, edited by Stanley E. Porter and David Tombs, 77–128. Sheffield: Sheffield Academic Press, 1995.

Ryken, Leland. "The Creative Arts." In *The Making of a Christian Mind: A Christian World View and the Academic Enterprise*, edited by Arthur Holmes, 105–131. Downers Grove: InterVarsity Press, 1985.

Saxe, John Godfrey. *The Poems of John Godfrey Saxe*. Boston: James R. Osgood & Co., 1873.

Scheub, Harold, and Elizabeth Ann Wynne Gunner. *African Literature*. http://www.britannica.com/art/African-literature#toc57038.

Schreiner, Thomas. *Galatians*. Zondervan Exegetical Commentary on the New Testament. Grand Rapids: Zondervan, 2010.

Seto, Wing-Luk. "An Asian Looks at Contextualization and Developing Ethnotheologies." *Evangelical Missions Quarterly* 23 (April 1987): 138–141.

Sire, James W. *Naming the Elephant*. Downers Grove: InterVarsity Press, 2004.

Sternberg, Meir. *The Poetics of Biblical Narrative: Ideological Literature and the Drama of Reading*. Bloomington: Indiana University Press, 1987.

T. Desmond Alexander et al., eds. *New Dictionary of Biblical Theology*. Downers Grove: InterVarsity Press, 2000.

Taylor, E. K. *Using Folktales*. Cambridge: Cambridge University Press, 2000.

Thiselton, A. C. *The Two Horizons: New Testament Hermeneutics and Philosophical Description with Special Reference to Heidegger, Bultmann, Gadamer, and Wittgenstein.* Carlisle: Paternoster, 2005.

Tullock, John H. *The Old Testament Story.* Upper Saddle River, NJ: Pearson Prentice Hall, 2001.

Tullock, John H., and Mark McEntire. *The Old Testament Story.* 8th edition. Upper Saddle River, NJ: Pearson Prentice Hall, 2009.

Turaki, Yusufu. *Foundations of African Traditional Religion and Worldview.* Nairobi: WordAlive, 2006.

Tutu, Desmond. *No Future without Forgiveness.* New York: Doubleday, 1999.

Ukachukwu, Chris Manus. *Intercultural Hermeneutics in Africa: Methods and Approaches.* Nairobi: Acton Publishers, 2003.

VanGemeren, Willem A., ed. *New International Dictionary of Old Testament Theology and Exegesis*, vol. 2. Grand Rapids: Zondervan, 1997.

Vanhoozer, Kevin J., ed. *Dictionary for Theological Interpretation of the Bible.* Grand Rapids: Baker Academic, 2005.

Waiyaki, James M. *The Story of Muhang'u: A Precolonial Look.* Forthcoming.

West, Gerald. "African Biblical Hermeneutics and Bible Translation." In *Interacting with Scriptures in Africa*, edited by Jean-Claude Loba-Mkole and Ernst R. Wendland, 3–29. Nairobi: Acton Publishers, 2005.

William, Klein W., Craig L. Blomberg, and Robert L. Hubbard Jr. *Introduction to Biblical Interpretation.* Revised edition. Nashville: Thomas Nelson, 2005.

Wolters, Albert M. *Creation Regained: Biblical Basics for a Reformational Worldview.* Grand Rapids: Eerdmans, 2005.

INDEX OF SUBJECTS

A
African context 5, 8, 18, 25, 53, 66–68, 91, 123, 124, 126, 154, 183, 190, 201, 202, 213
African diversity 25, 54, 111
African Initiated Churches 8, 209
African letters 192, 202
African songs 166, 167, 171, 172, 175, 178, 184, 186
African stories 110–112
afterlife 35, 40
Akamba 54
ancestors 25, 27, 28, 32, 33, 35, 36, 38, 40, 41, 49, 50, 54, 132, 142, 154
angels and demons 33, 34
apocalypse 99, 102, 197
application 5, 7, 18, 68, 70, 74, 80, 84–89, 133, 134, 159, 184, 190, 209
assumptions 9, 18, 22, 23, 47, 94, 132, 154

B
Bible stories 120, 128
biblical context 68, 69
biblical letters 191, 196, 197
"Blind Men and the Elephant" 21

C
colonial influence 4, 19, 47, 192. *See* also dichotomized thinking
communalism 36
contextualization 5–8, 10, 18, 86

cultural context 12, 80, 98, 103, 115, 131, 133, 159, 213
culture 9, 11, 18, 23–25, 48, 87, 110, 140, 169, 174, 211, 213
   African 6, 26, 27, 38, 45, 69, 70, 87, 88, 124, 211, 213
   biblical 69
   definition 6, 24. *See also* worldview
culture-bound 86–88
curse 55, 69, 132, 140, 199, 201, 202, 206, 207

D
dichotomized thinking 3, 8, 20, 22, 34, 91, 211
dichotomy 3, 20, 211
diversity 19

E
East Africa 19
Epicureans 10, 12, 13, 15–17
external reality 31, 34, 35, 48

F
feminist approach 9

G
Gikuyu 32, 49, 52, 79, 110, 112, 114, 116, 173
globalization 6, 24, 51, 68, 213

H
hermeneutical gap 6, 86
hermeneutical model 5

four-legged stool 6, 68, 70, 84, 89, 91, 114, 120, 123, 133, 153, 182, 191, 198, 212
hermeneutical spiral 66
hermeneutics 5, 6, 20, 30, 35, 67, 70, 79, 91, 107, 212
   approaches 18
   intercultural 7
   interpretation 5, 23, 24, 30, 31, 35, 47, 66, 71, 72, 81, 95, 105, 107, 123, 135, 173, 174
historical context 12, 42, 67, 80, 98, 103, 115, 131, 133, 144, 159, 173, 188, 189, 209, 213
history 56, 57, 58, 169, 178, 189, 190
holism 33
   African 27
holistic approach 72, 75, 84, 109, 112, 130, 147, 168
holistic thinking 22, 23, 26
honour 38, 50, 68, 87, 88, 122, 124, 141

I
individualism 37, 41, 42, 51
instruction 153
intercultural model 6, 20, 89

J
Jesus's teaching 6, 40, 135
   parables 6, 83, 120, 135
Johannine letters 196

K
knowledge 45–47

L
letters 191
literary context 73, 102, 126, 184
   flow 78–80, 188, 189
   genre 73, 74, 80
   grammar and syntax 73, 77, 158, 187

language 77, 78, 80
   of the Bible 96
   techniques 73, 75–77, 80, 114
literary device
   chiasm 128, 181, 185
   euphemism 176
   figurative language 119, 127, 144, 148, 156, 175
   hyperbole 119, 148, 176, 187, 207
   imagery 75, 76, 116, 119, 146, 147, 149, 175, 179
   intensification 157
   metaphors 76, 119, 127, 143, 148, 176, 179, 186
   parallelism 144, 156, 157, 172, 180, 181, 186
   repetition 76, 116, 127, 157, 165, 175, 181, 185, 207
   similes 76, 135, 148, 176, 179, 186, 187
   symbolism 24, 76, 110, 119, 120

M
meaning vs. application 85
memorability 139, 178, 180
merism 179, 187
missionaries 29, 211
missionary influence 4
modernization 6, 7, 24, 51, 68
morality 48–53, 55, 190
   African 50, 51
   biblical 50, 51
mutual interests 68, 69, 80
mythology 111

N
narrative 19, 71, 76, 77, 79, 85, 96, 97, 107, 109, 116–120, 127–129, 150, 165, 175, 176, 178
N'gai 79, 112–120

O

oral tradition 46, 47, 57, 68, 75, 76, 80, 85, 108, 130, 151, 168, 172
    Africa 19, 141, 183, 191, 192
    Bible 176, 178
    riddles 141, 142
    songs 46, 141, 166

P

parables 135, 136
Paul in Athens 10, 11
Pauline letters 196
personification 119, 179
poetry 73, 74, 96, 97, 128, 143, 151–153, 165–167, 169, 171–173, 176, 177, 179, 180, 185, 186
polygamy 3, 39, 68
prosperity gospel 28, 31, 201
proverbs 46, 74, 139–144, 146, 153–156, 160
    African 140, 143, 144, 155, 156
    biblical 140, 144, 154, 155–159, 188
punishment 28, 29, 35, 40, 50, 52–55, 68, 118, 124, 154, 155, 157–159, 162, 163, 183, 189, 190, 206

R

relationships 36, 39–41
    community 27, 36–42, 45, 46, 48–51, 53, 54, 69, 78, 110, 139, 141, 142, 146, 147, 150, 152, 154, 169, 174, 179, 182, 191, 192, 194, 202
    extended family 38, 40–42, 51
riddles 146–148, 152, 153

S

sanctification 101
Satan 33, 96, 155, 162, 163
shame 38, 50, 53, 68, 69, 88, 124, 125, 129, 133
spirits 32–35, 37, 39, 42, 48, 54, 55, 154, 209
Stoics 10, 12, 14–17
storyteller 85, 108, 114, 141
storytelling 75, 85, 108, 109, 117, 119, 143, 147
suffering 53–56, 124, 125, 129, 131, 134, 152, 162, 163, 173, 190
syncretism 3, 8, 19, 30, 86, 94, 202, 209, 212

T

theological context 70, 95, 99, 124, 184
theology 183
    African 8
    biblical 8, 95, 136, 155
    instruction 178
    relational 29
    retribution 29, 54, 55, 116, 121, 124, 154, 155, 163, 183
    transactional 28, 29, 31, 55, 116, 163, 174
time 56–58
trans-contextual 86–88
two horizons 70

U

ubuntu 36, 37
ultimate reality 25, 29–31, 53
    nature of 25
urbanization 24, 68

W

Wapangwa 31
Western education 34
wisdom literature 139, 140, 142, 146, 150, 153, 156, 159–162, 173, 180, 184, 185, 188
    African 148, 151, 152, 183
    biblical 150–152

wisdom sayings 148–150, 154
wisdom tradition 45, 86, 135, 140–142, 178, 190
witchcraft 3, 34, 54, 55
witchdoctors 3, 30, 55, 209
worldview 7, 9, 11, 15, 16, 18, 22, 25, 31, 36, 37, 42, 45, 53, 56, 67, 69, 115, 120, 121, 140, 142, 151, 162, 169, 174, 183, 201, 211, 214
   African 5, 7, 21, 24–30, 31, 32, 35–37, 39, 40, 43, 46, 47, 49, 50, 67, 69, 78, 93, 142, 152, 154, 162, 163, 183, 211
   biblical 20, 23, 26–28, 33, 34, 36, 39, 40, 46, 47, 50, 58, 69, 94, 121
   definition 22
   individual vs. communal 24, 36, 142
   secularism 30
   western 34

INDEX OF NAMES

A
Aratus 14
Augustine 4, 13, 94

B
Bujo, Benezet 49

E
Epimenides the Cretan 14

F
Fee, Gordon D. 83
Finnegan, Ruth 75, 80, 111, 146, 169, 171

G
Gehman, Richard J. 28
Gerald, West 70

H
Hillman, Eugene 4, 6
Hirsch, E. D. 74, 85

K
Kalugila, Leonidas 143
Kato, Byang 6, 8, 19
Kenyatta, Jomo 51

L
Loba-Mkole, Jean-Claude 18

M
Magesa, Laurenti 4
Mbiti, John S. 54
Mugambi, J. N. K. 38

N
Nash, Ronald N. 26

O
Origen 4, 94

S
Scheub, Harold 75, 146
Seto, Wing-Luk 24
Sire, James W. 22, 23
Stuart, Douglas 83

T
Turaki, Yusufu 33, 34
Tutu, Desmond 36

U
Ukachukwu, Chris Manus 6, 68, 85

W
Wanjiru 172–176
Wendland, Ernst R. 18

Y
Yarbrough, Robert W. 28

INDEX OF SCRIPTURE

Old Testament

Genesis
1:1....................26, 30
1:26–27........................51
1:27–28........................14
1:31..............................32
3....................................50
3:19..............................35
14:1–12......................196
19:30–38....................131
37..................................77
38:24–30....................133
45:8..............................77

Exodus
15................................177
15:21..........................176
20:1–17..................50, 87
20:12............................87

Leviticus
19:19............................87
23:22..........................125

Numbers
1:17–46......................196
21:17–18....................177

Deuteronomy
5:16..............................88
6:4–5............................26
6:5................................50
22:11............................86
22:16............................88

23:3–4........................132
23:6............................132
25:5–6........................133
25:5–10........................39
25:7–10......................133
27:26..........................201
28........................55, 155
31:11–13....................108
31:22..........................177
33:29..........................188

Joshua
1:8..............................188
7....................................50
7:24–25........................53
10:1–15......................196
15:16............................88
24:1–25........................76

Judges
12:9..............................88
14:14..........................152
17:6............................124
18:1............................124
19:1............................124
21:25..........................124

Ruth
1:1..............................130
1:1–2..........................131
1:2–3..........................125
1:4..............................127
1:6..............................128

1:13..................121, 130
1:16–17......................127
1:20............................130
1:20–21......................121
1:21............................128
1:22............................127
2:2..............................127
2:3–9..........................125
2:7..............................127
2:20............................128
2:23............................128
3:9..............................127
4:5..............................127
4:7....................127, 133
4:7–8............................83
4:10............................127
4:12............................133
4:14............................128
4:15............................125
4:16............................128
4:17–22......................132
4:18–22......................131

1 Samuel
1–2................................69
2:1–10........................177
24:3–7..........................42

2 Samuel
22................................176
23:1–7........................176

1 Kings
3:9 152
3 – 10 159
3:12 152
6 – 7 196

Nehemiah
8:1–8 108
8:9 109
26:1–62 196

Job
1:8 163
1:21 141
5:8–27 .... 56, 162
19:25 163
38:1 – 42:6 163
42:7–17 162

Psalms
1 .... 184, 188
1:1 188
1:1–2 180
1:2 185
1:3 .... 77, 185, 186
1:4 .... 185, 186
1:4–5 188
1:5 .... 186, 188
1:6 .... 186, 188
2 189
2:1 188
2:12 188
8 181
19:1 .... 27, 180
38:12 188
65:4 188
73 – 83 176
84:4 188
84 – 85 176
87 176
88 176
89 176
90 176

Proverbs
1:1 159
1:1–7 159
1:7 .... 46, 159
1 – 9 153
1:20–33 153
8:1–36 153
9:1–6 153
9:12 188
10:1 159
11 158
11:17 158
11:18 156
11:18–21 153
11:19 156
11:20 156
11:22 158
11:31 158
19:29 188
21:26 141
22:17 – 24:22 151
24:2 188
24:30–34 153
25:1 159
30:1 159
31:1 159
103:11–12 179

Ecclesiastes
2:13 161
2:24–25 161
3:12–13 161
3:22 161
4:13 161
5:18–20 161
7:11–12 161
7:19 161
8:15 161
9:7 161
9:13–18 161
11:1 181
12:9 161
12:13 161

Isaiah
29:20 188

Jeremiah
17:5–8 189

New Testament

Matthew
12:34 141
13:1–9 135
13:18–23 135
13:31–32 135
13:33 135
15 177
15:22–28 83
19:28 101
21:28–32 136
21:33–46 136
22:1–14 .... 135, 136
22:37–40 50
25:14–30 135
28:18–20 26

Mark
1:1 .... 71, 72
1:11 71
3:33 71
4:1–9 135
4:10–12 136
4:13–20 135
4:30–32 135
5:7 71
7:31–37 72
8:29 72

9:7 71	15:1 209	3:10–14 201
9:41 72	15:1–35 200	3:13 204
11:27–33 136	16:30–31 78	4:4 201
12:1–12 .... 135, 136	17 211	4:4–5 204
12:6 71	17:16–34 10	4:6 201
12:13–17 136	17:28 14	5:2–6 206
12:30–31 50	17:29 15	5:5 201
12:35 72	17:30–31 16	5:11 204
13:21 72	17:32 17	5:22 .... 201, 206
13:32 71		5:24 204
14:61 .... 71, 72	**Romans**	6:1 50
15:32 72	1:3–4 103	6:11 .... 200, 204
15:39 71	2:12–16 51	6:12 204
	3:23 36	6:12–13 206
Luke	3:25 16	6:14 204
1 177	9:25–29 103	6:15 205
6:38 31	10:18–21 103	6:16 204
6:43–44 140	11:36 177	6:17 204
6:45 141		6:18 204
8:4–8 135	**1 Corinthians**	
8:11–15 135	15:3 103	**Ephesians**
10:27 50	16:22 103	3:8 200
10:29–37 83		
13:18–19 135	**Galatians**	**Philippians**
14:15–24 135	1:1 .... 200, 204	2:5–11 103
16:22–26 35	1:1–10 .... 199, 201,	2:6–11 176
17:7–10 135	202, 204	4:20 177
19:11–27 135	1:2 .... 200, 203, 204	
20:1–18 136	1:3 .... 203, 204	**Colossians**
20:9–19 136	1:4 .... 201–203, 205	1:15–20 176
20:20–26 136	1–5 203	
	1:5 205	**1 Timothy**
John	1:6 203	1:17 177
7:53 – 8:11 68	1:7 205	
9 55	1:8 206	**2 Timothy**
13 82	1:9 205	2:15 213
15 40	1:11–17 208	
	1:16 201	**Hebrews**
Acts	2:3–5 206	1:1–2 198
1:6 105	2:8 200	1:5–13 103
2:20 208	2:20 201	9:22 28
7:38 200	2:20–21 204	9:27 35
9:4–6 204	3:1 .... 200, 204	11:6 101

12:1......................35, 69

James
1:27...........................47
5:19–20....................198

Revelation
5:9–10......................178
15:3–4......................178
20:13–15....................35